Today Khrushchev tends to be remembered for his 'buffoonery': as the man who banged his shoe on his desk at the assembly of the United Nations. This approachable introduction to Khrushchev displays another side, that of the serious politician attempting to reform the Soviet Union after Stalin's death.

Khrushchev was a key player in the Soviet experiment. He was a labour activist in the pre-revolutionary years, fought in the civil war, rose through the party ranks, denounced Stalin, and beat the United States in the space race. Once Khrushchev became Soviet leader, he realized that the system Stalin had bequeathed him needed to be modernized and reformed. And when those reforms in turn ran out of steam, he came to the conclusion that only further radical change could prevent the atrophy of the Soviet Union.

In this book, Geoffrey Swain offers an engaging account of Khrushchev's political career and his wider role in Soviet and world politics, arguing that Khrushchev was overthrown in 1964 not because of his incompetence, but because the radical reforms he had in mind threatened the interests of the communist party apparatus.

Geoffrey Swain holds the Alexander Nove Chair in Russian and East European Studies at the University of Glasgow, UK.

European History in Perspective

General Editor: Jeremy Black

European History in Perspective
Series Standing Order
ISBN 978–0–333–71694–6 hardcover
ISBN 978–0–333–69336–0 paperback
(outside North America only)

You can receive future titles in this series as they are published by placing a
standing order. Please contact your bookseller or, in the case of difficulty, write to
us at the address below with your name and address, the title of the series and the
ISBN quoted above.

Customer Services Department, Macmillan Distribution Ltd,
Houndmills, Basingstoke, Hampshire, RG21 6XS, UK

Khrushchev

Geoffrey Swain

macmillan education palgrave

First published 2016 by
PALGRAVE

Palgrave in the UK is an imprint of Macmillan Publishers Limited, registered in England, company number 785998, of 4 Crinan Street, London, N1 9XW.

Palgrave Macmillan in the US is a division of St Martin's Press LLC, 175 Fifth Avenue, New York, NY 10010.

Palgrave is a global imprint of the above companies and is represented throughout the world.

Palgrave® and Macmillan® are registered trademarks in the United States, the United Kingdom, Europe and other countries.

ISBN 978–1–137–33550–0 hardback
ISBN 978–1–137–33549–4 paperback

This book is printed on paper suitable for recycling and made from fully managed and sustained forest sources. Logging, pulping and manufacturing processes are expected to conform to the environmental regulations of the country of origin.

A catalogue record for this book is available from the British Library.

A catalog record for this book is available from the Library of Congress.

Printed and bound by CPI Group (UK) Ltd, Croydon, CR0 4YY

Contents

Introduction

Khrushchev's life was framed around Stalin. From their first meeting in 1925 until the completion of his memoirs shortly before his death, Khrushchev analysed and re-analysed his relationship with Stalin. This is the story of how a pre-revolutionary labour activist, one who flirted with Trotskyism, became a convinced Stalinist, was first mesmerised and then appalled by the personality of Stalin, and in the process of rejecting Stalin, rejected Stalinism as well, reintroducing towards the end of his rule debates about the role of the party in the economy that had not been current since the early 1920s. Khrushchev's evolution as a Stalinist was not untypical. He was a legal labour activist before the revolution; he did not join the revolutionary underground but preferred to be with the masses, organising at the work place, distributing literature, running a workers' retail co-operative. During 1917 he was a classic member of the revolutionary "sub elite", the middle rank activist who spread the word and served on a local soviet. As with many such activists, who favoured labour militancy, opposed the war, criticised the Provisional Government and welcomed the formation of the Soviet Government in October 1917, it was the civil war which forced them to identify fully with the Bolshevik Party rather than Bolshevik policies. Radicalised by the civil war, on returning to the Donbas mines destroyed in the fighting, he was frustrated by the near impossibility of getting things done and, unsurprisingly, railed against the incipient bureaucracy in the Communist Party identified by Trotsky. Nor is it surprising that such a radical hot-head should perform a radical zig-zag and be seduced by Stalin in 1925. Stalin made clear that "socialism in one country" was possible, and it was precisely the construction of socialism that Khrushchev was so keen to embark upon.

1

What was untypical about Khrushchev's career was its chance intersection with the lives of Lazar Kaganovich, perceived in the early 1930s as Stalin's deputy, and Nadezhda Allilueva, Stalin's wife. This meant that Khrushchev was not "building socialism" in a provincial backwater, but in Moscow itself, in charge, aged 40, of the most prestigious construction project in the country, the Moscow Metro. No wonder Khrushchev backed Stalin enthusiastically and shared none of the doubts of those who had experienced the famine of 1932–3. It was very easy for him to see any criticism of his herculean efforts in Moscow as the work of "enemies". Khrushchev never doubted that there were "enemies" opposed to the socialist construction in which he was engaged, but when Stalin's purges began, he was soon concerned that the policy of arresting people "just in case" they were enemies was leading to injustice. By the time Nikolai Ezhov was removed as Commissar for Internal Affairs towards the end of 1938, Khrushchev was convinced that arresting people "just in case" was a conscious policy of the Commissariat of Internal Affairs (NKVD) and was delighted when Stalin made clear that henceforth the NKVD should be firmly kept under party control. When this did not happen, for example during the annexation of Eastern Poland in September 1939, Khrushchev was quick to take up cudgels against the NKVD.

During the war, Khrushchev, unlike the other party leaders, was constantly at the front, involved in the two major turning points of Stalingrad and Kursk as well as other lesser battles. As a result, he began to question whether Stalin was always right. Administering Ukraine after the war, he was soon involved in a series of new clashes with the NKVD, renamed the Ministry of Internal Affairs (MVD) in 1946. Questioning Stalin's decisions and challenging the role of the MVD came together in Khrushchev's mind when Stalin summoned him back to Moscow in December 1949 to deal with an alleged "Moscow Affair". Stalin had recently dealt ruthlessly with the "Leningrad Affair", a purge of supposed Russian nationalist oppositionists, and he was convinced that Moscow was similarly infected. Khrushchev dismissed the "Moscow Affair" as a provocation, and spent the last years of Stalin's life trying to decide whether the security chief Lavrentii Beria was having a negative influence on Stalin, or whether Stalin was actually responsible for making Beria the monster that he was.

By the time Stalin had died in 1953, Khrushchev was convinced that Stalin had made Beria and it was Stalin's crimes that had to be atoned for. It took time to remove Beria and Georgii Malenkov from the post-Stalin leadership, but by the start of 1955 Khrushchev had begun his project of reforming communism. The first step was to end Stalin's invented conflict with Yugoslavia, then to inform the party membership about Stalin's true personality. The subsequent political crises in Poland and Hungary in 1956 almost unseated him, but he was strong enough to move on to the next great reform, decentralising the economy and establishing councils for the national economy (*Sovnarkhozy*). This radical departure from orthodox Stalinist economics prompted Malenkov, Kaganovich and Vyacheslav Molotov, the figureheads of the old Stalinist world, to attempt to overthrow Khrushchev. Their failure in June 1957 enormously strengthened Khrushchev's position, as did his rather reluctant decision three months later to dismiss Marshal Georgii Zhukov as Minister of Defence.

Once Khrushchev had combined the posts of party leader and prime minister, he could, from March 1958 onwards, push his reform of communism forward still further. Convinced that Stalin's talk of the class struggle getting more acute during socialist construction had been little more than a spurious justification for the purges, Khrushchev developed the concept of the all-people's state. In the Soviet Union, he suggested, the class struggle was over. All people whatever their social origins were equally engaged in starting to turn the Soviet Union from a socialist to a communist state, and that meant effectively the construction of a welfare state: pension reform, a social security blanket, higher wages and flats for all. In this process the old state apparatus would begin "to wither away" and communist self-administration would emerge in its place. These ambitions were formalised in the party programme endorsed at the 22nd Party Congress in October 1961.

The dream of reformed communism was soon hitting the twin buffers of economic shortage and *realpolitik*. Khrushchev was a reform communist at home, but he was very much a traditional communist when it came to confrontation with the West. Khrushchev had hoped that a combination of reductions in conventional military forces and the targeted development of rocket forces could reduce the overall spending on defence. As the international situation worsened over the future of Berlin and the Cold War arms race developed, it was clear that the consumer economy could not be stimulated by simply reducing expenditure on arms. The dilemma seemed insoluble. In June 1962 the price rises aimed at balancing the budget caused strikes and demonstrations in Novocherkassk, which ended with at least 50 demonstrators being killed. In October 1962, Khrushchev's plan to achieve nuclear parity on the cheap by deploying short range missiles in Cuba fell apart.

For Khrushchev, the reformed communist system promised in the party programme would now only be possible if the economy could be restructured so that it produced more from resources that already existed. That is what attracted him to the reform economists of the early 1960s, who suggested that productivity could be increased enormously if factories operated according to such concepts as profit rather than simply fulfilling plan targets. This, of course, involved questioning whether the economic mechanisms established by Stalin and associated with the successes of socialist construction were adequate to cope with the new demands of communist construction, with its new focus on consumer and welfare needs. The relationship between the party and the economy had been fixed by Stalin in the late 1920s, but when Khrushchev resumed the pressure for reform in the aftermath of the Cuban Missile Crisis, he was prepared to raise questions about how best to organise planning in ways that echoed Trotsky's discussions of such matters in the early 1920s.

Khrushchev was pushing towards the decision that the institution which many of his comrades, particularly those in the apparatus, took to be the very essence of socialist construction, *Gosplan*, had, in fact, served its time; it was now hindering the growth of productivity and would have to undergo root and branch change. When critics said that talking about the profit motive risked the restoration of capitalism, Khrushchev's response was – let's risk it. By 1964, it was already clear that the target announced in the new party programme of catching up with the west within 10 years was hardly going to be met, unless there was a truly dramatic increase in the productivity of the Soviet economy. After the Cuban Missile Crisis, Khrushchev had had to agree to a rather cobbled-together compromise reform of the Soviet economy; it was his decision early in 1964 to drop this compromise and return to the path of radical reform that led to his overthrow.

Khrushchev did not simply want to settle scores with Stalin, he wanted communism to have a viable future, and for that to happen it had to address the inter-related issues of consumerism and welfare. Stalinists believed that heavy industry should have priority in a socialist economy; that had been what the battle with Bukharin had been all about in the late 1920s. Khrushchev had always accepted heavy industry as the bedrock of the future, but he argued that if the Soviet economy ran at its true potential, counter-posing heavy industry to the consumer goods industry would be a thing of the past, since both would flourish. What was preventing the Soviet economy operating at its true potential was the way the planning apparatus had evolved from the dynamism of the early days to the bureaucratic conservatism of the present. He wanted communists to accept that there was more to communism than *Gosplan* and ideological platitudes. It is on this reform agenda that the case for Khrushchev the reformer rests.[1]

Writing on the theme of "Khrushchev as leader" in 2011, Ian Thatcher suggested that "Khrushchev's removal was a sign of how frightened the party *nomenklatura* had become by the leader's determination to bring it to account".[2] The notion that Khrushchev was removed not because he was incompetent but because he was a threat to important interest groups within the party apparatus inspired this study. It is not, of course, an entirely new idea. Khrushchev's son Sergei has written a series of studies to make the case for his father as a thwarted reformer, who began to face opposition from the apparatus almost as soon as he had established himself as undisputed party leader with the defeat of the Anti-Party Group in June 1957.[3] Academic writing, however, has tended to stick with the consensus that Khrushchev was engaged in ever more "hare-brained" schemes which risked rack and ruin for the Soviet state, a position essentially not so very different from the official explanation for his removal from office given by the Soviet Presidium in October 1964.

The two outstanding biographies of Khrushchev in English are those by William Tompson and William Taubman. Tompson's is the more focused and the more sympathetic. He understands Khrushchev's dilemmas, but he is not convinced by Khrushchev as a reformer. For him, Khrushchev was increasingly frustrated by the sheer difficulty of influencing events, and that frustration led to anger and impulsive initiatives which were reorganisations rather than genuine reforms. In sum, "Khrushchev had not yet come to understand that his endless reorganisation could not achieve the economic renewal he desired; constant re-arrangements of bureaucratic flow charts angered managers and administrators but did nothing to change either their work habits or the pressures which gave rise to the most destructive practices".[4] Taubman's biography, while fascinating on family details and authoritative on foreign affairs, is dismissive of Khrushchev's abilities as a domestic politician. The furthest he will go on the theme of reform is to acknowledge Khrushchev's "daring but bumbling attempt to reform communism".[5] It will be suggested below that Khrushchev's reforms were neither bumbling nor purely administrative.

The Tompson and Taubman biographies were written in 1995 and 2003 respectively. They were thus both able to benefit from the full version of Khrushchev's memoirs, which appeared some years after the dramatic publication of the initial version published before

Khrushchev's death in 1971.[6] However, neither author had the benefit of reading the series of documentary publications produced in Russia in the 2000s. These cover: Khrushchev's years in Ukraine from 1938 to 1949 and his subsequent time at Stalin's side from 1949 to 1953; the struggle against Beria in summer 1953; the process of rehabilitating the victims of Stalin; the Secret Speech in 1956; the Anti-Party Affair in June 1957; the removal of Zhukov in October 1957; and the dismissal of Khrushchev himself in 1964. Alongside these volumes, the same decade also saw the publication for the Khrushchev years of the rather erratically recorded Presidium minutes. In 2010, Matthew Lenoe's debunking of some of the myths surrounding the assassination of Kirov reproduced translated extracts from some of this material. These documents, when taken together, enable the researcher to gain a far richer insight into the disagreements and tensions within the Soviet leadership than was possible at the end of the twentieth century.[7] It is the contention here that this archival material confirms Khrushchev's twin ambitions of ending Stalinism and, thereby, reforming communism.

In the West, Taubman's biography prompted a revival of interest in the Khrushchev era. In the area of foreign policy, the Cold War International History Project run by the Woodrow Wilson Center for Scholars in Washington since 1991 has produced a wealth of new material. The pioneer in research into social and cultural policy under Khrushchev was Polly Jones, who in 2006 published a collection of essays on the Khrushchev era; this was followed by other collections edited by Melanie Ilič and Jeremy Smith, and these, in turn, prompted a number of monographs and more detailed explorations of what life was like under Khrushchev.[8] The scope of this biography, however, is not a consideration of what life was like for Soviet citizens as Khrushchev cajoled them into enjoying life under communism, but why Khrushchev envisaged communism in the way that he did, although the dividing line is not always easy to delineate since popular dissatisfaction with the delivery of much trumpeted improvements in the standard of living could inevitably impact on the issues faced by the ruling Presidium. Nevertheless, the focus of this biography is not the experience of satisfaction or dissatisfaction with life under Khrushchev, but how issues were addressed when they appeared in Khrushchev's in-tray; the focus is the man and the ideas which inspired his youth and which he was still struggling to implement at the age of 70.

A short political biography, to help contextualise the flourishing work of others on the Khrushchev era, seemed a worthwhile project.

What prompted this author to attempt it was a longstanding interest in the concept of national communism. When writing about the Yugoslav communist leader Tito and his struggle to identify a specifically Yugoslav road to communism, the on-off nature of his relationship with Khrushchev was striking: in this story Khrushchev emerged in a positive light, willing towards the end of his career to consider learning from Tito's experiment in constructing an alternative model for communism. When, however, it came to national communism in Latvia in 1959, Khrushchev was very much the ogre, in the traditional account at least, publicly humiliating the Latvian party leadership and instigating a thorough-going purge. Reconciling such an apparent contradiction through a more detailed exploration of Khrushchev's life seemed a suitable challenge.[9]

Chapter 1: Becoming a Party Apparatchik, 1894–1929

Youth as a Legal Activist

Nikita Khrushchev was typical of the radicalised workers of his generation. He was born on 15 April 1894 in the village of Kalinovka, situated some way to the west of the Russian town of Kursk but scarcely 10 miles from what would become, as the Russian Empire disintegrated, the border with Ukraine. Owing to a clerical error when the Russian calendar was changed on 1 February 1918, his birthdate was recorded as 17 April and that is the date which he celebrated. The Khrushchev family home was primitive, an earth floor, an area where the livestock were brought in and a stove without a chimney. "When the fire was burning and the food was being cooked, you could not stay inside; the smoke went out the door", he recalled. Kalinovka was big enough to have a school run by the local administrative council but Khrushchev was frequently absent from school because he was needed in the fields – one summer he joined his mother and father in working on the estate of a wealthy local landowner, Khrushchev being put in charge of the oxen team used for ploughing. However, like so many peasants of that era, Khrushchev's father supplemented his income with migrant work in the growing network of mines and ironworks on the River Donets, the Donets Basin or Donbas. As he grew older, Khrushchev often accompanied his father in his search for temporary work and so he supplemented his village education in a school close to one of the miners' settlements. His first spell of work "as a kid" was to help a Jewish metal fitter employed in a Donbas factory, fetching and carrying for him. In this way Khrushchev had only some four years of intermittent education.[1]

Even as a youngster, Khrushchev was exposed to the political tur-
moil of Imperial Russia. In 1905 he was with his father in Yuzovka, the
largest town in the Donbas, later known as Stalino and ultimately as
Donetsk named after its founder, the Welsh engineer John Hughes.
Khrushchev was returning from a local school when he heard
rumours that a pogrom had taken place against the Jews; he later
recalled witnessing "rows of corpses" laid out on a street. Not surprisingly, his father sent him back to his grandfather's village so he missed
the wave of strikes which subsequently shook the Donbas in that
revolutionary year which almost saw the Tsar overthrown. However,
in 1905 even village life was far from quiet: as happened throughout
much of Southern Russia, the villagers of his native Kalinovka were
involved in a rebellion against the local landlords, attacking and pil-
laging the local estates.[2]

In 1908 the family decided to move lock, stock and barrel to
Yuzovka. At that time the town had 55,000 inhabitants: the centre
of town, known as the "English Colony", was where local society
gathered; but to the north, south-east and west were settlements of
workers' shacks. The Uspenovskii mine where the family settled was
some three miles to the south and here they squeezed into the two
rooms of a one-storey barrack-like flat. Unlike his father, Khrushchev
did not work in the mine itself but, aged 14, took an apprenticeship
with the nearby German firm Bosse and Genefeld Engineering, which
repaired and maintained the machinery used in the local mines –
hoists, conveyors and the like. Khrushchev trained as a metalworking
fitter, a skilled and relatively well-paid occupation which he chose
deliberately in the knowledge that "in the proletarian circles in
which I spent my youth, the skilled metal workers enjoyed the high-
est authority".[3]

Linking that authority to political action began for Khrushchev
in 1911. His exposure to the Social Democrats began while he was
still an apprentice with Bosse and Genefeld. His initial mentor was
Artem Skachko, a political activist who had moved from Petersburg to
the Donbas to avoid arrest. Under Skachko's guidance, Khrushchev
became an avid reader first of the weekly *Zvezda* and then of the
daily *Pravda*, the newspapers of the Social Democratic deputies in
the Imperial Duma, the legislative assembly established by the Tsar
after 1905; Khrushchev used to follow the accounts of their work
with interest. When on 17 April 1912 troops in Siberia opened fire
on unarmed workers of the Lena Goldfields Company who were
protesting that they had received no pay for several weeks, killing at
least 150 of them, the whole of Russia experienced a wave of protest

strikes. Khrushchev's plant was one of those to be affected, and he helped organise the one-day protest strike called by Skachko and other militants. Khrushchev was assigned two roles, first to ensure his fellow apprentices took part and second to organise a group of comrades who would prepare to resist the possible use of strike breakers. He also organised a collection to support the families of those killed, and it was this action which brought him to the attention of the authorities.[4]

As a result of his actions organising the protest against the killings at the Lena he was promptly sacked from Bosse and Genefeld. However, as a skilled metalworker at a time of rapid industrial expansion on the eve of the First World War, Khrushchev was not out of work for long. He moved from Yuzovka and sought work unsuccessfully in Mariupol, then for a short time he moved to Kharkov and worked in the Berlizov plant there but before the end of the year, old friends had found him a job and he was back in the Yuzovka mining complex, working at the French owned Rutchenkovo mines. Since this new job was some distance from his father's mine, he moved in with the family of a friend.[5]

Recalling his first political act during the Lena protest, Khrushchev noted that the local strike organiser was someone respected within the factory not only for his activism "but also because he was a highly skilled worker". Khrushchev was rapidly adopting the mind-set and lifestyle of an aristocratic worker. "Skilled metal workers", he remembered, "tended to look down on construction workers", who rarely took part in strikes; their class consciousness "was not at a high level". Khrushchev's own class consciousness, however, was developing as his contacts with other Social Democrats grew. When in 1913 the Social Democrat Duma Deputy for the local Ekaterinoslav Province, Grigorii Petrovskii, came to visit Yuzovka, Khrushchev was one of those informed where a secret meeting of activists would take place, a meeting which, in the event, had to be cancelled when the police found out about it. Khrushchev was thus one of the many "legal activists" of the years between 1905 and 1917 who were key players in the Social Democrat movement, but operated on the fringes of the underground Social Democratic Party.[6]

Like many such "legal activists", Khrushchev both distributed the Bolshevik daily *Pravda* before it was closed down with the start of the First World War, and organised readings of the newspaper in workers' circles. He became chairman of the local Sobriety Society, a frequent cover for workers' educational activity in Imperial Russia, and during the First World War, from which he was excused as a skilled essential worker, Khrushchev became active in the local workers' trading co-operative, being a member of its ruling board and accounting commission as well as sometimes serving in the shop. He was also involved in what he later called "workers' self-defence": because the only local policeman was a Cossack who liked to drink, workers kept order themselves, "beating up" those who transgressed accepted norms – "I grew up among hooligans", he later recalled in 1961. Like many "legal activists", Khrushchev was rather proud that he could sing the workers' version of the Marseillaise, but was "rather weak" on the theoretical fundamentals of Marxist doctrine; what mattered for him was "understanding the need for workers to unite against the factory owners".[7]

Equally, as a skilled metalworker Khrushchev was moderately well off. He would often recall that he had been better off in material terms as a skilled worker on the eve of the First World War than he was as Moscow party secretary in the 1930s. When he got married in 1914, he could afford a flat with a separate bedroom and living room-kitchen, and he could afford to stock it with the fruit and vegetables which grew in abundance nearby. There were even small bourgeois affectations: lemons were cheap, so tea with lemon was regularly consumed in the Khrushchev household, which soon grew as first daughter Yulia was born in 1916 and then son Leonid in 1917. Khrushchev was particularly proud of the camera he bought at this time, but after his marriage there were no more references to the motorcycle he had assembled from spare parts to impress his laddish friends.[8]

During the war, he moved jobs fairly often, but always within the same complex; this was partly to increase his salary, but also because he was engaged in strike activity in 1915 and 1916. In March 1915 he was involved in a strike in the Rutchenkovo complex, which began in the mechanical workshop; according to later accounts, he made a speech denouncing the war and when the authorities tried to detain him, a crowd of supporters protected him, enabling him to make good his escape. The 1916 strike took place in May and this time Khrushchev's role was a major one: Khrushchev "came to our shop and talked to the workers for a long time", one later recalled, remembering the preparations for the strike. Between these two wartime strikes, in October 1915, Khrushchev attended a miners' meeting addressed by the Bolshevik underground activist Lazar Kaganovich, a central figure in the Bolshevik underground hierarchy in the Donbas and someone with whom Khrushchev's career would become closely entwined.[9]

Kaganovich also addressed a local rally not long after the Tsar's overthrow in February 1917, which Khrushchev again attended, but the Bolshevik Party did not have much support in Yuzovka. When Khrushchev chaired a session of the newly formed Rutchenkovo Soviet on 29 May 1917, the agenda was thoroughly reformist: the eight-hour day, the housing shortage and whether administrative buildings could be used for housing, the free coal allocation to miners and medical services; these were the issues discussed, along with criticism of a worker for refusing to return to his military unit, an awkward topic for the anti-war Khrushchev. Those who met him at that time referred to his "popularity" and "authority": he was the only Bolshevik elected to the soviet, and he often had to explain why he was opposed to the war and the "capitalist" ministers in the Provisional Government, and why the Bolsheviks believed the mines and factories really belonged to the workers. During the July Days – summer demonstrations in the capital when the Bolsheviks were both accused of trying to seize power and condemned as German agents – Khrushchev forced his way onto the platform at a local meeting and, against objections from the Bolsheviks' Menshevik opponents, put the Bolshevik case.[10]

In the August 1917 elections for the Yuzovka town council, the Bolsheviks won only 6 seats out of 73, while in the September local soviet elections the Bolsheviks gained only a third of the seats. Khrushchev was still the classic "legal activist" of the Bolshevik cause, identifying more with class than party. Although he defended Bolshevik policies, he saw no need to join the party, while always acting in its interests. When in August 1917 General Lavr Kornilov, the Supreme Commander of the Army, tried to stage a counter-revolutionary military coup in the capital, Khrushchev was immediately elected to the local military revolutionary committee established to defend the revolution in Yuzovka; significantly, the local military revolutionary committee was entitled the United Military Revolutionary Committee, reflecting the strong presence in it not only of Mensheviks but of the Bolsheviks' other socialist opponents, the Socialist Revolutionaries (SRs).[11]

As elsewhere in the Donbas, the Bolsheviks' October seizure of power was not immediately welcomed and Khrushchev later recalled his clashes with the SRs at this time. The Yuzovka Soviet opposed the Bolshevik seizure of power and Khrushchev was part of a workers' lobby which urged the soviet to change its stance. On 31 October, the Yuzovka Soviet backed a Menshevik resolution calling for the formation of a coalition soviet government rather than one formed by Bolsheviks alone, and as late as February 1918 the Bolsheviks controlled only 45% of the seats on the Yuzovka Soviet. Khrushchev moved his activity from the soviet to the trade unions and by December 1917 he was chair of the Council of the Mining and Metalworkers Unions which sought to co-ordinate the growing factory committee movement; the leadership of the union as a whole, however, remained in SR hands.[12]

Red Army Commissar

It was when the Donbas sank into a cycle of civil war, foreign occupation and more civil war, that Khrushchev decided to join the Bolshevik Party. He explained his motivation in his memoirs: "Then came the civil war. It drew a line of demarcation between people and simplified the struggle. Who was on what side, where the Whites were, and where the Reds, were all immediately evident. Life itself drew a clear class line of demarcation."[13] And following that class line, Khrushchev sided with the Reds. On 22 December 1917 General Aleksei Kaledin began a counter-revolutionary advance from the Don region of South-East Russia, across the River Donets and towards the Bolshevik heartland of Russia; the miners of the Donbas formed a Red Guard to help the newly formed Red Army stop Kaledin in his tracks; the counter-revolutionary threat was real; in nearby Makeevka, Kaledin's bands had dissolved the workers' soviet and murdered 20 workers, dumping their bodies in cesspools. Khrushchev was one of the leaders of the Rutchenkovo Mine Workers' Detachment, which joined the First Donetsk Proletarian Regiment and on 31 December engaged Kaledin's forces near the Yasinovskii mine.[14]

   In March 1918, Lenin's Government signed the Treaty of Brest-Litovsk with Imperial Germany and under its terms the German Army was deployed to secure and effectively occupy the newly declared independent state of Ukraine. Yuzovka came under German administration and one of the first acts of the new authorities was to restore the pre-revolutionary managers to the mines, exacting revenge on labour militants like Khrushchev. As a result, Khrushchev and his family decided to return to Kalinovka where in April 1918 he finally joined the Bolshevik Party.[15] His first party assignment was to join a "committee of the poor". Although the Bolsheviks had seized power alone in October 1917, their action had forced a split among the SRs and by the start of December the Bolsheviks had agreed to form a coalition government with the newly established Left SR Party; the

Left SRs, a peasant party to the core, were tasked with introducing a land reform. The Bolshevik–Left SR coalition broke down when only the Bolsheviks were willing to sign the Treaty of Brest-Litovsk. Alone in government once more, the Bolsheviks decided to abandon the land policy of the Left SRs and introduce what they called a "socialist" policy for the land.

In February 1918, while the Bolshevik–Left SR coalition still held, the Bolsheviks had introduced the first "bourgeois" stage of the land reform, dividing land among the peasantry; from April 1918 the second, "socialist" stage would begin when individual peasant farmers would form large, collectively owned farms. Reflecting Lenin's class analysis of the countryside, the Bolsheviks argued that the poor peasants would be the key element in such a transformation of the countryside, carrying out a class war against the richer "kulak" peasants who would resist such a change. Reminiscing in 1960 when his Chinese rival Mao Zedong was busy establishing a network of agricultural communes, Khrushchev recalled how in 1918 he too "agitated for communes", but things had not gone well. Like many members of the committees of the poor, established at this time to undertake class struggle in the countryside, Khrushchev had precious little real agricultural experience, and class struggle proved difficult to ignite. The chairman of the local committee of the poor was soon "drinking with the kulaks" and had to be brought before a revolutionary tribunal. In practice the sole purpose of these committees of the poor was to co-operate with grain requisitioning brigades sent from the towns to seize grain desperately needed to feed the urban population. The strength of peasant resistance to this "socialist" policy forced Lenin to wind up the committees of the poor in December 1918.[16]

Mobilised into the Red Army towards the end of 1918, Khrushchev joined the Ninth Army in Tsaristyn and was soon a battalion-level political commissar. Initially he was based near Kursk, and involved in fighting half way between Kursk and Orel. This was not a battle with counter-revolutionary White forces, but action against the Bolsheviks' former ally, one of the many armed groups of Left SR insurgents which operated at this time; Khrushchev later recalled how difficult it was to combat the Left SR slogan "we are for soviets, but soviets without communists". Another early duty was to monitor the border with Ukraine, which remained under German control until early 1919; his task was to ensure that those wishing to leave Soviet Russia only took with them the limited number of possessions they were allowed. It was while he was stationed on the Southern Front, but not yet engaged in active fighting against the White General Anton Denikin, that he learned that his wife had caught typhus; she died just before he got back to Kalinovka to care for her.[17]

Khrushchev's active service against Denikin began towards the end of 1919 when his unit joined the forces in pursing Denikin to the edge of the Sea of Azov; by the end of the year he was in Taganrog, where his infantry division was transferred to the First Cavalry Army. From there, beginning in early March 1920 and continuing throughout April, Khrushchev's unit advanced along the coast of the Sea of Azov reaching the Black Sea at Anapa, capturing Novorossiysk on 27 March with the help of local partisans and then turning back to seize Taman on 1 May. Then it was mopping up operations further south along the Black Sea shore from Tuapse to Sochi.[18] During this campaign, Khrushchev was selected to attend a political course organised by the Political Department of the Ninth Army in Krasnodar. Delegates were housed in a former school for daughters of the nobility, with "a park, beautiful hallways and salons, separate bedrooms and a bedside table beside each bed". To his embarrassment, the Red Army men, unused to such luxury and the water closets provided, had wrecked the facilities within a few days. Khrushchev was very conscious of his lack of schooling and general lack of culture. While in Sochi he was briefly billeted with one of the many aristocratic families of Russia who had taken refuge there from the horrors of Russia's civil war. His landlady had graduated from the St Petersburg Institute of Young Maids of Gentle Birth, one of the most privileged schools in the capital. Nevertheless, she seemed to take a genuine interest in Khrushchev and the new regime he represented. He recalled in 1959: "They came to respect me ... We were still unpolished, uneducated workers at that time, but we wanted to receive an education, to learn to govern the state ... I remember the landlady asking me, 'Tell me, what do you know about the ballet? You're a simple miner, aren't you?' To tell the truth, I didn't really know anything about ballet at that time ... but I said to her, 'just wait, we're going to have everything and ballet too' ... I was certain there was a better life ahead."[19]

For the remainder of 1920, Khrushchev was involved in counterinsurgency operations in the north Caucasus. The speed of the White collapse in late 1919 and early 1920 was in part the result of an SR-led insurgency on the Black Sea coast. Once the Whites had been defeated, some of these insurgents turned their fire on the Bolsheviks. Khrushchev attended another conference of political commissars to prepare for action against "the rebel bandits swarming" through the area. Finally, in 1921, his unit was deployed in Georgia as part of the Bolshevik forces which between 15 February and 18 March overthrew the Menshevik Government which had been established there since May 1918, declaring the formation of the Soviet Republic of Georgia on 25 February 1921. Khrushchev was stationed near Kutaisi, but occasionally travelled to Tbilisi for briefings from the political department. On these journeys he noted the sullen attitude of Georgians to the occupying forces.[20]

The Rising Apparatchik

By autumn 1921 Khrushchev was back in Rutchenkovo as deputy director (political affairs) of the mine complex in which he had previously worked. Initially he was there as a member of the Labour Army, and he was not officially demobilised until 1922. As a member of the local party committee, he was involved in October 1921 in an initially unsuccessful attempt to re-open local coking ovens, as well as missions to send troops out into the countryside to bring in grain. In spring 1922 he recalled touring villages to urge peasants to sow grain, even though they were so weak from hunger "they literally swayed in the breeze".[21]

After just a few months of this work, Khrushchev decided he had to get a proper education, so that autumn he was part of the first intake to the workers' faculty of the Donetsk Mining and Technical College. In a move that he would later repeat, it was no time before he became the technical college's party secretary. In these roles he soon became a general trouble shooter. Not long after his return from the war, there was a strike at one of the mines and Khrushchev used bluff and common sense to get the strike called off. He recalled later how the workers "gave us hell even though they knew us inside out [because] we had worked with them before the revolution at that very mine". This was also a period of great personal happiness for Khrushchev. Nina Kukharchuk arrived in Yuzovka to teach political economy in the district party school in 1922; she also served as a party propagandist in the Rutchenkovo mine. Khrushchev attended some of her lectures and soon they were living together. They would later have three children, Rada (born 1929), Sergei (born 1935) and Elena (born 1937).[22]

Defusing the strike and similar successes meant Khrushchev's star rose. On 23 December 1923, he was chosen to represent the technical college at the Yuzovka Regional Party Conference; at that meeting he was elected to the party's Yuzovka Regional Committee and made a delegate to the Provincial Party Conference.[23] For all that he had taken a first small step up the ladder of the party apparatus, Khrushchev still had some of the attitudes he had acquired as a labour activist. During 1923 he began to be concerned at what he saw as violations of internal democracy within the local party, concerns shared by a certain Trofim Kharechko. Khrushchev remembered Kharechko as "having fought for the people during the revolution" and he was someone Khrushchev had known even before the revolution, someone he had helped to settle in Yuzovka. Khrushchev joined Kharechko in a campaign for inner-party democracy, even though Kharechko had openly backed the Declaration of 46, a document signed by those who supported Trotsky's call for the party to adopt the New Course. Khrushchev "actively and rather sharply spoke out against the secretary and other party workers" and later conceded that "objectively" this coincided with "the discussions provoked by the Trotskyists". Thus, to use his own words, "although in essence I never spoke together with Trotskyists, objectively my speeches were a support to the Trotskyists".[24]

At the time this incident had little resonance, but it would be significant later and, as Khrushchev confided to Kaganovich, his "Trotskyist" activity continued into 1924. Little evidence of this Trotskyist phase of Khrushchev's remains, but residual labour activist attitudes, and arguably also of Trotskyist concerns, came across in his handling of labour unrest in 1924. Early in 1924, when Mensheviks were trying to organise strikes in the region about low pay and difficult working conditions, it was Khrushchev who was, as a man of the people, sent once more to defuse the situation. This he did with a combination of firmness and humour. When the regional party leadership met to discuss the aftermath of the incident, harsh measures were called for against the Mensheviks, but Khrushchev could not agree. He argued that the party was not doing enough to talk to the miners, nor taking enough interest in the details of their daily life. The logic of such criticism was that the party was becoming an introverted bureaucracy, divorced from its working class base, a key element of Trotsky's stance.[25]

After two years of study, Khrushchev left the workers' faculty in September 1924. He had been so involved in political work – he had, for example, formed part of the Yuzovka delegation sent to attend Lenin's funeral in January 1924[26] – that he did not get awarded a diploma. Although he toyed with the idea of returning to factory work, the party had little difficulty in persuading him to take up full-time party work and his career was soon progressing.[27] In April 1925 he was part of the delegation which attended the

14th Party Conference in Moscow; at the conference he had the temerity to criticise the "petty bourgeois ideas and contacts" of his regional party secretary. Khrushchev and the other members of the delegation were photographed with Stalin, in honour of Yuzovka being renamed Stalino. This was an important turning point for Khrushchev. He had been enormously impressed with Stalin's conference speech, in which for the first time it was clearly stated by a Soviet leader that socialism could be constructed "in one country", without waiting for the anticipated world revolution. Yet he was even more impressed with Stalin's behaviour while the photograph was being taken. The photographer issued a series of instructions about where to look and when to smile and Stalin joked: "you cannot order us around". This comment, Stalin's speech and Stalin's general demeanour towards worker delegates like himself convinced Khrushchev that "Stalin really was a democratic-minded person" and so he became "filled with more and more profound respect for this individual".[28]

In July 1925 Khrushchev's career advanced further when he was made secretary of the newly formed Petrovo–Mariinskii District, which included one of the largest Donbas mines, and he represented this district at the 1st All Ukrainian Party Conference on 18 October 1926. Much of this work was essentially routine. He recalled in his memoirs his role in overseeing the work of consumer co-operatives, drawing on his pre-revolutionary experience, and his frustration that private shops did better because they were prepared to offer credit and "paid more attention to customers". However, although at a junior level, Khrushchev was also beginning to play an active role in the factional politics of the second half of the 1920s, always defending Stalin. Khrushchev's Stalin was not the Stalin of historians, of Machiavellian intrigue, of attacking first the Left and then the Right; Khrushchev's Stalin was the Stalin the regional party secretaries saw, the Stalin who was patient, who strove "to demonstrate his desire for party unity, and to show, if not respect, at least patience towards the views of other members of the collective in which he worked as a part".[29]

Khrushchev attended the 14th Party Congress in December 1925, the 15th Party Conference in October 1926 and the 15th Party Congress in December 1927. At the first of these assemblies he supported Stalin's attack on Zinoviev. Back in spring 1925, the Stalin–Bukharin leadership had decided to give tax concessions to the peasantry in order to try and boost agricultural production: Zinoviev and Kamenev argued that this was a concession too far, and that the only peasants to really benefit from it were the rich "kulaks". As this row developed, the 14th Party Congress was at first postponed, and then it was summoned only after it had been agreed that Zinoviev would be allowed to give an alternative report to the congress. Stalin wanted Zinoviev's report to be soundly defeated and the Ukrainian delegation, including Khrushchev, were carefully briefed as to which way they should vote: "even today," Khrushchev mused in his memoirs, "I think that our ideological struggle was fundamentally correct." When delegated to the 1st All Ukrainian Party Conference in October 1926, Khrushchev warmed to this role of scourge of the opposition, demanding on that occasion that "repressive measures" be taken against them. At the 15th Party Conference held the same month, Khrushchev vociferously praised the policies being pursued by Bukharin as government leader.[30]

Khrushchev's involvement in factional politics was strengthened by the reappearance in his life of Kaganovich. Kaganovich had been working in Stalin's office since 1922 and would join the Politburo as a candidate member in July 1926. Appointed to head the Ukrainian Communist Party in April 1925, it was inevitable that his path should cross with Khrushchev's. At a district party conference attended by Kaganovich, Khrushchev decided to approach him and make his formal acquaintance. He explained to Kaganovich how, back in early 1917, he had attended a rally which Kaganovich had addressed, and then asked point blank if Kaganovich was prepared to help him with his party career; Khrushchev explained that his ambitions were constantly being thwarted because of his brief flirtation with Trotskyism. Kaganovich was non-committal, but when, shortly afterwards, Khrushchev travelled to Kharkov, then the capital of Soviet Ukraine, and turned up at Kaganovich's office to make the request for a second time, Kaganovich, impressed by Khrushchev's openness, did indeed offer him a job.[31]

In December 1926 Khrushchev was given an apparatus post, he became head of the Organisation Department of the Stalino Regional Party Committee, which effectively made him Stalino deputy party secretary. As such, nine months later, he was the key player in the ouster of the Stalino First Secretary, which was demanded at a closed meeting of the Stalino Regional Committee on 12 September 1927. Khrushchev called for a Central Committee investigation into the affairs of the Stalino organisation, which Kaganovich promptly agreed to, and he was present at the meeting of the Ukrainian Politburo which decided that a new First Secretary be appointed. At the 15th Party Congress in December 1927 it was Khrushchev who publicly denounced the disgraced former Stalino First Secretary's "dissipation and corruption"; inappropriate behaviour probably had taken place, but Khrushchev had criticised the First Secretary back in 1923 during his Trotskyist phase, and the First Secretary liked nothing better than to remind Khrushchev of his errant past.[32]

Khrushchev's "Trotskyism" seemed far in the past. At the 14th Stalino Regional Party Conference on 10 November 1927 he challenged Trotsky's view that the party had become bureaucratised, by arguing that elections were held regularly and that the party was working hard to engage with the non-party masses through a variety of organisational forms. But it was not all party intrigue. In 1927 Khrushchev was involved in drafting plans to "green" Stalino. The city's bridge had been restored after the civil war, the sewage system was working, a tram system was under construction and the time had come, Khrushchev told the chairman of the Stalino City Executive Committee, to improve the appearance of the city with trees and green spaces which should be incorporated into the city's reconstruction plan. At a more mundane level, Khrushchev also introduced a clear timetable of meetings so that party, trade union, Komsomol and soviet meetings did not clash and were regularly spaced.[33]

Khrushchev's reward for the ouster of the Stalino First Secretary was not a regional party secretaryship for himself, but a further step higher within the apparatus. In March 1928 Khrushchev moved to Kharkov to take on the key post of head of the Organisation Department for the whole of Ukraine. This was a clear promotion, but the world of the apparatus did not suit him, he liked to be out and about. By July he had been offered the post of Second Secretary in Kiev and accepted it. Soon Khrushchev was mixing with the people again. There were demonstrations by the unemployed to deal with, demonstrations that were encouraged by his old enemy the SR Party, as well as a new enemy, the "bourgeois nationalist"; it was this struggle with "Petlyuraite teachers" that stuck in his memory. Nor had the Trotskyists entirely gone away; on 28 September 1928 he spoke out against the "counter-revolutionary tendency" which was trying to persuade workers not to buy industrialisation loans and thereby sabotaging the first five-year plan.[34]

However, a new and rather different enemy was on the horizon by the autumn of 1928. Back in spring 1927, Britain had broken off diplomatic relations with the Soviet Union. The subsequent "war scare" over summer 1927 had persuaded Stalin that the defence needs of the Soviet Union demanded more speedy industrialisation than Bukharin, with whom he effectively shared power, would accept. At the July 1928 Plenum of the party's Central Committee,

Stalin organised a showdown with Bukharin, out-voted him and condemned him as the leader of a Right opposition, resistant to the call for rapid industrialisation. Even before this, Khrushchev had moved to back Stalin: at the 2nd Conference of the Ukrainian Communist Party on 9–14 April 1928, it was Bukharin, whom he had so recently praised, that Khrushchev now criticised. The Rightists, he claimed, were refusing to take up the new posts assigned to them by the centre and thereby breaking party discipline; of course, these new posts took the Rightists away from positions of influence and into a backwater.[35]

On 14 July 1928 Kaganovich was moved back to Moscow to take up a post as a Central Committee secretary and Stanislav Kosior took over as First Secretary of Ukraine. Although during the civil war, Kosior had headed the political department of the Ninth Army, Khrushchev had been too junior a figure to know him well. Partly because he had lost his patron in Kaganovich, but also out of a genuine desire to do something about his lack of education, Khrushchev asked for permission to be sent "back to school".

Chapter 2:   Stalin's Favourite, 1929–41

From Student to City Father

In September 1929 Khrushchev moved to Moscow to take up a place in the Industrial Academy. It is clear that the academy itself had reservations about taking Khrushchev on, given his lack of formal qualifications, but after he had sought the intervention of Kaganovich it was all arranged. At the academy he did indeed struggle academically – the embarrassing "fail" for his English was tactfully erased from his transcript – but he was immediately thrown once again into party work and factional struggle. As Khrushchev recalled in his memoirs, within the Industrial Academy there was every sort of oppositionist. There were still supporters of Zinoviev, as well as the Right Opposition of Bukharin, but soon a third opposition group had emerged, the "Right-Left Bloc of Syrtsov and Lominadze".[1]

In 1929 Stalin not only pushed ahead with his industrialisation campaign, but the winter of 1929–30 saw the first, disastrous wave of forced collectivisation of the peasantry, accompanied by the deportation of alleged "kulaks" to Siberia. Poorly prepared, with no clear guidance issued on how extensive collectivisation should be or whether it applied only to peasant land or to peasant livestock as well, Stalin was forced to backtrack and on 2 March 1930 wrote an article in *Pravda* entitled 'Dizzy with Success'. Its theme was to blame overzealous local officials for what had gone wrong, rather than the policies which Stalin had himself pushed through. Not surprisingly, many who had supported Stalin in responding to the war scare of 1927 and pushing ahead with industrialisation in 1928, began to wonder whether with his approach to collectivisation Stalin was not going too far too fast. Wavering Stalinists, like Sergei Syrtsov and Vissarion Lominadze tried to use the 16th Party Congress on 26 June–15

July 1930 to commit the party to slowing the pace of both industriali-sation and collectivisation.

It was in this atmosphere of factional struggle that Khrushchev took his first move in Moscow politics. On 4 November 1929 he tried to get elected to the ruling committee of the communist cell in the Industrial Academy; he was not successful. "I remember how my com-rades kept proposing my candidacy for the presiding committee, but two or three times I lost the vote and was never elected … Finally I was elected to the inspection commission, but the truth is that later I lost the vote there again." Lack of success had no impact on Khrushchev's Stalinist loyalties. He defended Stalin's line in 'Dizzy with Success', even though he visited a collective farm near Samara around this time and found listless peasants begging for bread, "a situation of literal starvation" he later recalled. Not long after his return from Samara, Khrushchev's loyalty meant his Moscow career took a sudden and dramatic turn for the better when he was mysteriously summoned to the *Pravda* editorial offices and briefed on what he should do next. [2]

Kaganovich had been made secretary of the Moscow Party Committee on 22 April 1930, and on 26 April *Pravda* published the text of a short speech Stalin had made to the first graduates of the Industrial Academy. The published version of Stalin's speech was bland, but in the actual speech he had urged the academy to do more to combat the Right, since the policies once advocated by Bukharin were still defended there and, in the climate after "Dizzy with Success", the recovery of the Right seemed likely. *Pravda* planned a press campaign against the academy and the paper's editor saw Khrushchev playing a major role. On 26 May 1930 *Pravda* published an article repeating the line that not enough was being done to combat the Right in the Industrial Academy. In preparation for the 16th Party Congress, the Rights at the Industrial Academy had proposed nominating a slate of candidates headed jointly by both Bukharin and Stalin. On 28 May Khrushchev organised a meeting which "recalled" this delegation and instead nominated just Stalin; that same meeting elected Khrushchev secretary of the Industrial Academy Party Committee. Although Khrushchev was not elected as a delegate to the 16th Party Congress, he was provided with a guest pass and was thus able to hear Stalin's speech, which once again he found inspiring. Loyally, he at once organised a campaign to rout the Right within the academy, making clear that silent acquies-cence was no longer enough; all party members had to make a clear statement in favour of Stalin's policies or risk expulsion. By November 1930 Khrushchev could assure Stalin when they met and talked for the first time, that the situation at the Industrial Academy was secure.[3]

The Industrial Academy was located in the Bauman District of Moscow and in January 1931 Khrushchev took over as Bauman District secretary; once again he moved against surviving Rightists in the organisation. He recalled that at his first Bauman District Conference he was "greeted rather coldly by the delegates" and that during his speech "disapproving voices could be heard". One of those involved in the "tumult" was Lenin's widow, Nadezhda Krupskaya, whose "speeches did not fit in properly with the party's general line". However, if his activities in the Bauman District did not go down well locally, they went down well in the Kremlin. As Bauman District secretary he was invited to an expanded Politburo session at which Stalin spoke: Khrushchev was impressed: "the brevity of expression and the precision of the formulation of the tasks that were being posed won me over, and more and more I was filled with respect for Stalin, recognising his special qualities as a leader".[4]

This process was repeated in summer 1931 when *Pravda* got up a campaign about the Communard Co-operative in Krasnopresnenskii District, which was also reputed to be a hotbed of Right activity. After the paper's report of 13 July 1931, Khrushchev took over as Krasnopresnenskii District secretary, replacing the confirmed Rightist Martemyan Ryutin. By January 1932, Khrushchev was deputy secretary of the Moscow Party Committee under Kaganovich and a member of the key "architectural-planning" commission charged with the reconstruction of Moscow; by the autumn he was having regular face-to-face meetings with Stalin. Ryutin, by contrast, drafted and began to circulate a two-hundred-page programme calling not only for the slowing of the industrialisation drive and an end to forced collectivisation, but the removal of Stalin by force. He was arrested on 23 September 1932.[5]

Clearly Kaganovich had a lot to do with Khrushchev's advancement. Kaganovich recalled in his memoirs how he discussed the matter with Stalin and mentioned Khrushchev's early flirtation with Trotskyism and how he had outgrown it. At this point in the conversation, Stalin turned to his wife and said: "Nadya, that Khrushchev from the Industrial Academy who you mentioned as a good worker, is that right?"[6] Khrushchev's rapid rise in influence was not only down to Kaganovich's long standing support. As Industrial Academy party secretary he was bound to meet one of its most prestigious students, Nadezhda Allilueva, Stalin's wife. She and Khrushchev were roughly the same age; he seems to have become very fond of her and it was inevitable that comments on Khrushchev's activities should get back to Stalin. When Khrushchev took over as party secretary in summer

1930 she chose to come and see him, and soon they were working closely together, "she saw me almost every day", he recalled, and he addressed her as Nadya rather than the more formal Nadezhda. The association with Stalin's wife explains how he became an intimate of the Stalin household. He recalled attending dinner parties with Stalin and his wife and meeting "old man Alliluev", Nadezhda Stalin's father. These were pleasant meals; he recalled: "those family meals took place in such a relaxed atmosphere, with jokes and such like; Stalin was very human at those meals". Khrushchev and Nadezhda Stalin stood next to each other on the Lenin mausoleum on 7 November 1932, scarcely 24 hours before she committed suicide when she learned of her husband's infidelity.[7]

Khrushchev was not only a delegate to the 17th Party Congress in February 1934 but was elected on that occasion as a full member of the Central Committee, without going through the usual candidate stage. On the eve of the congress, on 24 January 1934, he was made Moscow party secretary. Although by the time of the 17th Party Congress he had witnessed Stalin's temper as well as his democratic spirit – he had been upset to overhear Stalin's vitriolic attack on a junior during a congress session – he was still "literally entranced by Stalin, his attentiveness, his considerateness, how well informed he was, and his caring and nurturing attitude". "I honestly had great admiration for him", he remembered.[8] Khrushchev's speech to the 17th Party Congress showed his absolute loyalty to Stalin. In Stalin's report to the congress he had addressed what he called "Questions of Ideological and Political Leadership". Accepting that the "party today is united as it has never been before", he asked "does this mean, however, that the fight is ended ... that we can rest on our laurels?" His answer was a firm "no". "We have smashed the enemies of the party, the opportunists of all shades ... but remnants of their ideology still live in the minds of individual members of the party and not infrequently they find expression." One clear example of this was the attitude of some party members to the formation of a classless society. "They began to reason in this way," he said, "if it is a classless society, then we can relax the class struggle, we can relax the dictatorship of the proletariat, and get rid of the state altogether since it is fated to wither away soon in any case." Communists who argued in this way "fell into a state of foolish rapture".[9]

Khrushchev echoed Stalin closely: "we must struggle against the incorrect understanding of some concerning the process of building a classless society. Some understand this problem in this way, that, they say, we can be happy, classes soon will not exist and there will be no need to undertake class struggle. Class struggle is not coming to an end and we must mobilise the strength of the party, the strength of the working class and strengthen the organs of the proletarian dictatorship for the final destruction of the class enemies, all remnants of the Right, Left and every other opportunist, who wanted and still want to slow our further successful movement forward."[10] Khrushchev was clearly not one of those advocating reconciliation with former oppositionists, something that other delegates to the congress favoured.[11]

Khrushchev could do more than simply be loyal. He was the practical man who delivered the goods. First as Kaganovich's deputy and then as Moscow secretary, Khrushchev's main concern was the construction of the Moscow Metro, which began early in 1934. Mining engineers were brought from the Donbas to dig the tunnels and the project was soon taking up more than three-quarters of Khrushchev's time. His control of the project was total. The chief US technical adviser recalled how Khrushchev would resolve differences of opinion between engineers by getting them to submit their ideas personally to him on no more than two sides of paper. Although the original target was to open the first line by 7 November 1934, that was allowed to slip and the revised target of 1 May 1935 was met. At this time Khrushchev worked closely with the chairman of the Moscow soviet, Nikolai Bulganin. When in 1935 Kaganovich was appointed to head the Commissariat of Transport, Khrushchev took over the post of Moscow Province party secretary.[12]

Khrushchev was revelling in his success. He recalled how, at this time, if there was ever an issue he was unsure about, he would phone Stalin and Stalin would nearly always agree to see him. Although not a member of the Politburo, Central Committee members had the right to freely attend Politburo meetings and he "made frequent use of this right". Often Stalin would invite out Khrushchev, as Moscow party secretary, and Nikolai Bulganin, as chairman of the Moscow soviet, saying "Hey, you two city fathers, come over to dinner". Then there were trips to the Bolshoi Theatre with Stalin and Prime Minister Vyacheslav Molotov, sitting in the government box. According to an NKVD report he was shown when he officially took over from Kaganovich, the political situation in the capital was stable with just a few wildcat strikes and the odd Menshevik-inspired leaflet to undermine the calm. Although he had clashed with Lenin's widow when in charge of the Bauman District, now he had to work with her since it was her job to investigate complaints against party members. Khrushchev would receive the complainants, do what he felt he could and report back to Krupskaya, sometimes in person; he therefore felt ambivalent when later, in 1937–8, she came under fire from Stalin.[13]

The Purges in Moscow

As Moscow party chief Khrushchev had no choice but to comment on the trial of Zinoviev and Kamenev held in August 1936. The speech he made was a standard piece of propaganda, which condemned the accused, demanded the death penalty for Trotsky as well as the accused, and broadened the net of conspiracy further by noting how Bukharin, supposedly through intermediaries, had been in contact with Zinoviev; the party had been indulgent towards Bukharin, Khrushchev recalled – a lot had happened since 1919 when he remembered being "enchanted" by a speech Bukharin made to the soldiers of the Ninth Army.[14] Khrushchev's speech on this occasion gave some glimpses into the views of a convinced Stalinist. Khrushchev did not deny that 1932, the year when the failings of collectivisation had helped create famine, had been "the most difficult year", but for him it was then that the party had overcome its difficulties and had gathered in strength; Stalin's opponents, on both Left and Right, saw 1932 as the year when Stalin's refusal to acknowledge the reality of the famine meant he had gone too far and needed to be removed. Consistent with his views expressed at the 17th Party Congress that the party should mobilise against its enemies, Khrushchev argued that now, in 1936, when it had been decided to strike out at the party's enemies, the party should strike hard. He joined the call for more vigilance in the hunt for enemies, but he also introduced a significant note of caution by criticising those people who decided to expel members from the party "to be on the safe side".[15] As the purges developed, Khrushchev continued to see this as an important distinction as he became increasingly critical of those whose zeal for combatting enemies led them to discipline the innocent, just to be on the safe side.

By the beginning of 1937 Stalin was determined to remove from the Central Committee those who he felt were conciliators at heart, those who at the time of the 17th Party Congress had experienced "foolish rapture" and talked about how the class struggle could be relaxed. Throughout the autumn of 1936 a vigilance campaign had been underway, targeting Trotskyite wreckers, and on 16 January 1937 Pavel Postyshev was dismissed as the First Secretary of the Kiev Party Committee and the Ukrainian First Secretary, Kosior, was criticised for a lack of vigilance in this regard. Postyshev had clashed with Stalin once before. Back in January 1933, at a time when Stalin was first beginning to argue that "the growth of power of the Soviet state will intensify the resistance of the last remnants of the dying classes", Postyshev had suggested that "shouting about kulaks, wreckers, officers and Petlyuraites" did nothing to address such practical tasks as getting the harvest in. Postyshev was more and more convinced that the problems the country faced had little to do with Trotskyite wreckers. Sergo Ordzhonikidze, the Commissar for Heavy Industry, felt the same: he had publicly questioned whether wrecking was the problem it seemed and had intervened with Stalin when his deputy, Georgii Pyatakov, had been arrested and made the key defendant in the second great show trial of 23–30 January 1937. Instructed by Stalin to give a report on wrecking to the February–March 1937 Plenum, Ordzhonikidze committed suicide on 18 February. At this plenum, at which Molotov attacked "limiters of tempo" and "wreckers" and Ezhov called for a vigilance campaign, Postyshev again expressed his reservations.[16]

Khrushchev expressed no such doubts at this time in public. At a mass rally in Red Square on 30 January 1937 he denounced Pyatakov and the others accused in the second show trial; he called for vigilance and then condemned "Judas Trotsky and his band who are preparing to sell to the German and Japanese imperialists Ukraine and the Far East".[17] However, in private at the February–March 1937 Plenum he was more measured. Stalin repeated his mantra that "it is necessary to shatter and discard the rotten theory to the effect that with every step of progress which we make the class struggle here is bound to die down ... this is not only a rotten theory, but also a dangerous theory, for it lulls people to sleep ... On the contrary, the greater our progress, the greater our successes, the more embittered the remnants of the smashed exploiting classes will become, the more quickly they will resort to sharper forms of struggle." Vigilance was essential, since "the real wrecker will show success in his work from time to time".[18] One of the key issues discussed at this plenum was whether or not Bukharin should be put on trial and executed. Despite this almost hysterical atmosphere created by Stalin's speech, Khrushchev engaged in none of the baiting or aggressive interrogation of Bukharin that characterised the behaviour of Molotov and Kaganovich. He simply sought factual clarifications: had there been talk between Bukharin and his alleged supporters of establishing "a second Central Committee", and why had Rykov failed to report the appearance of an anti-party document to his local party cell? When it came to the fate of both Bukharin and Rykov, Khrushchev voted for expulsion from the party and a trial, but, like Postyshev, he opposed the imposition of the death penalty.[19]

Stalin still had work to do before the mass purges could begin. In spring 1937 internal party elections took place and an "oral order" went out to the effect that the NKVD had to approve all those nominated for party posts. As Khrushchev would repeatedly stress when looking back on these events "the security agencies that were supposed to be under the control of the party instead became higher than the elective organisation, and they did what they wanted".[20] The result was that when the next Central Committee Plenum was held on 23–29 June it both expelled 31 members of the Central Committee and endorsed the report on the "Plot Propagated in all Structures of the Party and State" prepared by Stalin's recently appointed security chief, Nikolai Ezhov. On 2 July the Politburo initiated the first of a series of "mass actions" against potential members of a fifth column, and on 31 July the third show trial of Bukharin, Rykov and others was agreed. As the first mass operation began, Khrushchev reported to Stalin on 10 July that 41,305 criminal and kulak elements had been identified in Moscow and its province, of whom 33,436 were actively criminal; of them 6,500 deserved the death penalty and 26,936 exile; the requisite troika, on which Khrushchev would sit, had been established to implement summary justice.[21]

At the time Khrushchev had no reason to question the role of the NKVD and carried out his duties unquestioningly. He was responsible for organising conferences of both the Moscow and Moscow Provincial party organisations in May and early June. During the Moscow Conference he was the consummate Stalinist. Boris Treivas had worked with Khrushchev since 1931 when he was in Bauman District, but in April 1937 Treivas was found not only to have issued party cards to 19 people later discovered to be Trotskyists, but had tried to protect his associates and thus "hinder" the work of the NKVD; Khrushchev expelled him from the ruling bureau of the city party and denounced him as an enemy of the people; he was then arrested.[22]

As the proceedings of the Moscow Conference began, Khrushchev was telephoned by Ezhov and told that one of the delegates proposed for election to the committee was about to be arrested and that he should ensure therefore that measures were taken to avoid the embarrassment of that person being elected; Khrushchev did what was required. However, shortly afterwards he was contacted by Georgii Malenkov, then the head of the Department of Party Administration, and told that the prominent Old Bolshevik, Emalyan Yaroslavskii, a one-time scourge of Trotsky, was to be arrested and so he too should not be elected to the committee. This was more difficult, Yaroslavskii was a well-known and popular figure, and when Khrushchev began to lobby against him, some delegates stubbornly insisted on voting for him and even wrote to Stalin complaining about Khrushchev's behaviour. Since Khrushchev had been careful to consult with Stalin at every stage of this affair, nothing came of the complaint, and Yaroslavskii, although elected to the committee, was arrested shortly afterwards.[23]

Khrushchev's behaviour was rather different at the Moscow Provincial Conference. Here he decided to confront a case of expulsion "to be on the safe side". One of those to be elected to the provincial committee had the same, unusual surname as the organiser of the counter-revolutionary uprising in Kaluga in 1918. Rumours began to circulate that the Brandt who had organised that uprising nearly 20 years previously was the father of the Brandt who now stood for election to the provincial committee. Khrushchev took the case to Stalin, vouched for Brandt and explained that it was just a silly rumour; Brandt was duly elected to the provincial committee. A rather similar incident even occurred with Malenkov. Malenkov was summarising his party career, as was required, when he mentioned that he had spent some time during the civil war in Orenburg. A delegate jumped up and said that Orenburg had been full of Whites, and perhaps Malenkov was a secret White. It took Khrushchev some time to persuade delegates that this was not the case.[24]

Khrushchev's dividing line between vigilance and a paranoid revelling in excess was also apparent in his attitude to the tone of the resolution on vigilance that was supposed to be passed by the Moscow Provincial Conference, since it included the phrase "sharpening knives against masked enemies". So he went to see Stalin and asked Stalin whether he would consider editing the wording. As Khrushchev recalled: "The political evaluation of the resolution was unrecognisable. All the 'not yet defeated enemies of the people' had been crossed out by Stalin. Passages about the need for vigilance remained, but they would have been considered fairly moderate for those times." The text of the resolution was "not in keeping with the tone of our party press". Khrushchev's speech on this occasion was nevertheless blood curdling enough, telling delegates "this is a struggle with the man who sits next to you, who hails your successes and our party's achievements, while at the same time squeezing the revolver in his pocket".[25]

It was in the climate of growing hysteria between the Moscow and Moscow Provincial conferences that Khrushchev thought it wise to inform Stalin himself of his own brief association with Trotskyists in 1923 and 1924. Unaware that Kaganovich and Stalin had already discussed this some time ago, Khrushchev first sought the advice of Kaganovich, who suggested that Khrushchev should simply keep quiet about the matter. However, Khrushchev decided to ignore Kaganovich and not only tell Stalin but ask if he should mention it in his own speech to the Moscow Provincial Conference. Stalin at first advised against mentioning it, but Molotov, who was also present, thought he should; in the end Stalin agreed with Molotov. Stalin's only question was for reassurance that these activities had been limited to 1923–4; Stalin also claimed that he had once known Kharechko, Khrushchev's mentor in Trotskyism.[26]

Khrushchev's belief that purging people "to be on the safe side" was wrong can be seen from his behaviour during the purge of the Komsomol. At this time, Khrushchev confidently informed the female friend of an activist who had been arrested that there was no reason for her to fear her own arrest since, when she had been acquainted with the arrested man, it had been before the start of his alleged spying career for Germany; the woman was nonetheless arrested shortly afterwards. Khrushchev made a similar error of judgement when in 1937 he arranged for Rykov's daughter to be given a teaching job; she was arrested in 1938.[27] On 10 August he told the Moscow Provincial Committee about his concerns. The Komsomol had been a bit "holier than thou" when it claimed that, unlike the party, it had not been penetrated by enemies. There was a problem with the Komsomol, it did need to be purged, but every case had to be investigated properly, contacts had to be proved: "we have incidents", he said, "when they begin to investigate a connection 'ten knees away', someone somewhere once walked along the same street". He gave as an example of how things should be done the case of the director of the Moscow tram system: he had once worked in Belgium, had joined the Belgian Communist Party and had come to Moscow as part of a workers' delegation; at first that seemed to be the only reason for his arrest, and since Khrushchev knew the man, he had decided to investigate; yet when Khrushchev went to visit him after his arrest and saw the evidence that he had given information in return for money, he was convinced. Arrests needed to be based on facts like these, he said, and sometimes the NKVD's evidence needed to be checked.[28]

As a member of the Central Committee, Khrushchev did not receive materials relating to Politburo meetings, but he did receive material sent out by Stalin and in 1937 this was, as he later recalled, an "entire books' worth" of verified confessions. "No doubts arose in my mind at that time about the authenticity of the documents" for "when Stalin was exposing 'enemies of the people' I had thought him very perspicacious". As he later pointed out, the confessions he was shown, like that of Vlas Chubar', had been signed by the accused on every page. The arrest of General Iona Yakir, however, did surprise him. Yakir had been an assistant commander of Red Army forces in Ukraine and Crimea in 1928 and Khrushchev had known him then and considered him a friend. Not long before his arrest Yakir had visited Khrushchev in his dacha and the two men had gone for a long walk. Khrushchev's response to Yakir's arrest is telling. He recalled both sadness that his comrade had turned traitor, and concern lest "I also might be affected". Since Khrushchev knew himself to be innocent, he was already aware that the principle of arresting people "to be on the safe side" might involve him in the affair. That impression must have been reinforced when, at a meeting with Stalin about this time, Stalin casually dropped into the conversation that the recently arrested Commissar for Posts and Telecommunications had given evidence against Khrushchev; Khrushchev answered Stalin firmly that this could not be the case, since there was nothing for him to testify about.[29]

As more and more arrests took place in Moscow, it was inevitable that others he considered his friends were arrested. Grigorii Kaminskii had been rector of the Industrial Academy when Khrushchev was party secretary, and so they met virtually daily; thereafter, like Khrushchev, he had served as Bauman, and Krasnaya Presnya District Secretary, so their close acquaintance continued. Looking back in later life, Khrushchev considered "Grisha" one of his closest friends of the day. Kaminskii had gone on to become Commissar of Health and in that capacity had signed the false death certificate which stated that Ordzhonikidze had died of heart failure. At the 23–29 June 1937 Plenum Kaminskii, partly echoing the hysteria of the time, had reported on rumours dating back to the civil war years that Lavrentii Beria, then the Caucasus First Secretary but soon to replace Ezhov as security chief, had been a spy in 1919 when the British had occupied Azerbaijan. After a break in proceedings, it was announced that Kaminskii had been expelled from the party and arrested. Allegations like this could not be made about those close to Stalin.[30]

Khrushchev was equally surprised by the arrest of his former Moscow Second Secretary, Natan Margolin, who had gone on to become Dnepropetrovsk First Secretary: "I simply could not accept that Margolin was an enemy of the people", he recalled. Another of those arrested and executed was an old comrade from the Donbas workers' faculty, Vasilii Simochkin, who had also served as a district secretary in Moscow, then as the Ivanovo Voznesensk First Secretary. It is not clear if Khrushchev raised this case with Stalin, but Stalin raised it with him. Stalin confided somewhat later that the arrest and execution of Simochkin had been an error and that he had been innocent of all charges. NKVD error seems to have been sufficient explanation for Khrushchev. As he recalled, "I saw things through the eyes of Stalin and repeated arguments I had heard from Stalin"; there were enemies, but the NKVD could not always be trusted to get the job done properly when blinded by its own blood-curdling rhetoric.[31]

The Purges in Ukraine

In August 1937 a high level delegation, led by Molotov and including Khrushchev, was sent to Kiev to attend the plenum of the Ukrainian Communist Party. Molotov criticised the mistakes of the leadership and called for dismissals; the Ukrainians refused to respond.[32] Their refusal to act led to Stalin's decision of 27 January 1938 to send Khrushchev to Ukraine. Stalin was clearly convinced that the purge in Ukraine had not been carried out with sufficient vigour. Whereas in most parts of the country the arrest targets for the mass operations had been agreed and reached by the start of 1938, in the second week of February Stalin and Ezhov imposed new quotas for arrests in Ukraine. At the end of January a new NKVD chief was appointed by Ezhov for Ukraine, Aleksandr Uspenskii, and by the middle of February the two men were in Kiev; as Khrushchev told the 14th Ukrainian Party Congress in June 1938, once Ezhov got to work "almost the whole party leadership turned out to be hostile". The purge of the Ukrainian party could have involved as many as 54,000 executions since NKVD documents showed how the proportion of those arrested who received the death penalty increased to nearly 100% after Khrushchev's arrival in Kiev.[33] When Khrushchev arrived in Kiev he learned that there were no first secretaries in Chernigov, Vinnitsa and Moldava regions, no second secretaries in Odessa and Dnepropetrovsk regions, and that only one region had a third secretary; nine people's commissar posts were also vacant.[34]

Between February and June 1938 all 12 provincial first secretaries in Ukraine were replaced, as were most second secretaries. In the army all corps and division commanders were replaced. At rank-and-file level expulsion rates reached 18–20%; between June 1937 and June 1938 over 50% of party cell secretaries were replaced. Khrushchev himself recalled that as he tried to establish his new administration "there were no party provincial secretaries left, nor chairmen of provincial soviets"; he travelled from Moscow with a ready-made team of some 20 administrators. When called back to consult with Stalin, Khrushchev was told he should take on, in addition to being Ukrainian First Secretary, the posts of Kiev and Kiev provincial secretary, which he did on 17 April.[35] Just before Khrushchev's assignment to Kiev, at the 11 January 1938 Plenum, Khrushchev was made a candidate member of the Politburo.

The main business of that January plenum was to support a resolution of which Khrushchev whole-heartedly approved, since it would ostensibly end the practice of expelling party members "just in case". Postyshev, who in February 1937 had been removed from Ukraine to the provincial backwater of Kuibyshev for questioning whether innocent party members were being expelled, was now used as a scape goat. He was charged with having gone to the other extreme and, "to be on the safe side", he had decided to disband some 30 party district committees. Postyshev was called on to defend his actions and was subjected to aggressive grilling by Kaganovich, Malenkov, Molotov, Beria and Ezhov; Khrushchev once again eschewed histrionics and tried to clarify the accuracy of Postyshev's claim that he had struggled to find suitable people to promote in the place of those dismissed for political unreliability. Khrushchev knew Postyshev slightly; in April 1925, at the time of the 14th Party Conference, he had shared accommodation with Postyshev in Moscow.[36]

Once established in Kiev, Khrushchev stood by his policy and that adopted at the January plenum. Correct procedure was important since it was essential not to arrest the innocent: "comrades, we must unmask and relentlessly destroy all enemies of the people; but we must not allow a single honest Bolshevik to be harmed, we must conduct a struggle against slanderers". Khrushchev's report to the 14th Ukrainian Party Congress, 13–18 June 1938, included the fact that between January and May 1938 3,135 people had been restored to the party's ranks when accusations against them had been dropped.[37] When Mikhail Kostenko, the Kiev Second Secretary, was arrested Khrushchev decided to investigate and went to the NKVD interrogation centre where Kostenko was brought from his cell; Kostenko, however, simply confirmed his confession. Before he died, Kostenko had left testimony incriminating Tikhon Cherepin, the Second Secretary for Kiev Province. Khrushchev contacted

Malenkov and argued that, as far as he was concerned, Cherepin was innocent and the testimony untrustworthy. This intervention saved Cherepin: on Malenkov's advice he was transferred out of Kiev, but no other action was taken against him; he died fighting the German Army at Odessa in 1941. At about the same time, Khrushchev intervened to prevent the NKVD from arresting the newly appointed Dnepropetrovsk regional secretary. The NKVD had discovered that the man concerned had given false information when he had joined the party: the NKVD assumed that this was because he was hiding a secret Polish background, but Khrushchev was aware of the truth of this, and eventually persuaded the NKVD that it was actually his Jewish ancestry that he was trying to conceal. As "Uspenskii literally flooded the Ukrainian Central Committee with memoranda about enemies of the people", Khrushchev's interventions were inevitably few and far between but they did reflect an unease about what was taking place.[38]

That unease was even clearer when it came to the role played by a certain Nikolaenko. One of the sources of information Stalin used for his assessment that vigilance was lax in Ukraine were the denunciations sent to him by a woman called Nikolaenko. When Khrushchev was appointed to his new post in Ukraine, Stalin called him in and said: "you pay attention to Nikolaenko". When Khrushchev met Nikolaenko he was not impressed: "She began telling me about the enemies of the people. It was just some kind of mad rambling [and] ... I began cautiously to correct her." Since both Stalin and Kaganovich seemed to value her opinions, she was difficult to turn away and became a frequent visitor to Khrushchev and soon, he recalled, she was "discussing her personal affairs with me" – "it was absolutely impossible to believe her". When, back in Moscow, Khrushchev explained to Stalin that he had not found her information in any way useful, "Stalin flared up, got very angry and came down hard on me – 'not to have confidence in such a person is wrong ... ten per cent of the truth is still the truth', Stalin said". Khrushchev, however, still took no notice of her denunciations, prompting her to write a letter to Stalin denouncing Khrushchev. That letter seems to have changed Stalin's attitude towards Nikolaenko and later he would joke with Khrushchev about how they had both survived her denunciations.[39]

Khrushchev certainly continued to monitor NKVD activity warily. On at least three occasions he investigated cases where relatives had insisted to him that the accused were innocent. In one case he checked, the person concerned had confessed so there was nothing more that could be done, while in the two others cases, he witnessed a "confrontation" between the accused and the accusers in which, on both occasions, the accused admitted their guilt. But sometimes such investigations were vindicated. Addressing KGB workers in 1954, Khrushchev recalled how "before the war" the Second Secretary of Voroshilovgrad Province had been accused of taking part in a conspiracy. Khrushchev felt it was so unlikely that he had asked to see the evidence. Having seen the evidence, he agreed to the arrest but continued to monitor the investigation, regularly asking for updates. He was pleased when the NKVD accepted that "a mistake" had been made, but then horrified to learn six months later the man had still not been released.[40]

When Khrushchev arrived in Ukraine there was no Commissar for Trade. In consultation with Stalin, a certain Ivan Lukashov was appointed, but then arrested almost at once; Lukashov had previously worked with Khrushchev in Moscow, and so Khrushchev was "badly shaken" by the arrest, since he "trusted him, respected him". He was therefore delighted when Lukashov was suddenly released, but shocked to learn that the case against him had rested on Khrushchev's decision when in Moscow to send Lukashov to Poland on a trade mission; this had been portrayed by the NKVD as secret contacts with Polish intelligence. When Khrushchev reported on the affair to Stalin, Stalin agreed that "such perversions and distortions do happen".[41] On another occasion, a man came to see Khrushchev and explained that he had been arrested, tortured, had confessed and had then been released; his confession had been to the effect that the newly appointed Ukrainian prime minister, Demyan Korotchenko, was a Romanian spy. Khrushchev informed Stalin, "who got very angry" and when they discussed the matter later, Stalin explained how the NKVD officials responsible had been executed. This prompt action by Stalin, Khrushchev recalled, "helped dispose me more favourably than ever" towards Stalin. As far as Khrushchev was concerned, his own misgivings about the role of the NKVD at the height of the purges seemed to be shared by Stalin himself.[42]

In autumn 1938 Stalin suddenly contacted Khrushchev and told him to drop everything and return to Moscow. His task was very specific, to build up the necessary reserves of vegetables to see Moscow through the winter. However, there was another side to the matter. After Khrushchev had left Moscow, the purge of the Moscow party organisations had continued. Aleksandr Ugarov, who had taken over from Khrushchev as Moscow secretary when he left for Ukraine, had proved unable to get on top of supplying the city with basic foodstuffs and for this reason had been unmasked as an enemy of the people;

he would be arrested in November. Khrushchev was instructed to handle this issue as well.[43] He organised a joint plenum of the Moscow and Moscow Province Party committees on 15 October and explained that although while he had been in charge he had "striven with all his strength" to expose enemies, many had remained. As a result, Ugarov was sacked and replaced by Aleksandr Shcherbakov; however, it was Khrushchev not Shcherbakov who on 2 November read out the Politburo decision on "The Errors of the Moscow Organisation". While he was in Moscow, Stalin asked Khrushchev to leave his Ukrainian posting and return to the capital as deputy prime minister. It was with some difficulty that Khrushchev persuaded Stalin that, since he had only recently found his feet in Ukraine, it made greater sense for him to return to Kiev.[44]

Despite willingly purging Ugarov as requested by Stalin, on the flimsiest of pretexts, Khrushchev still had reservations about the work of the NKVD. While in Moscow, he learned of the arrest of two of his assistants. When Stalin mentioned it, Khrushchev defended them as "good men, honest fellows", to which Stalin said that not only had these good honest fellows already confessed but they were giving testimony against Khrushchev himself, suggesting, in Stalin's words, "that you are not Khrushchev at all but someone else". Ezhov had convinced himself by this time that Khrushchev was actually a Pole.[45] In the circumstances, Khrushchev did not insist, but immediately on his return to Ukraine, he took up another case. When he learned of the arrest of the First and Second Secretaries in Gorlovka, he had immediate concerns. Although the case put before him seemed watertight, he noted that "the confessions were phrased in very similar ways". When he convened the Gorlovka District Committee to break the news about the arrests, some of the older comrades objected that one of those arrested was a local boy who had grown up in the workers' settlement. Khrushchev asked the NKVD to double check and the local boy was released. There was no intervention from Khrushchev, however, for those former Komsomol activists accused of plotting to shoot Khrushchev as he stood on the podium for Kiev's 7 November march-past.[46]

The NKVD and Western Ukraine

In the middle of November 1938, Khrushchev was told that Uspenskii was to be removed as head of the Ukrainian NKVD and arrested; shortly afterwards Ezhov resigned as Commissar of Internal Affairs.

When Ezhov's replacement, Beria, formally took over control of the NKVD on 8 December 1938, he had already discussed with Khrushchev the need to do something about the innocent people being arrested. Khrushchev later recalled that when Uspenskii was arrested, "something dawned on us".[47] Khrushchev was quick to join in the denunciation of the NKVD under Ezhov and the way it had acted irresponsibly, when it had acted beyond the power of the party. On 11 December 1938 he addressed a plenum of the Ukrainian Komsomol about an investigation into abuse of power by a certain NKVD operative, Usenko: "I am now convinced that those bastards in the NKVD", he said, had covered up the actions of Usenko. In his view "honest people" were needed in the leadership of the NKVD.[48]

On 13 December Khrushchev raised similar issues when he addressed NKVD personnel: some unsavoury types like "former traders" had been recruited to the NKVD; there was clear evidence of anti-Semitism among some of them; and "many people now in leading work in the NKVD would not have been allowed to undertake party work or go into battle", he said. On this occasion he referred to a letter he had received from a Komsomol activist who had been unjustly imprisoned but then released. Incidents like this happened, Khrushchev declared, "because most of the Bolsheviks sent to work in the NKVD lost their Bolshevism, they learned the ways of the Chekist and lost their party spirit". To correct this he suggested a simple organisational change, the party secretaries in the NKVD should be paid by the Central Committee and not the NKVD itself. "Comrades, an incorrect policy is being conducted, innocent people are being arrested, things must be checked, this sort of thing must be ended and actions taken which raise the authority of the party."[49]

Were these genuine concerns about the NKVD, or was Khrushchev simply parroting the new party line? For on 9–11 January 1939 a Central Committee Plenum had criticised the provocative methods of the NKVD under Ezhov. His concerns seem to have been genuine enough. At the 18th Party Congress on 22 March 1939 Khrushchev was promoted to full membership of the Politburo, but a couple of months later he put his career in jeopardy by speaking frankly to one of his old friends. In summer 1939 he received in his Kiev office Petr Kovalenko, an old friend from the 1920s, one of those who had been arrested during the purges but then released. Khrushchev listened to his tale of interrogation and torture and commented: "Do you think I understand what is going on in this country? Do you think I understand why I am sitting in this office as Ukrainian First Secretary rather than in a cell in the Lubyanka? Do you think I can be sure that they won't drag me out of here tomorrow and throw me in prison? Nonetheless we must work, we must do everything possible, everything in our power, for the happiness of the people."[50]

On 23 August 1939, the day the Nazi Soviet Pact was signed, Khrushchev was in Moscow and spent the day hunting; he was an excellent shot. What he and his comrades had "bagged" was served up for dinner that evening, with Stalin in an excellent mood: "there's a game going on here to see who can best outwit and deceive the other", he said, referring to his pact with Hitler.[51] Immediately Khrushchev had a new job to do. The signing of the Nazi–Soviet Pact opened up the way for the "liberation" of Western Ukraine from Polish rule. Khrushchev was closely involved in the operation to annexe to the Soviet Union the Ukrainian-inhabited part of Poland's eastern territories, following at the heels of the troops and arriving in Lvov on 22 September. He then took the lead in organising the vote of 22 October which called for unity with the rest of Ukraine, as well as the new Ukrainian Supreme Soviet elections of March 1940. Khrushchev later recalled encountering no resistance to the process of sovietisation, although when the collectivisation of agriculture began, he was careful to ensure that it was introduced at a modest pace. There was also a personal aspect to these operations. Khrushchev's parents-in-law came from Chelm Province, which under the Nazi–Soviet Pact was to be part of the Soviet sphere of influence, but under the German–Soviet Boundary and Friendship Treaty of 28 September 1939 was re-allocated to Germany. Khrushchev was involved in a dramatic dash to rescue his parents-in-law and get them to Soviet territory.[52]

However, not everything went smoothly during September 1939, and the target of Khrushchev's concerns was once again the NKVD which he continued to berate, both for incompetence and for a bullying attitude to party officials. At the end of September 1939 he had a massive row with Ivan Serov, Beria's deputy and the new head of the NKVD in Ukraine, someone who would eventually become a close associate. In a report to Beria of 27 September, Serov explained how Khrushchev had ranted to him about the NKVD "falling back into its old ways" and trying to bring party workers under its control. Serov had stressed that the NKVD "had grown out of the old methods" and where these continued "they would swiftly be brought to an end".[53] The question of the relationship between the party and the NKVD, and the role of the NKVD in arresting the innocent, was clearly still on his mind. When the Ukrainian Communist Party held its

15th Congress on 13–17 May 1940, Khrushchev forcefully re-asserted the leading role of the party: "the party is responsible for everything, whether it is army work, chekist work, economic work, soviet work – all is subordinate to the party leadership and if anyone thinks otherwise, that means he is not a Bolshevik". He also repeated his message to the 14th Congress in June 1938, that "slanderers" making false accusations had to be carefully watched; on this occasion he ridiculed those who "write names down in a notebook and proceed alphabetically", rather than carry out serious investigative work.[54]

Khrushchev was in Moscow in June 1941, rather frustrated because the purpose of this visit to Stalin seemed unclear to him. On 20 June he got Stalin's permission to return to Kiev, but no sooner had he arrived than the very next day he was summoned at eleven in the evening to the headquarters of the Kiev Special Military District. Here he was informed from Moscow that it seemed probable war was only days, possibly only hours away. The fighting started a few hours later at three in the morning of 22 June. After Kiev airport had been bombed, Khrushchev phoned Stalin to say that this had to be a real war and not a local provocation; Stalin agreed.[55]

Chapter 3:   Questioning Stalin, 1941–53

War Commissar

Although his precise designation changed during the war, Khrushchev was effectively a "chief political commissar" throughout the fighting, a middle man between his Politburo colleagues in Moscow and the commanders in the field. It was an uncomfortable position because he got the wrath of both. His immediate task when the Nazi attack began was the defence of Kiev. The Nazi invasion began on 22 June 1941 and tank units of the German Army were already nearing Kiev on 11 July. However, the infantry were far behind, so mounting an effective defence of Kiev seemed quite possible. The Red Army's resistance hardened and local propaganda spoke of Kiev being "a second Tsaritsyn", the town that in the Russian Civil War had never fallen to the Whites. As the Nazi forces drew nearer, the call went out to form a volunteer people's militia, but although the militia was very active, weapons were in short supply. When Khrushchev phoned Moscow to ask for extra arms he was told: "there are no rifles, cut some pikes; the rifles are only for Leningrad and Moscow".[1]

Worse was to follow. Khrushchev discovered that Stalin's dictum "not one step backwards" made the rational redeployment of forces impossible. It was clear to the generals on the ground that the Germans intended to "roll up" the Red Army forces still operating to the west of the River Dnieper. Stalin, however, refused to allow those forces to retreat across the river, and as a result by the beginning of August most of the forces originally based in Western Ukraine had been destroyed. Then, in the last week of August, the German Army crossed the Dnieper both to the north and south of Kiev; encirclement seemed imminent but when Khrushchev asked Stalin for permission to pull troops out of Kiev to prevent them being encircled,

Stalin would not agree. In the end, Khrushchev's order to evacuate Kiev on 15 September 1941 was given without Stalin's agreement, but effectively it was too late. By 15 September the encirclement was complete and on 19 September Kiev was occupied by the German Army; 103,000 Soviet prisoners of war were taken in "the most devastating encirclement of the Second World War".[2]

This was the first of many tactical disagreements between Khrushchev and Stalin which occurred during the war. The next concerned Kharkov. Initially Kharkov had been evacuated by the retreating Red Army, but by the end of 1941 the front had begun to stabilise. In the south Khrushchev's forces were able to retake Rostov on Don, and in late March 1942 Khrushchev attended a meeting at Supreme Headquarters which agreed to launch an offensive to retake Kharkov; this was the most ambitious of a series of local offensives planned at this time. There was concern among some generals, including General Georgii Zhukov, that these local offensives would dissipate resources, and the planning of the Kharkov offensive got muddled since for a while it was thought it might evolve into a more general offensive; the victory at Rostov on Don had opened up the so-called Barvenkovo Salient, which at its furthest point was only 25 miles from Kharkov. The offensive began on 12 May, but progress was slower than anticipated.

The Kharkov operation was based on the assumption that Hitler's target was still Moscow, but actually it was now the oil fields of the south. When on 17 May the Germans launched a pre-planned operation to the south it soon became clear that the advancing Red Army forces would have to retreat to the Barvenkovo Salient or risk being cut off. Khrushchev's generals called for the offensive to be cancelled, Khrushchev, fearing Stalin's response, delayed until the afternoon of 19 May before accepting his generals' advice and agreeing to contact Stalin. Khrushchev had hoped to talk to Stalin in person, but Malenkov answered the phone and Stalin refused to speak to him. Khrushchev could hear Stalin instructing Malenkov to inform him that the Kharkov offensive was essential and must continue.[3] More than the retreat from Kiev, Khrushchev saw this as a turning point in his relations with Stalin. "I had had occasion more than once to get into an argument with Stalin on one or another question of a non-military nature and sometimes I had succeeded in changing his mind", he recalled. "This was something I liked about Stalin, that in the end he was capable of changing a decision if he was convinced that the person he was talking with was right, if that person stubbornly continued to argue and defend his point of view, and that person's arguments had solid ground beneath them. In such cases Stalin would finally agree." On this occasion, however, Stalin would not budge and it was Khrushchev who had to face the consequences. After the inevitable and disastrous defeat of the Red Army on 29 May, Khrushchev was summoned to Moscow and he feared that Stalin "could not overlook this catastrophe". In the event, all Stalin did was to make an oblique reference to the First World War when the Tsar had put the commander of an encircled army on trial. Later, when Stalin suggested that the Germans were lying about the number of prisoners they had taken at Kharkov, Khrushchev told him firmly that the German numbers were completely accurate. The Red Army acknowledged 171,000 prisoners taken, but the Germans claimed 214,000.[4]

As over the summer the front retreated once again, moving ever closer to Stalingrad, Khrushchev went with it, being recalled to Moscow only for discussions on whom to appoint to defend the city. By August 1942, "with the entire city in flames", he was organising the transfer of key staff to the east bank of the River Volga, except for a small operational headquarters which would remain on the west bank, within the city centre. Stalin interpreted this redeployment as an attempt to evacuate the city and he rang Khrushchev to protest; shortly afterwards a delegation headed by Malenkov was sent to Stalingrad on a visit of inspection. The inspection did at least bring home to Stalin the seriousness of the situation. Not long after Malenkov had returned to Moscow, Stalin rang to ask if Khrushchev could hold on for just three more days: Khrushchev insisted he could hold out for far longer than that. This prediction of Khrushchev's turned out to be true, but that did little to smooth over relations with Stalin and irritations and disagreements continued. Often the issue was appointments: Stalin had doubts about the reliability of General Rodion Malinovskii because of his role in the Kharkov operation, but for the very same reason, viewed from the opposite perspective, Khrushchev favoured appointing Malinovskii to lead the Stalingrad counter-offensive: Stalin finally agreed, but only on condition Khrushchev watch Malinovskii closely.[5]

After the momentous victory at Stalingrad, Khrushchev was moved from the Military Council of the Southern Front to the Military Council of the Voronezh Front. He was surprised by this, because while he had been in Stalingrad, Stalin had told him to leave Ukrainian affairs to others, in particular the oversight of the Ukrainian partisan movement. However, his appointment to the Voronezh Front clearly meant that his responsibility for Ukrainian affairs was restored, not only for the partisan movement, but as the front moved westwards, for the liberation and reconstruction of Ukraine as well.[6] Disagreements with Stalin were fewer in 1943, but as preparations began for the Battle of Kursk, 5–23 July, there were several tense conversations about the need for reserves and where they would come from. Against expectations, the fighting in Kursk turned out to be more serious in the southern sector where Khrushchev's Voronezh Army Group was based than in the north, and although plenty of reserves stood in readiness over 70% of the casualties were in Khrushchev's sector. Later, Khrushchev felt once again that one of Stalin's orders needed to be adapted in the light of circumstances. The generals with him all believed that the angle of attack needed to be reconsidered, but in the light of previous experience no-one wanted to take responsibility for adapting the plan agreed with Stalin. Khrushchev eventually decided to send Stalin a coded telegram on the matter but, as before, Stalin refused to do anything other than insist on repeating his original order. As Khrushchev told political workers in the Ministry of Defence some 15 years later, "people need to be listened to".[7]

Khrushchev later recalled that he could not remember a single instance during the war when he took the initiative, contacted Stalin, and went to Moscow to talk things through. Yet on the occasions he was summoned to Moscow he witnessed the changes that took place in Stalin's demeanour as the war progressed. On 8 July 1941 he was "shell-shocked", "completely unrecognisable" and looked "apathetic and limp, his face expressing nothing". After the successful defence of Moscow at the end of 1941, he was "completely different ... and walked around like a soldier". By February 1943 he was "standing tall" and his mood quite different. And on the eve of the Battle of Kursk he was "glowing with confidence".[8] However, the combination of witnessing Stalin's frailty, and his pig-headed refusal to recognise military realities on the ground, meant that by the end of the war Khrushchev's hero-worshipping of Stalin was over.

Liberating Ukraine

As early as summer 1943 Khrushchev was actively preparing for the liberation of Kiev, in particular he was involved in planning and supplying the partisan operations which would ease the Red Army's return. As soon as Kharkov was liberated on 28 August 1943, Khrushchev was there to set up a temporary administration for Ukraine. He recalled addressing crowds together with General Zhukov, even though German reconnaissance planes were still circling the city. At once the organisational committees for party and soviet administration, prepared long in advance, were slotted into place; food supplies were organised, water systems restored and power plants repaired.[9] Despite such careful preparation, however, there was always a shortage of personnel and while still in Kharkov, Khrushchev took a decision which would lead him once again to have doubts about the activities of the NKVD; because of the shortage of suitable personnel he decided to seek to employ people arrested by the NKVD. On 31 October 1943 he asked the Ukrainian People's Commissar for State Security to release 41 intellectuals, including 23 writers and scholars, 10 historians and assorted composers, actors and artists. Earlier in 1943 he had chosen Vasilii Kostenko as the future leader of the Ukrainian Komsomol, and asked him for the names of fellow Komsomol activists from the 1930s. Khrushchev then sent those names to the NKVD, asking about their present circumstances; on being told that none of them had survived the purges, he commented to Kostenko: "they destroyed people for no reason".[10] He still had no faith in the way the NKVD had implemented the purges, and his relationship with Stalin was no longer what it had been.

Khrushchev was there as Kiev was liberated on 5–6 November 1943, meeting on a street a man who claimed to be the only Jew left alive in the city. Khrushchev set to work at once, the government offices were quickly transferred from Kharkov to Kiev, and Khrushchev managed to persuade a reluctant Stalin that the only way to restore the Donbas economy was to excuse miners and metalworkers from military service just as he had once been excused military service during the First World War. From February 1944 onwards Khrushchev was again both head of the Ukrainian Communist Party and head of the Ukrainian Government. One of his main concerns was the reconstruction of Kiev, and in his view this was one of his greatest achievements, particularly rebuilding the *Kreshchatik* complex in central Kiev. This was more than a simple restoration project: "beautiful buildings", he said, "resulted from our work".[11] A less attractive achievement was the resettlement of Crimea after the deportation of the Crimean Tartars on 18–20 May 1944. The Tartars were accused en masse of collaboration with the Germans and in their place Khrushchev was given the task of settling Ukrainians and some Russians on the vacated land. The settlers had to be persuaded, even bullied, to make the move and in the end some 9,000 Ukrainians took advantage of the resettlement programme. Khrushchev was also responsible for reconstructing Crimea's naval base at Sevastopol, and when this led to clashes with the Russian Ministry of Construction in Moscow, Khrushchev proposed that the peninsula should formally become part of Ukraine. Stalin refused.[12]

One of Khrushchev's key responsibilities was the restoration of Soviet power in Western Ukraine, where, in his view, the situation was "far more complex" than it had been in 1939. The Germans had encouraged Ukrainian nationalism, armed nationalist groups and formed a Galician SS Battalion within the German Army. However, the Germans had also taxed and exploited the Ukrainian peasantry, prompting the Organisation of Ukrainian Nationalists to establish a Ukrainian Insurgent Army (UPA) led by Stepan Bandera. The UPA, joined by veterans of the Galician SS Battalion, was determined to resist the return of the Red Army to Western Ukraine. However, the Red Army would also meet opposition from those who saw Western Ukraine as Eastern Poland. As soon as the Red Army crossed into territory that had been the eastern part of Poland until September 1939, it faced opposition from the pro-London Polish Home Army.[13] In this way Khrushchev found himself dealing with both Ukrainian and Polish affairs. When the Germans decided to evacuate Lvov, Khrushchev was there to act at once and prevent Ukrainian nationalists establishing a hostile administration there. From his base in Lvov, Stalin ordered Khrushchev to maintain contact with the new pro-communist administration established for Poland in Lublin. Khrushchev was thus actively involved in resolving such issues as the Polish–Ukrainian population exchange agreement signed at this time, and the future of Chelm Province which the Soviet Union had briefly annexed in September 1939 but now agreed should be part of Poland. In January 1945 Khrushchev was summoned to Moscow and ordered by Stalin to fly to Warsaw and help restore the basic infrastructure of the city, recently liberated by the Red Army.[14]

Those courses Khrushchev had taken during the Russian Civil War on counter-insurgency operations in the north Caucasus had not been in vain. Visiting Lvov on 19 September 1944, he called on the party not to be afraid of the armed Ukrainian nationalists. The party needed to act firmly and to establish good contacts on the ground; but when necessary, it should be ruthless and deport those who were clearly hostile – such a combination of carrot and stick would defeat "the Banderites". A month later on 11 October he again called for firm action against "this old and tempered enemy". He condemned the "bureaucratic approach" of those who thought that simply sending in the security services was enough; it was essential to work on the ground and that meant using the Ukrainian language which "should be used everywhere". Nationalist slogans and propaganda had to be carefully studied in order to be effectively opposed. Even if, as he conceded, an absolute majority of the local population might support Bandera, their views could be changed. Khrushchev's theme was the same in early January 1945. The key to security was not troops but locally recruited Destroyer Battalions, since "one local is better than ten outsiders". There should be no random burnings or arbitrary shootings, he suggested, even if it was time "to drop all liberalism" in combating the Banderites.[15]

The Banderites proved to be a stubborn enemy, and continued to occupy much of Khrushchev's time in the second half of 1945 and the first half of 1946. Dropping liberalism not only meant regular, small-scale offensive operations against armed national-ists, but also the detention of "bandit families". To speed up such arrests Khrushchev demanded that the requirement that two pieces of evidence were needed before arrests could take place should be dropped. These extreme measures had some success, and at the time of the Supreme Soviet elections in February 1946 the "bandits" seemed to have been defeated. When in summer 1946 persistent, smaller-scale operations were resumed, Khrushchev used a speech of 19 September to put the blame on the security services, in particular the fact that the Ministry of State Security (MGB) and the MV did not co-ordinate their activity in any way and only met when the party leadership brought them together. At about this time Khrushchev's own family was caught up in the anti-bandit struggle: his wife's uncle was captured by the "bandits" and killed.[16]

Governing Ukraine

Although the nationalist insurgency would rumble on at a low level for several more years, the worst was over by the end of 1946, allow-ing Khrushchev to focus on other urgent matters. Of these the most important was the harvest of 1946 and the growing signs that a famine threatened. In this context Khrushchev's relations with Stalin wors-ened dramatically as 1946 came to an end. By then it was clear that the harvest in Ukraine was going to be terrible. Although Khrushchev claimed he "did everything to make sure Stalin understood this" and warned him that under half of the planned grain delivery was likely to be made, Stalin's attitude was as implacable as it had been during

the famine of 1932: in Stalin's view the grain was there and the peasants were hiding it; Stalin simply refused to accept Khrushchev's
figures. As a pre-emptive measure, Khrushchev asked permission
to issue ration cadres, Stalin responded with a telegram describing
Khrushchev as "a suspicious element" and, when he reported to
Stalin in person, he got "the angriest reprimand imaginable". The
more Khrushchev tried to explain, the angrier Stalin got. "I reported
on everything to Stalin, but the only response was more anger: 'This
is spinelessness. They are playing tricks on you'." In this situation it is
not surprising that Khrushchev insisted to his subordinates, like the
Odessa party secretary, that their grain quotas had to be fulfilled even
though they too were in despair.[17]

   In response to the growing threat of famine, Stalin called a Central
Committee Plenum on agriculture on 21–26 February 1947. He asked
Khrushchev to give the key report, but Khrushchev refused saying
he knew a lot about agriculture in Ukraine but nothing about the
other republics. Foolishly, when Khrushchev heard the plenum report
on agriculture given by Andrei Andreev, he was quick to criticise it.
Stalin snapped at him protesting: "first you refuse to give the report,
and now you criticise it". But Khrushchev ploughed on, making the
situation worse, because he believed his point was a serious one: the
primary task, he argued, was for farms to harvest and retain the best
seed to be used for the following year's sowing; only after the seed corn
had been collected and put on one side should state grain deliveries
begin. Stalin insisted, as he had since the start of the collectivisation
campaign in the winter of 1929–30, that state deliveries should come
first and only once that duty had been met should consideration be
given to future supplies of seed corn, which would be distributed from
state reserves when necessary. When the plenum established a commission on agriculture, Khrushchev disassociated himself from two of
its decisions, repeating his views on seed corn and also arguing that
while spring wheat was suited to Siberia, it was not suited to Ukraine.
As he later recalled, "I was soon being accused of being against grain
requisitioning just because I had proposed retaining seed".[18]

   Given the suggestion that Khrushchev had opposed Stalin's policy
of grain requisitioning, it is perhaps not surprising that Stalin decided
to send Kaganovich to Ukraine to check up on him. Khrushchev was
removed from his post as Ukrainian First Secretary on 3 March 1947
and then three weeks later from his post as Kiev secretary, retaining
only his post as Ukrainian prime minister. Kaganovich arrived in Kiev
at the end of February, taking over as Ukrainian First Secretary on
3 March, by agreement with the plenum of the Ukrainian Central

Committee which was then taking place; the plenum dutifully accepted Stalin's view that the only way out of the current agricultural impasse was for seed corn to be distributed from state reserves and made available to the state and collective farms of Ukraine.

While Kaganovich began his investigation into the state of the Ukrainian Communist Party, Khrushchev "stayed in Kiev as a telephone dispatcher, to push through the seed and other cargo necessary to ensure good crops". In a slightly surreal atmosphere, the Khrushchev and Kaganovich families would meet and dine together at apparently happy gatherings, while Kaganovich tried to unearth evidence of Ukrainian nationalist intrigue amongst Khrushchev's entourage.[19] Some 15 years after the event, Khrushchev's supporters would recall how Kaganovich surrounded himself with "toadies" and purged cadres loyal to the party, terrorising the Ukrainian leadership; members of the Ukrainian intelligentsia were a particular target, as Kaganovich assembled a plenum to discuss the question of nationalism, a plenum held on 25 June at which Kaganovich lambasted the failure of the Ukrainian party to take "bourgeois nationalism" seriously and accused the Academy of Sciences of allowing someone "who welcomed the Germans as liberators" to write works of supposed scholarship. This was not the first time that Stalin had suspected Khrushchev of being soft on Ukrainian nationalism: when General Vatutin had been killed by Banderites at the end of February 1944 Stalin had initially objected to the inscription on the statue Khrushchev raised in his honour. It read: "To General Vatutin from the Ukrainian people"; Stalin felt this smacked of nationalism.[20]

In mid June 1947 Khrushchev fell ill with pneumonia. Treated with oxygen at a sanatorium near Riga, it was not until August that he was back on his feet and well enough to recuperate on the Baltic coast in Kaliningrad, before returning to Kiev at the end of that month. By September, Stalin's trust in Khrushchev seemed to have been restored. He decided that Khrushchev should co-sign all Kaganovich's memorandums, and on 26 December 1947 Khrushchev was back as party leader, although he now ceded his role as Ukrainian prime minister to Demyan Korotchenko, a long-term supporter.[21] Once Kaganovich had left Kiev, the campaign against nationalism was toned down. In particular, Khrushchev arranged the release of the "nationalist" poet Maksim Rylskii. Khrushchev also claimed that at about this time he came under pressure to explain why there was no statue of Stalin in Kiev; he responded that he believed it was wrong to put up a statue to people who were still alive.[22]

Once back in charge, Khrushchev continued to develop his own leadership style. Back in 1927 he had insisted that his Stalino party organisation was not bureaucratised, and Khrushchev was proud of the fact that, unlike at national level, in the post-war years normal party life continued: in 1946 and 1947 there were four meetings of the Central Committee, with three in 1948 in the run-up to the 16th Ukrainian Party Congress on 25–28 January 1949; over the same period Stalin held only two Central Committee plenums, in March 1946 and February 1947. Vladimir Semichastnyi, the Ukrainian Komsomol secretary from 1947 to 1950, recalled how easy it was to work with Khrushchev. Khrushchev constantly told him to be more forceful, to demand to meet ministers if problems arose and the needs of the Komsomol were ignored; if there were no suitable films for young people, summon the Minister of Culture – that was Khrushchev's advice. When Semichastnyi later clashed with Khrushchev over an issue concerning the Komsomol press, "at first he did not agree, but then became convinced that he had made a mistake, that the decision should not have been made without consulting the Komsomol leadership". As a result, Khrushchev "never signed a paper relating to the Komsomol without me having sight of it". At the Ukraine Komsomol Congress he refused to vet the speeches in advance, and said that, if they were good, he would say so at the congress, and if they were bad, he would say that too. Semichastnyi found that approach open and democratic.[23]

However, Khrushchev soon found himself involved in another clash with the security services. In a speech delivered in Lvov on 23 April 1947, Khrushchev had put the blame for a resumption in low-level Banderite activity on the decision to transfer all operations against nationalist groups to the MGB. Giving the MGB clear authority in this was an improvement over responsibility being shared between the MGB and the MVD, but the MGB's transformation from an essentially intelligence-gathering organisation to one engaged in active combat had created a hiatus which the "bandits" had been able to exploit. Khrushchev's concern about the new powers of the MGB was the same as his earlier objection to the role played by the NKVD; would the MGB assume it was superior to the party? Khrushchev was absolutely clear that the MGB's operations against "bandits" should be under the oversight of the party. A year later his fears seemed to be justified. In April 1948 the Ukrainian security chief complained to Minister of State Security Viktor Abakumov that Khrushchev was insisting that the security services should share all their intelligence information with the party leadership, something the MGB refused to do. There was then a direct confrontation between Khrushchev and Abakumov, and eventually Abakumov telephoned Khrushchev to back down.[24] On 22 February 1949 the Ukrainian Politburo condemned the actions of four MGB "special groups" which in the course of 1948 had beaten up and robbed innocent citizens accused of supporting the nationalists.[25]

In a speech given on 23 April 1948, Khrushchev explained how important this principle was, putting it in the context of the purges of a decade earlier. Khrushchev reminded his audience that "traitors like Ezhov" had been unmasked within the NKVD at the end of 1938, after which party control over the security service had been reasserted. That decision had never been rescinded and "was not a matter for discussion"; anyone who did not accept party control over the security services could contact the Central Committee and "get guidance there from Comrade Stalin". Khrushchev complained about the way the MGB spoke and expected others to listen and, moving from the general to the particular, he then described a case where he had insisted on reviewing the evidence presented by the MGB and had successfully shown to the security personnel how that evidence could have a very different interpretation put on it to the one favoured by the security services. This clash with the MGB perhaps explains why when he was summoned back to Moscow at the end of 1949, he did not act in line with Stalin's expectations.[26]

Moscow Again

Khrushchev's star was certainly in the ascendancy when he was appointed to head the Moscow party once again on 16 December 1949. At the same time he was appointed a secretary to the Central Committee and at the celebrations of Stalin's 70th birthday, on 21 December 1949, Khrushchev sat on one side of Stalin with Mao the new ruler of communist China on the other. Khrushchev quickly formed the impression that his return to Moscow and sudden pre-eminence resulted from Stalin's desire to reduce the authority in Moscow of Malenkov and Beria, and for the last years of Stalin's life Khrushchev was almost as frequent a visitor of Stalin's office as Malenkov. Kaganovich confirmed that at this time Khrushchev "together with Malenkov and Beria became frequent guests at Stalin's dacha".[27] Until the death of Andrei Zhdanov in August 1948, Stalin had allowed two groups to compete for his favour, a Zhdanov interest group, which tended to push the party's authority, and a Malenkov interest group, which favoured the pre-eminence of state institutions. In bringing Khrushchev to Moscow after 18 months in which the Malenkov group had faced no competition, Stalin was signalling the appointment of a new Zhdanov, a new person to speak for the party. It was no accident that on 16 December 1949 Khrushchev was appointed to the party's Organisation Bureau, a body that had always been Malenkov's preserve.

Within this general context, however, Stalin had a very specific reason for bringing Khrushchev back to Moscow. Since the summer of 1948 Stalin had become increasingly obsessed with a new foreign security threat posed by Tito's Yugoslavia and its supposed agents. Although Yugoslavia had initially been the most loyal of satellite states, that had all changed towards the end of 1947. It was then that Tito revived ideas, which had been abandoned in 1945, about establishing a Balkan Federation. The Bulgarian leader Georgii Dimitrov rallied to the notion, and soon plans were being developed for a new super-confederation which would unite not only Albania, Bulgaria and Yugoslavia but also Greece, where communist guerrillas were engaged in a civil war against a government supported by the West.

Stalin was ambivalent about the idea of a Balkan Federation, and certainly did not want to engage in a confrontation with the West over Greece, so he insisted that if a federation went ahead it should be firmly under Soviet control and not become a regional super-confederation owing allegiance to Tito. When in spring 1948 Tito refused to be disciplined by Stalin, Yugoslavia was expelled from the communist umbrella organisation the Communist Information Bureau (Cominform) at its 2nd Conference in June 1948. By the time of the 3rd Cominform Conference in November 1949, "the Tito clique" was being accused of having "openly gone over to the imperialist camp", having "sold Yugoslavia to the American monopolists" and having completed "its transition to fascism". The key to this transformation from people's democracy to fascist state was supposed "evidence" unearthed during the trial in Budapest in September 1949 of Lázló Rajk.[28]

Just as, in Stalin's eyes, Trotsky had moved in the 1930s from being a dissident communist to a plaything of foreign intelligence services, so he now argued that Tito was not just a troublesome communist with grandiose plans for a Balkan Federation but a plaything of British intelligence; any communist associated with Yugoslav communism was seen as a Titoist agent and therefore an imperialist agent. Purge trials quickly followed in Albania and Bulgaria, where Yugoslav influence had been strong and genuine in the period 1944–7, and then spread to Hungary where the Hungarian leader Mátyás Rákosi was keen to curry favour with Stalin by unmasking Hungary's own Titoite. Rajk, who had been both Minister of the Interior and Minister of Foreign Affairs, had indeed had links with Yugoslavia, although these were extremely tenuous; in the minds of those preparing the show trial, however, these links proved that Rajk had been a loyal disciple of Tito and a foreign intelligence agent.

Looking for evidence of disloyalty closer to home, Stalin's security services believed they had unearthed something rather similar to Titoism within the Leningrad party organisation. During the 900-day siege of Leningrad it was almost inevitable that the local party leadership should have developed a sense of independence from Moscow, a willingness to show initiative and exhibit a critical spirit – when a Yugoslav communist delegation visited Leningrad immediately after the war it noted that spirit and the greater freedom exhibited by Leningrad communists when compared to their comrades in Moscow. Understandably, Leningrad communists tended to support each other after the war in an informal network, particularly once some of them had been transferred to Moscow. To Stalin, this behaviour was very suspicious, particularly when the Leningraders started to advance ideas which he distrusted. The prime minister of the Russian Federation, Aleksei Kuznetsov, formerly the Leningrad regional party secretary from 1945 to 1946, and the *Gosplan* chairman, Nikolai Voznesenskii, a key figure in the Leningrad soviet executive before the war, had both advanced the idea of establishing a Russian Bureau of the Central Committee to ensure that purely Russian issues were not lost sight of; although Zhdanov had once proposed this idea before himself, it was now perceived as "opposing the Leningrad Party organisation to the Central Committee", the charge on which Kuznetsov, Voznesenskii and many other "Leningraders" were detained, tried and executed.[29]

Khrushchev's summons to Moscow was prompted by Stalin's fear that the Moscow party organisation had equally been penetrated in the same way as the Leningrad organisation. Khrushchev maintained that, at the time, he had no reason to doubt Stalin's security concerns. "On the whole I felt no lack of confidence in Stalin, I felt that excesses had been committed, but for the most part everything had been done correctly." However, his experience with the security services in Ukraine was clearly that statements originating from their investigations could not always be taken at face value. On the other hand, it is clear from his memoirs that he saw nothing unusual in a telling comment made by Stalin at about this time. Stalin's comment was prompted by the statement of the Czechoslovak Communist Party leader, Kliment Gottwald, assuring Stalin that there were no "Rajks" in his country: "What a blind kitten that Gottwald is," Stalin said, "he does not understand that it is impossible not to have enemies inside the party." Nor did the confessions of the arrested "Leningraders" make a great impression on him, at the time, although he did recall reading them. However, when Stalin handed him the supposed evidence against the Moscow First Secretary, Georgii Popov, he reacted just as he had done during the Nikolaenko affair in 1938 when he arrived in Kiev: "my immediate sense was that the document had been deliberately fabricated or had been written by a madman or scoundrel".[30]

Shortly after Stalin's 70th birthday celebrations, Khrushchev was asked for his views on the Popov case. Remembering later that he "really did take a risk then", Khrushchev made clear to Stalin that the Popov case was "either madness or a provocation". Although Stalin cursed and swore, and later frequently came back to the question asking Khrushchev repeatedly if he was really certain about Popov, ultimately Stalin accepted Khrushchev's judgement. Khrushchev had Popov demoted to a junior ministerial post as Minister of Urban Construction, and later he was demoted still further to be a factory director in Kuibyshev, but he survived and after Stalin's death was made ambassador to Poland. A massive purge of the party organisation was not part of Khrushchev's agenda for Moscow.[31]

Khrushchev's agenda was in fact very different. Speaking on 29 December 1949 he announced that "Comrade Stalin has turned my attention to living conditions", and he was soon involved in two related campaigns, to improve housing and to improve food supplies. There was little progress with housing. Stalin had told the Politburo in 1949 when it considered the reconstruction plan for Moscow that the Soviet Union needed "a beautiful capital in which everyone stands in awe". He called for no more four- or five-storey blocks of flats but blocks with eight to ten storeys as the norm and up to a quarter of blocks twelve or fourteen storeys high. Building complexes like these should surround Moscow and be "a delight to the eye". As the future would show, such an approach was entirely alien to Khrushchev.[32]

Agriculture, therefore, took priority. In Ukraine, Khrushchev had taken a variety of initiatives in this area. An attempt in summer 1948 to interest Stalin in the development of livestock farming had foundered, but he had had more success when he had experimented with merging collective farms into bigger and more productive units. After his move to Moscow this policy was extended nationwide; during 1949–50 the number of collective farms was reduced from over 6,000 to 1,500.[33] Khrushchev was always an enthusiast, and soon he was suggesting that this policy of merging collective farms should be taken even further, to the point where "agrotowns" had been established, agricultural units big enough to bring all the benefits of urban living to rural communities. This proposal proved controversial. It was criticised in the state newspaper *Izvestiya*, which pointed out that forming agrotowns could mean households being uprooted and re-settled at their own expense, and all those being re-settled having the additional cost of building a new house in the agrotown. Khrushchev defended his views in a *Pravda* article on 4 March 1951, but this time Stalin had decided to back Malenkov and the supporters of the state apparatus. After pressure was exerted from on high, a subsequent *Pravda* editorial made clear that Khrushchev's proposal was simply "for discussion". On 2 April Khrushchev was sent a letter from the Central Committee, drafted by Malenkov, condemning his proposal; he at once wrote to Stalin acknowledging his mistake.[34]

Such a public snub, especially after Khrushchev had gained the distinct impression that he had been brought to Moscow to act as a brake on Malenkov's power, must have given Khrushchev pause for thought about Stalin's capricious nature and the byzantine world of intrigue that Moscow had become. His fingers burned, he concentrated more on Moscow's need for housing, introducing for the first time the use of prefabricated reinforced concrete to build apartment blocks. Even before the war, when working with Bulganin in the mid 1930s, he had made an early experiment with what he called "block construction" or prefabricated units, but the technology had not worked at the time and it was not then a high priority. At the start of the 1950s these experiments resumed with much greater success.[35]

A Mad Time

In March 1963, Khrushchev told a meeting of writers and artists that the last years of Stalin's life were "madness after madness". In the prologue to his memoirs he was more cautious and wrote the following: "In the final period of Stalin's life, the time leading up to the 19th Party Congress and especially just after it, some doubts began to arise in our minds. I am speaking of those who were in his immediate circle, myself, Bulganin, Malenkov and to some extent Beria." Whatever the individual doubts Khrushchev had had for some time about the activities of the security services, he had not thus far located the source of the problem with Stalin himself. However, from autumn 1951 this seems to have changed. It was then that fellow Politburo member Anastas Mikoyan shared with Khrushchev some of the bizarre incidents which had occurred while Mikoyan had been holidaying with Stalin in Novyi Afon on the Abkhaz coast of the Black Sea. The Hungarian communist leader Rákosi, the most servile of the Soviet satellite leaders, became suspect in Stalin's eyes. While in Novyi Afon, Rákosi had telephoned Stalin to ask if he could join him for a few days. How, Stalin wanted to know, had Rákosi learned where Stalin was on holiday? Stalin became obsessed with the notion that Rákosi had used some sort of clandestine intrigue to obtain secret information about Stalin's holiday plans. Another story Mikoyan shared with Khrushchev about that holiday was Stalin's remark: "I do not even trust myself".[36]

Where he could, Khrushchev tried to mitigate the impact of Stalin's capricious whims. The affair of the economist L D Yaroshenko is a case in point. In November 1951 Stalin had launched a discussion on the Soviet economy centred around his own pamphlet *The Economic Problems of Socialism in the USSR*. On 20 March 1952 Yaroshenko wrote to the Politburo complaining that his own writings on economic matters had not been taken into consideration in this discussion, and he went on to outline his ideas. Stalin then wrote an addendum to *The Economic Problems of Socialism in the USSR* which denounced Yaroshenko's "erroneous and un-Marxist views". However, the public humiliation of Yaroshenko was not enough. Stalin became convinced that an early draft of his pamphlet had been "leaked" and picked up, copied and bowdlerised by economists such as Yaroshenko. At first Stalin blamed Khrushchev for this leak, and then he decided that it must have been one of his longest-serving associates, his secretary Aleksandr Poskrebyshev, who was summarily sacked at the end of 1952. Khrushchev, on the other hand, did not consider that Yaroshenko had done much wrong, so when the Moscow Party Committee met to decide his fate, he was, of course, subjected to criticism, but Khrushchev insisted that "we are a strong and united party; we shall be magnanimous; we shall not impose any penalties". Yaroshenko was not punished but was transferred to a post in Siberia. Only later, once he was beyond Khrushchev's authority, was he arrested. Another act of compassion in 1951 led Khrushchev to respond favourably to another letter from the daughter of Rykov. Despite Khrushchev's earlier intervention she had been imprisoned, but she had recently been released and was now asking for help in finding suitable work. Khrushchev wrote that he would do what he could.[37]

Probably because he already had in mind preparations for the 19th Party Congress, Stalin contacted Khrushchev in June 1952 about his fear that "unworthy cadres" had been appointed to posts within the Moscow Party organisation. Whatever reservations Khrushchev might have had about Stalin's behaviour he still accepted the importance of vigilance and so he duly investigated. He discovered that while the picture was generally satisfactory, almost unbelievably given the extent of the Ezhov purge in 1937–8, a former Rightist from 1928 to 1929 had been discovered holding down a party job, as had a former supporter of Trotsky in the early 1920s; a former supporter of the 1932 Riutin Programme was also uncovered.[38]

In preparing for the 19th Party Congress Khrushchev felt he was doing what Stalin had asked him to do and that was to revive the party, and there was more to reviving the party than tracing the last remnants of the pre-war oppositions. From August 1952 *Pravda* began a campaign against failings within the party. Where local committees were poorly organised or rarely met and lacked discipline, such ill-discipline was denounced. Equally, those party bodies which violated the "principle of collegiality" and avoided criticism and self-criticism were denounced; as part of this campaign it was made clear that the study of ideology was essential and that no party member should concentrate on economic work to the exclusion of ideological consid-erations. Khrushchev could now use his control of *Pravda* to print a special supplement on the issue of the new party rules and to criticise the "smugness" of those who used references to democratic central-ism to suppress criticism.[39]

In late September 1952 he organised the Moscow Regional Conference and here again he attacked those who "painted over criticism" and called for the "broad development of party democ-racy" and denounced "bosses" and "humbug communists". The new party rules, it was explained, required party members to be "active fighters". When the 19th Party Congress took place on 5–14 October 1952, the agenda balanced the two pillars of Stalinism: the congress would discuss the Fifth Five-Year Plan and it would renew the party's rules; Malenkov would give the report on the first, Khrushchev the report on the second. A report on the state of the party endorsed by the Central Committee immediately after the congress denounced the "office-bureaucratic" approach which it felt permeated much of the party. When reporting to the Moscow party organisation on the success of the 19th Party Congress, Khrushchev repeated his condemnation of a bureaucratic approach to criticism and self-criticism, criticised himself for his agrotown proposals, and argued that bureaucracy inevitably arose where "mass control over the activities of an organisation was weak".[40]

However, as the 19th Party Congress came to a close, Stalin's obsessive behaviour was visible for every member of the Central Committee to see. In the traditional way a Central Committee Plenum was held immediately after the close of the congress, on 16th October. At that plenum Stalin gave Molotov and Mikoyan what Khrushchev called "a thorough going over". He called into question their honesty and made clear he had no political confidence in them and suspected "some sort of political unreliability on their part". Although the two of them were included in the 25 names of the newly established Presidium, which replaced the Politburo, neither of them featured in the nine-member Presidium Bureau which in theory had executive authority, nor the actual group of five who ran the country – Stalin, Malenkov, Beria, Bulganin and Khrushchev. As Khrushchev recalled, "we were concerned about the fate of Molotov and Mikoyan", and he, Malenkov and Beria encouraged the two of them to continue to attend the informal night-time dinners at Stalin's dacha where most important decisions were made.[41]

At the time of the 19th Party Congress, Stalin's security fears focused on the "cosmopolitan" nature of the Soviet Union's Jewish community. Again, the origins of this were in Stalin's obsession that Tito-like ideas may have somehow penetrated into the Soviet Union. His target was the Jewish Anti-Fascist Committee which had been set up during the war to publicise in the US the anti-Semitic crimes which the Nazis had perpetrated in the Soviet Union. When the Crimean Tartars were exiled in May 1944, the Jewish Anti-Fascist Committee proposed to Stalin that Crimea might become an area of settlement for Jews. Stalin rejected the proposal out of hand, as did Khrushchev, who said later that it would have led to the establishment of "an American base in the south of our country".[42] No more discussion took place on the matter, but later it appeared suspicious to Stalin, especially when linked to the way the newly created state of Israel so quickly fell in with the US, even though the Soviet Union had worked hard to back its establishment in May 1948. Linked to this was the behaviour of Golda Meir, the first Israeli ambassador to Moscow, who over the summer of 1948 demonstratively insisted on attending synagogue in Moscow, and making contact with leading members of the Jewish Anti-Fascist Committee, in particular Molotov's wife. The Jewish Anti-Fascist Committee was closed down in November 1948 and by early 1949 hundreds of Jewish activists had been arrested, including the committee's leading figure, Solomon Lozovskii, a veteran Bolshevik and former Deputy Minister of Foreign Affairs. Although Lozovskii was first detained on 13 January 1949, the trial of the Jewish Anti-Fascist Committee did not begin until May 1952.

Then, on 13 January 1953, *Pravda* carried the headline "Vicious Spies and Killers under the Mask of Academic Physicians" and accused leading Jewish doctors of being responsible for the death of Zhdanov. When Khrushchev had been ill with pneumonia in 1947, one of the doctors who cared for him was Moisei Vovsi, now one of those accused of being a member of what became known as the Doctors' Plot. During the 19th Party Congress, Khrushchev had fallen ill once again and this time he was treated by another of the accused doctors. This second illness coincided with the very moment when, as a Presidium member, he was presented with the allegations levelled at the doctor treating him. As Khrushchev commented later: "I believed him [the doctor], but what could I do as a member of the Presidium? We were sent the evidence ... then he confessed ... None of the members of the Presidium, apart from Beria, had the right ... to cast doubt on the protocols of the interrogations."[43]

Despite understanding Stalin's personal responsibility for the absurd suspicions against Molotov and Mikoyan, and the implausible machinations of the Doctors' Plot, Khrushchev's personal relations with Stalin remained good until the very end. On the very eve of his fatal illness, on 28 February 1953, Khrushchev recalled that Stalin was joking boisterously, jabbing him in the stomach and calling him "Mikita", the Ukrainian version of his name Nikita. This was something Stalin always did when he was in a good mood; Khrushchev's son-in-law remembered frequently answering the telephone and hearing Stalin's voice ask for "Mikita". For the final three nights, while Stalin lingered between life and death, slipping in and out of consciousness, Khrushchev was at his bedside. When Stalin was pronounced dead, his daughter burst into tears and Khrushchev remembered how he too "sincerely wept".[44]

Chapter 4:   Dethroning Stalin, 1953–6

The Beria Danger

Despite Khrushchev's efforts since the 19th Party Congress to restore the authority of the party, it was those in favour of the state's authority who benefitted at first from Stalin's death. It was no accident that Khrushchev was the only member of the new ruling Presidium who was not a member of the Council of Ministers. The key figures in the new government announced at a joint meeting of the Central Committee Plenum, the Council of Ministers and the Supreme Soviet Presidium on 5 March were. Malenkov, as prime minister; Beria, as Minister of Internal Affairs; Molotov, as Minister of Foreign Affairs; and Bulganin, as Minister of Defence. Khrushchev, it was suggested, would "concentrate on work in the Central Committee"; he would not, however, have any title other than "Secretary" for the post of general secretary was abolished. The implication was fairly clear, Khrushchev's role was to mobilise the party into supporting the implementation of government decisions. This situation was reinforced when on 14 March a Central Committee Plenum relieved Malenkov of his party responsibilities and gave Khrushchev leadership of the Secretariat; at the same time Khrushchev gave up his responsibility for Moscow's party organisation.[1]

The new government was determined to address some of the issues of Stalin's rule at once. Malenkov told a Presidium meeting on 10 March, the day after Stalin's funeral, that under Stalin there had been serious breaches of normal procedure and that "it was essential to stop the policy of the cult of personality". At the Central Committee Plenum on 14 March Malenkov reassured members that now the party had a collective leadership.[2] As to breaches of normal procedure under Stalin, on the eve of the 14 March Plenum Beria announced that there would be a re-investigation of the Doctors' Plot and on 16 March he arrested Mikhail Ryumin, the Deputy Minister of State Security and Head of Special Investigations; on 1 April the arrested doctors were all rehabilitated.[3] An amnesty declared on 27 March released those serving sentences of under five years who had displayed "a conscientious attitude to work" and who "did not pose a threat to the state"; and it also halved the sentences of those serving more than five years. This began a process which would see the prison camp population reduced by two-thirds by the start of 1956.[4]

At the Presidium meeting on 10 March 1953, Khrushchev took a much more forthright view than his colleagues on the question of Stalin's breaches of normal procedure. He made his anxieties about the way the purges had been handled very clear indeed, stating bluntly: "I, Khrushchev, you Klim [Voroshilov], you Lazar [Kaganovich], you Vyacheslav Mikhailovich [Molotov] – we should offer repentance to the people for 1937." His colleagues would not go that far, but on 3 April the Presidium called on the new Minister of State Security to draw up a report on past law breaking within the MV. Shortly afterwards leading members of the Central Committee were privately briefed by Beria that "during the last two years" Stalin's "illness" had resulted in a variety of crimes. Clearly it was only Stalin's most recent breaches of normal procedure which were to be considered.[5]

Another of the breaches of normal procedure which quickly came under the spotlight of the new government was the Russification of the republican party and state apparatuses which had taken place during Stalin's last years. Beria reported to his Presidium colleagues on the situation in Lithuania on 8 May and on 16 May raised the situation in Western Ukraine. These were not the only republics affected; at the start of May the leadership of the party in Uzbekistan received a letter on the nationality issue from Beria which called for the sacking of many existing leaders perceived as being too pro-Russian. The Uzbek leadership at first refused to agree to these changes, but then caved in to Beria's pressure. These moves by Beria gave Khrushchev some concerns. As party leader he objected to some of the Uzbek changes and he overruled Beria's suggestion that the new Ukrainian party secretary be the playwright and Deputy Premier Aleksandr Korneichuk; Khrushchev appointed his long-standing ally from Ukraine, Aleksei Kirichenko.[6] What concerned Khrushchev most about Beria's moves at this time, however, was that he was using his own MVD workers to gather material about party activists and thus bypassing the Central Committee apparatus; indeed the report on

Lithuania was prepared without the knowledge of the Lithuanian Central Committee.[7]

Khrushchev was determined that the party apparatus take on this issue itself and it was he who prepared a report on the situation in Latvia for discussion in early June. He then summoned the Latvian leadership to Moscow for a dressing down, warned them of the dangers of Russification and ordered then to hold a plenum on 23 June to appoint a new, more Latvian leadership; back in Riga excited party activists started throwing Cyrillic typewriters out of the window. As Khrushchev noted later, Beria's proposals "could by no means be considered incorrect in every respect", but it was the way they were being implemented that was alarming, since Beria was not only bypassing the party but undermining it.[8] On the day of Stalin's funeral, 9 March, Beria made a speech on the Lenin mausoleum promising "to preserve the rights written into the Stalin Constitution" and stressing that the people were now more than ever united around "the Soviet Government and the Party Central Committee". The order – government first, party second – was quite deliberate. Beria's son remembered that "in their plans my father and his colleagues had agreed to abolish the post of general secretary, and free the economy from party tutelage". Beria felt that, after some three generations of communist rule, the population was loyal and economic affairs were too complex to be entrusted to "apparatchiks who should confine themselves to activity in their cells; it was not up to the Central Committee to run the country, that was the job of the Council of Ministers". From Khrushchev's perspective, when, on 15 June, Beria sacked the Belorussian Minister of the Interior without involving the Presidium, he was seriously treading on toes.[9]

In beginning to investigate certain of Stalin's crimes, and in endeavouring to reduce national antagonisms in the constituent republics, Beria could claim to be keeping within his brief as Minister of Internal Affairs. However, on 2 June he submitted proposals "on measures to restore to health the political situation in the GDR". These put forward various economic and political measures to improve the lot of German Democratic Republic (GDR) citizens, but also talked of the need for "a flexible tactic" to work for "the main task … [of] a united Germany on democratic and peace-loving foundations". With this proposal, Beria was not only straying into Molotov's territory of foreign affairs, but suggesting that the communist regime in East Germany (GDR) could be abandoned, which Khrushchev could hardly accept. Khrushchev supported Molotov in opposing the proposal and Beria's initiative was abandoned – Molotov was so grateful for Khrushchev's support that he proposed that he and Khrushchev should in future address each other using the intimate term for "you" used between friends.[10]

Although the East German regime was not abandoned, it was told that it had to abandon plans "to build socialism" and, instead, introduce what became known as the New Course, a more modest economic programme which would improve the standard of living for East German citizens. This instruction was not welcomed in Berlin, where the local communist leadership tried to resist moves to cancel a previously announced decision to raise production norms by 10%. The result was confusion. When on 16 June the Berlin press made clear that the increased work norm was indeed to be introduced, despite earlier reports that it would not, a spontaneous strike wave hit Berlin and other cities. Only the deployment of Soviet tanks saved the East German regime.

Beria was again treading on Khrushchev's toes when he took the lead in instructing the Hungarian communists about the reforms they needed to undertake. On 13 June a delegation from the Hungarian party was brought to Moscow for talks on economic and political affairs, and Beria criticised Rákosi for his Stalin-inspired obsession with security – could it be normal, he suggested, that from a people of just nine and a half million, one and a half million had legal proceedings taken against them. Beria proposed that the roles of party leader and prime minister should in future be separate, with Imre Nagy, whom Rákosi had imprisoned in 1949, becoming prime minister and Rákosi staying on as party leader. At this meeting Beria put across his own political credo by stressing that the role of the party should be to undertake agitation and propaganda in order to support the government in carrying out its programme. "Let the Council of Ministers decide things and the party worry about cadres and propaganda", he reportedly said. This was the very opposite of Khrushchev's view.[11]

On May Day 1953 careful observers noted that there were no slogans attacking Yugoslavia. Beria was planning to launch another foreign policy initiative: reconciliation with Tito. On 31 May 1953 Beria was provided with a report from a supporter in the Ministry of Foreign Affairs which suggested that Yugoslavia should no longer be given the status of a "fascist" state but a "normal bourgeois state". As a result, on 16 June the Soviet Union suddenly appointed a new ambassador to head its Belgrade mission. Beria was keen to push the normalisations of relations with Yugoslavia one stage further and see if relations between the Soviet and Yugoslav Communist Parties could not be restored. On 25 June, Beria, supported by Malenkov, authorised the newly appointed representative of the MVD within the

Soviet Union's Belgrade embassy to approach the Yugoslav Minister of Internal Affairs, Aleksandar Ranković, with the following message: "Greetings from Comrade Beria, who remembers you well. Comrade Beria asked me to inform you personally and in strictest confidence that Malenkov, Beria and their friends are firmly in favour of a reassessment and improvement in mutual relations between our two countries. In that connection Comrade Beria asks you personally to inform Comrade Tito of this and if you and Comrade Tito share this point of view, then it would be expedient to organise a confidential meeting of those delegates for this purpose."[12]

It was Khrushchev who decided that Beria had to be stopped. He was not against ending Russification – he had moved to end it in Latvia – nor was he against reconciliation with Tito – he would take over that policy too. It was not what Beria was trying to do, but how he was doing it that Khrushchev objected to. In his memoirs Khrushchev recalled how he increasingly sensed that "an offensive was under way against the party and that the party was being subordinated to the Ministry of Internal Affairs".[13] This was what he had fought against so consistently throughout his time in Ukraine, the party had been subservient to the NKVD at the height of the purges and such a circumstance should not be allowed to arise again. Beria talked about observing the constitution, but if he succeeded in usurping the party, the powers he acquired could be used to establish his personal dictatorship.

Apart from obvious naked ambition and years of intriguing with Stalin, was there any evidence that Beria was moving towards his own dictatorial regime? On 25 June Beria informed Malenkov that the interrogation of Ryumin about the Doctors' Plot had revealed that the Leningrad Affair was also a frame-up. Beria's immediate proposal was that he arrest the former Minister of State Security, but opening up the Leningrad Affair was not good news for Malenkov, who had been closely involved in certain stages of that purge. Beria's move might not have been a direct challenge to Malenkov's position, but it did suggest that Beria would be in a position to blackmail him and exert pressure over the new leader; Beria was rumoured to hold incriminating evidence on all his Presidium colleagues.[14]

As Khrushchev prepared to make his move, he was suddenly struck by a possible justification for his action. "There came back to me some words uttered by [his old friend] Kaminskii [at the 1937 February–March Plenum] that during the civil war, when the British occupied Baku, Beria had been an agent of Britain's counter-intelligence service". Fortified by this very Stalinist understanding of the threat which Beria posed, Khrushchev pressed ahead, Mikoyan being the only member of the Presidium with serious reservations about removing Beria; on the day Khrushchev acted he spent much of the morning alone with Mikoyan on the bench at his dacha in earnest conversation.[15]

Khrushchev's plan was relatively simple. A meeting of the Council of Ministers would be called on 26 June to discuss routine matters. The agenda would not arouse Beria's suspicions, but at a certain point during the meeting Malenkov would suggest moving on to party business and turning the meeting of the Council of Ministers into a meeting of the Presidium; at this point he would propose that Beria be dismissed from all his posts. To be on the safe side, Khrushchev sent the usual Kremlin guards on manoeuvres, called the Kremlin commandant away on business, and asked his wartime friend the Chief of Moscow Air Defence to provide some back-up; Malenkov asked General Zhukov, just appointed Deputy Minister of Defence, to be involved in Beria's physical detention. At one point during the confrontation, Beria reached for his briefcase, and Khrushchev, fearing it contained a gun, grabbed his arm. The British spy story was never more than a pretext; it was Beria's avoidance of party procedure that was recorded in the minutes. "Enemies wanted to put the organs of the Ministry of Internal Affairs above both the party and the government. The task is to put the Ministry of Internal Affairs at the service of the party and government, to take these organs under the control of the party." Later the minutes noted laconically: "on the question of Hungary, we did not agree in advance". Explanation came in a letter Beria wrote to Malenkov from his prison cell agreeing that he should have let Malenkov nominate Nagy as prime minister of Hungary – "I jumped forward in an idiotic fashion", Beria wrote.[16]

When the Central Committee held its plenum on 2–7 July, Malenkov set the tone when he informed members that Stalin's "cult of personality" had meant that no collective discussions had taken place and that criticism and self-criticism had been abandoned: "nothing justifies the fact that we did not call a congress for thirteen years, that for years there was no plenum of the Central Committee, that the Politburo did not function properly but was replaced by groups of three or five, working under Stalin's instructions on separate tasks and questions". All this led to considerable harm being done to the party. Khrushchev, however, won an important victory, for the meeting resolved that "the party is the organising and directing force of Soviet society", logically, therefore, all ministries were under its oversight. The party's supremacy had been reaffirmed, although, as things turned out, it would take Khrushchev a while to formalise this more securely.[17]

Khrushchev was keen not only to berate Beria's ambition, but to get back to the way Stalin had breached normal procedure. He told delegates how he had stood with Bulganin at Stalin's bedside immediately after his death, saying that Beria would do everything to become Minister of Internal Affairs so that he could control positions throughout the state and even establish an espionage system over the Presidium. And that is what had happened; Beria's steady extension of his powerbase beyond internal security matters was proof of his malign intentions. But Khrushchev was quick to remind members of the last time the NKVD had stood above the party, the Ezhov years, when "in 1937–38 there were many questionable cases". Khrushchev had believed for many years that Stalin bore no responsibility for the arbitrary acts of the NKVD, and he had acted to discipline the security services when errors came to light. Khrushchev's experience in Moscow since 1949 made such a view untenable and he now suggested to the Central Committee, that Beria had been able "to play" Stalin, to sow doubts in his mind, first with a vague hint, then something more definite, until Stalin would suddenly turn on a formerly trusted comrade. Khrushchev added: "we all respected Stalin, but the years took their toll, and in the last years Stalin did not read papers, did not receive people ... and that scoundrel Beria used this very skilfully".[18]

Khrushchev versus Malenkov

Although the removal of Beria and the July Plenum greatly strengthened Khrushchev's position, Malenkov remained for now in a position of superiority. His power rested in the state apparatus and one of his first moves on Stalin's death had been to streamline the number of ministries by reducing them from 45 to 13; a decree of 11 April 1953 gave these 13 new super ministers additional powers. Malenkov consciously bypassed the party apparatus by using a session of the Supreme Soviet, rather than a Central Committee Plenum, to launch a programme of reduced spending on heavy industry, increased spending on consumer goods and new investment in agriculture. In his 8 August report to the Supreme Soviet on the proposed 1954 budget he not only talked about the New Course towards consumer goods spending but announced a dramatic agricultural reform, which cancelled the outstanding debts of collective farmers and drastically lowered the compulsory delivery targets. While careful to talk about continuing to develop heavy industry, he nevertheless referred to "temporarily forcing the development of light industry", without adjusting the five-year plan.[19]

Khrushchev and Malenkov had worked together on these agricultural proposals, and Khrushchev would have preferred it if they had been agreed at a Central Committee Plenum before being presented to the Soviet people at the Supreme Soviet. For Khrushchev, Malenkov's method was back to front; the Central Committee should agree a reform and then present it to the Supreme Soviet, rather than vice versa; as it was, the September Plenum simply endorsed Malenkov's proposals on agriculture. Khrushchev was determined to strengthen his hold on the party apparatus and used that plenum to ensure he was in future designated "First Secretary", rather than the very vague designation he had had since March of being the person running the Secretariat. This was not a concession Malenkov agreed to willingly; he accepted it only after Bulganin had threatened to propose a motion to this effect from the floor of the plenum if Malenkov refused to do it. This change had an immediate impact; after the September Plenum documents began to appear under the signatures of both Malenkov and Khrushchev.[20] Khrushchev had dug his heals in at this time because he felt he was the party leader who understood agriculture; he had clashed with Stalin on the matter, and he had been the first to say out loud what everybody knew deep down, that if the country needed bread, collective farmers would have to be paid properly.[21]

Khrushchev was quick to trump Malenkov's agricultural reform by developing the idea of the Virgin Lands Campaign, launched at the 23 February 1954 Plenum. Khrushchev told members that the quickest way to increase the production of grain was to exploit "virgin land" in Kazakhstan and western Siberia. The scheme offered "quick results on the cheap".[22] Khrushchev had calculated that even if there was not a good harvest every year, developing the agricultural potential of Kazakhstan and parts of Siberia was an attractive prospect and would significantly increase grain supplies. In his view, at least in the short term, the extensive development of agriculture was a much cheaper option than its intensive development, and even into the 1960s he felt the Virgin Lands offered better value grain than that grown in other parts of the country.[23] What is more, the Virgin Lands Campaign offered the opportunity to show the party's power for popular mobilisation; for several years the Komsomol mobilised the youth of the country to spend their summers in Kazakhstan.

The struggle between Khrushchev and Malenkov was not just about the relative strengths of the party and state apparatuses; it was also about the relative claims of heavy and light industry. Khrushchev and the party apparatus championed the traditional strengths of the Soviet economy, heavy industry and defence; Malenkov, on the other hand, followed the logic of his New Course to its natural conclusion and favoured the development of consumer goods, denying the need for any increase in defence spending. During speeches made for the March 1954 Supreme Soviet elections, this difference became very clear. Khrushchev called for the modernisation and strengthening of the armed forces, linked to the expansion of machine building seen as essential to harvesting the new Virgin Lands; Malenkov made no mention of heavy industry, or of defence, and even argued that in the nuclear era a world war could only end in "the destruction of world civilisation". This intellectual honesty turned into humiliation when Molotov protested, Khrushchev supported Molotov, and Malenkov was forced to issue a "clarification" on 26 April 1954 to the Supreme Soviet; and it was Khrushchev who made clear to the Supreme Soviet after Malenkov's retraction that "if the imperialists attempt to unleash a new world war, it will result in the final destruction of the capitalist system". Significantly, it was also Khrushchev who reported to the Supreme Soviet on the coming year's budget.[24]

The removal of Beria opened up a new, more rigorous phase in the process of rehabilitating Stalin's victims, and this too worked against Malenkov. This process began when a former military prosecutor wrote to the Central Committee's Department of Party Administration outlining the failings of the Procurator's Office during the Stalin years. This letter was forwarded to Khrushchev. It made the simple case that, although at the end of the Ezhov purges the Central Committee had decided on 17 November 1938 that the procurator had the right to oversee all arrests, the policy of arresting first and gathering evidence later had continued right up to the present and the Soviet Procurator General had done nothing about it. Khrushchev used this letter as a justification for starting a systematic investigation of illegal actions during Stalin's lifetime. He immediately appointed a new Procurator General, Roman Rudenko, a man of great experience who had served as Chief Procurator for Ukraine under Khrushchev and before that as one of the prosecutors in the Nuremburg War Trials. On 1 September 1953, the Supreme Court was empowered, at Rudenko's request, to review all decisions taken during Stalin's 1937–8 mass actions by troikas or other extra-judicial committees which had bypassed the procuracy. By the end of October, Rudenko was regularly sending Khrushchev ad hoc requests for clemency or rehabilitation, and by 8 December he had sent Khrushchev a list of those condemned by troikas set up by the Commissariat of Internal Affairs (later MVD) between 5 November 1934 and 1 September 1953. Of 442,531 cases considered: 10,101 people had been sentenced to death; 360,921 people had been detained; 67,539 people had been exiled; and 3,970 people had received other forms of punishment.[25]

Within this broader picture, Khrushchev himself took an interest in the Leningrad Affair, the case that, indirectly, had brought him back to Moscow and the case that could be used to blacken Malenkov's name. In November 1953 he visited Leningrad in person to attend a joint meeting of the city and provincial party committees. Using his new authority as First Secretary, he removed those appointed in 1949 after the Leningrad Affair by Malenkov and appointed a new Leningrad First Secretary, Frol Kozlov, someone on whom, initially, he could rely. He also used the occasion to challenge the message from Malenkov that party activists should confine their interests to party matters; there was no such thing as purely party work, Khrushchev argued. Party officials needed to be able to tackle concrete issues of industrial and agricultural production. Undermining Malenkov's views and linking him to the Leningrad Affair clearly went together in Khrushchev's mind.[26]

On 10 December 1953 he was presented with a detailed report on the Leningrad Affair, but he did not act at once. At the start of March 1954, Rudenko asked the Presidium for permission to move beyond the troikas of the mass actions and establish a commission to investigate the cadre purges in order to identify those party members with a case for rehabilitation after an unjust court trial. No sooner had this commission been set up, than the Supreme Court rehabilitated those involved in the Leningrad Affair. This move enabled Khrushchev to act, and on 15 April 1954 the Presidium decided that Khrushchev should return to Leningrad in person to explain to party activists there just why it now appeared that the Leningrad Affair had been a falsification. The speech Khrushchev delivered made clear that, although Kuznetsov and Voznesenskii had "broken state discipline", and for that had been issued with a party reprimand, there had never been an anti-state conspiracy.[27]

While in Leningrad on 7 May 1954, Khrushchev gave his first public speech criticising Stalin. He was clear that "Stalin was a great man, a Marxist of genius", but even people like that should not have been given the powers Stalin exercised. Stalin would call Abakumov, tell him what to do, but none of the Presidium members, other than Beria, could query Abakumov and challenge the veracity of the interrogations he carried out. Stressing the role played by Beria, Khrushchev explained that Stalin had been ill in his last years and that Beria had played on his suspicions: "it depended on the state of his health, he sometimes went to extremes, he might praise someone or just as likely arrest him". He insisted that "before the war Stalin was not like this", but then qualified this by adding that "we must consider a lot of cases from 1937–8". It would be wrong, he suggested, to think that there were no enemies in those years, "there were enemies and bitter ones", but "clearly Beria, Ezhov and others had arrested and shot many innocent people". In response to a written question, Khrushchev confirmed that the Presidium had recently set up a commission to investigate the cadre purges of 1937–8. A month later, addressing KGB workers from across the Soviet Union, he said that Ezhov and others had "behaved criminally" and turned the NKVD into an organisation "standing above the party". However, as he told the Leningrad activists, when "I am asked, how will we bring this to the attention of party members, I find it difficult to say".[28]

There was to be no let-up in the rehabilitation campaign however. Back in November 1937 Khrushchev had endorsed the arrest of Olga Shatunovskaya, then the acting head of the Moscow Party Administration Department. She had friends in high places; her childhood playmate had been Lev Shaumian, son of one of the heroic Baku commissars with whom Mikoyan had worked during the civil war. In 1945 Mikoyan had got her released from prison but Stalin would not agree to her returning to Moscow. As the rehabilitation of cadres proceeded in March 1954, the head of the Azerbaijan Communist Party, the man who had denounced Shatunovskaya in 1937, was arrested as an associate of Beria. Shatunovskaya then petitioned Khrushchev and by May 1954 she had an apartment in Moscow, a car and a senior position in the Party Control Committee, which had been instructed by Khrushchev to push forward the process of rehabilitation.[29]

By summer 1954 the signs that Malenkov's position was being undermined were clear. After June, the names of the Presidium members were given in the press in alphabetical order, not with Malenkov first. When in the middle of August a big expansion of the Virgin Lands scheme was proclaimed, the announcement was made, as usual, in the name of both the Central Committee and the Council of Ministers, but for the first time since Stalin's death the Central Committee was listed before the Council of Ministers. Less than a fortnight later, *Pravda* called on all party organisations to intensify their scrutiny of government departments, very definitely a victory for Khrushchev's views. At the same time, lower down the party hierarchy, Khrushchev had engineered a series of new appointments since becoming First Secretary. During the autumn and winter of 1953–4 two-thirds of provincial party secretaries in the Russian Federation were replaced, while at republican level Zinovii Serdyuk, one of Khrushchev's closest associates while in Ukraine and throughout the war, was appointed party secretary in Moldavia. From September 1954 Malenkov no longer chaired Presidium meetings.[30]

During his summer break in Crimea in August and September 1954, Khrushchev held a series of meetings with Presidium allies Mikoyan and Bulganin, and with the party chiefs of Leningrad, Moscow and Ukraine; meetings with the party leaders from the Far East and Siberia followed shortly afterwards. The ground was being prepared for a direct confrontation with Malenkov and this began on 6 November when *Pravda* published an article by the head of *Gosplan* which stressed the importance of Lenin's dictum that heavy industry was the cornerstone of a socialist economy. Thus far, despite Malenkov's championing of light industry, heavy industry had continued to expand, but the plan for 1955 would, for the first time, see a significant shift towards light industry. On 21 December 1954 the different priorities of Khrushchev and Malenkov became visible to all. Both *Pravda* and *Izvestiya* produced articles celebrating 75 years since the birth of Stalin, but *Pravda* stressed the Stalinist orthodoxy of concentrating investments in heavy industry, while *Izvestiya* praised the measures taken to boost light industry and the production of consumer goods. When the Presidium met on 31 December 1954 it heard a report on the "deeply mistaken economic views" which gave priority to consumer goods. By 5 January 1955 *Izvestiya* had conceded that the "all-out development of all branches of heavy industry" was essential for a socialist economy, and on 24 January *Pravda* carried an editorial against "vulgarisers" of Marxism who questioned the priority of heavy industry.[31]

"The question of Malenkov" was discussed at a Presidium meeting on 22 January 1955, and three days later, when a Central Committee Plenum gathered on 25 January 1955, there was some talk of removing him from the government completely; but Khrushchev was concerned at the impact this might have on the international standing of the Soviet Union. At the plenum, Malenkov's policies were compared to those of the Right Opposition of the late 1920s, to the policies of Bukharin and Rykov who had opposed Stalin's commitment to full-scale industrialisation at break-neck speed; there was also much talk of "pseudo-economists" and "opportunism". However, Khrushchev was determined to extend the charge sheet to Malenkov's "moral responsibility" for the Leningrad Affair. When the Presidium met on 31 January 1955, ostensibly to discuss Malenkov's future, much of the discussion revolved around Beria, his misdeeds and how they had impacted on other members of the leadership.[32]

During these discussions, Kaganovich expressed his personal anguish concerning the arrest and execution of the innocent: "the facts relating to Beria are true, I am suffering inside over this, but what is more important, the interests of the party or of personal interests"? Clearly Kaganovich still felt Stalin's crimes were justified by the greater good. Voroshilov asserted that "the party must know the truth" and maintained that Malenkov had not properly distanced himself from Beria. Khrushchev raised again the point that he had already raised in Leningrad, how should the party be informed of Stalin's crimes and the actions of his closest associates. No decision was reached. It was clearly decided that no public link should be made between Malenkov's dismissal and the growing criticism of Stalin. On 7 February 1955 the Presidium resolved to keep Malenkov on as deputy prime minister and Minister of Power Generation; at the same time Zhukov became Minister of Defence and Bulganin prime minister.[33]

Despite the decision not to link Malenkov and Stalin, Khrushchev made clear when he addressed a plenum of the Ukrainian Central Committee on 18 February 1955 that one of the main reasons for Malenkov's dismissal was his Stalinist past. He explained that, while Abakumov had organised the Leningrad Affair, Beria had provided information on Abakumov's findings to Moscow, where Malenkov had received and endorsed that material on behalf of the Central Committee. Malenkov and Beria were close friends and acted together. Investigations had shown that, after interviewing both Kuznetsov and Voznesenskii at his dacha, Stalin had thought that modest punishments were in order, an academic job for Voznesenskii and a Far East posting for Kuznetsov; it had been Beria who had opposed this and Malenkov who "could have adopted an independent position and proposed a thorough investigation" but did not and instead acted as "a blind man in Beria's hands".[34]

Restoring Relations with Tito

Coming to terms with Stalin's crimes was also evident in Khrushchev's push to restore relations with Tito's Yugoslavia. From early February 1954 Khrushchev was working for some sort of resolution of the Yugoslav issue, but meeting constant frustration from Molotov and the Ministry of Foreign Affairs. On 8 February 1954, taking advantage of Molotov being out of the country, a Presidium commission was established to assess what sort of state Yugoslavia was. A fortnight later Mikhail Suslov, the secretary responsible for links with foreign communist parties, reported to the Presidium that, although disguised by "socialist phraseology", Yugoslavia was in fact a "bourgeois" state. The report did, however, also recognise that efforts to undermine Tito's authority through the Cominform had been entirely unsuccessful, and that a basis did exist for improved relations between the two countries. Khrushchev let things rest there for a bit, but, after Tito had made a public statement to the effect that Yugoslavia would welcome a normalisation in relations, he returned to the issue in May and June 1954; Yugoslavia was discussed in the Presidium on no less than six occasions.[35]

On 4 May, the Presidium looked again at Suslov's report and instructed him to rework it. This reworking produced a draft issued on 18 May, which suggested for the first time that the Soviet stance in 1948 had been "mistaken". It suggested that, while there had been an issue between the two states in 1948 which needed to be addressed, the sudden break in relations had been a mistake and had actually backfired since it had strengthened Tito's position. Looking for those responsible, the report blamed Beria on the Soviet side, and on the Yugoslav side singled out Tito's young firebrand colleague Milovan Djilas, who, conveniently, Tito had just excluded from the Yugoslav leadership because of his demands for a more democratic style of government in Yugoslavia; Djilas had seriously upset Stalin in autumn 1944 by complaining about the behaviour of Red Army officers in Yugoslavia. This second Suslov report concluded by proposing that the Soviet Communist Party should approach its Yugoslav counterparts for talks. Once again, Molotov was out of the country when this decision was made and protested about it angrily on his return, insisting that only state channels should be used to maintain contact between the two countries.[36]

Ignoring Molotov's objections, the Presidium decided on 27 May to prepare the other socialist states for a change in policy towards Yugoslavia, pointing out that the possible return of Yugoslavia to the "democratic camp" would be "a serious victory for the international communist movement". Molotov's opposition continued and it was only on 22 June that Khrushchev finally signed the proposed letter to Tito, which called for inter-party talks, criticised the actions of both Beria and Djilas and accepted that in 1948 not all the possibilities for defusing the situation had been taken. Tito's response to Khrushchev's letter was cautious. His close colleague Kardelj informed the Soviet ambassador in private that the initiative was welcome, but that was all. Keen to speed things up, the Presidium sent another letter, referring to Kardelj's comment and urging a prompt response. When Tito did respond, on 11 August, his attitude was disappointing. He welcomed the tenor of Khrushchev's letter with its reference to "non-interference in the affairs of other countries", and acknowledged the need for more trade and improved relations in general; however, the issue of inter-party contact was rejected as premature. Tito added that he had no idea if Beria had played a role in the events of 1948 on the Soviet side, but he was clear that Djilas's role in 1948 had had no significance within Yugoslavia.[37]

Between 17 and 23 September 1954 the Presidium held further long discussions on the question of Yugoslavia. As a gesture of good will, it decided to close down the Union of Yugoslav Patriots and the radio stations "For a Socialist Yugoslavia" and "Free Yugoslavia". Then Khrushchev sent a third letter, clearly addressed this time to "Comrade Tito". He repeated his assurances about "non-interference in the internal affairs of other countries" and urged renewed contact between the two parties, since, he noted, Tito's letter had raised "no principled objections" to such a move. If such a move was simply premature, he explained, the Soviet side would not insist on immediate implementation, although it believed it inexpedient if personal contacts were delayed for too long; the cause of socialism demanded every effort was made to restore friendly relations, Khrushchev concluded. Tito still played hard to get. It was only on 24 October that he responded, and then simply to say that a closed session of the Yugoslav party would debate the issue in November; this was not "dragging things out", he suggested disingenuously, but consulting broadly. However, Tito did concede that personal contact was essential in resolving these issues and that a meeting would be possible once he had returned from planned visits to India and Burma. On 23 November the Yugoslav Central Committee duly met and concluded that Yugoslavia should accept the invitation to talks.[38]

The Presidium met on 25 November and welcomed Tito's response, which was then circulated to the leaders of the other socialist countries. On 28 November 1954, Yugoslav National Day, Malenkov, Molotov,

Khrushchev and Bulganin all attended a party at the Yugoslav embassy and toasted "Comrade Tito". Khrushchev told Western journalists present that they could toast "Comrade Tito" because both the Soviet Union and Yugoslavia were "led by the teachings of Marxism–Leninism". However, at a similar diplomatic gathering precisely one month later to mark the progress in trade talks, Khrushchev was not so emollient. He responded furiously when one of the Yugoslavs present used the term "Stalinism": "There is no such concept as 'Stalinism'. Stalin was a Leninist! All of us here today worked with him and learned from him. He lived and died a communist! We stand or fall together with him! Is that not the case, comrades?"[39]

This speech was part of a deliberate attempt by Khrushchev to keep Molotov on board, but Molotov's intransigence on Yugoslavia was soon a matter of public knowledge. On 8 February 1955 Molotov addressed the Supreme Soviet and made critical comments on Yugoslavia, stressing that "in 1948 Yugoslavia moved away from the stance it adopted in 1945". The Yugoslav press was quick to denounce the views of "Mr Molotov". When the Presidium resumed its discussion of Yugoslav matters on 22 February, it decided to send a further letter of explanation to the leaders of the socialist countries, this time being very cautious about the prospects for "unity on the basis of Marxism–Leninism". It was not until 14 March 1955 that the Presidium agreed the text of a letter in reply to Tito's acceptance of 24 November 1954. This reply again urged a personal meeting and one "not long delayed". Tito made Khrushchev sweat for another month before responding on 16 April and suggesting a meeting in the middle of May; Khrushchev accepted at once.[40]

As the Presidium met to plan Khrushchev's visit, Molotov fought a rearguard action to prevent the planned reconciliation. On 19 May he repeated his view that in 1948 the Yugoslav communists had rejected Marxism–Leninism and that if they wanted to make amends they should join the Warsaw Pact and re-sign the Soviet–Yugoslav Treaty of Friendship in operation between 1945 and 1948. Molotov also expressed outrage that an article by Zhukov in the 9 May Victory Day issue of *Pravda*, which praised the Yugoslav partisans, had not been discussed in the Presidium. Molotov, however, was alone. Mikoyan, Bulganin and Kaganovich all rejected his assertion that in 1948 the Yugoslavs had adopted a course of "bourgeois nationalism", but this row continued at Presidium meetings on 23 and 25 May as the final version of Khrushchev's speech was hammered out.[41]

Khrushchev's speech at Belgrade airport on 26 May famously began with "a sincere apology" for what had happened and "the extraneous developments of that period". Khrushchev called for "a joint understanding on the basis of Marxism–Leninism", but repeated the notion, which Tito had already rejected, that Beria had been responsible. To Khrushchev's surprise and fury, Tito cut short the start of the translation of Khrushchev's speech with a curt "we all understand Russian" and got into his car. It was with some difficulty that Khrushchev overcame an instinctive urge to return straight home after such an open snub. When the talks began on 27 May, Khrushchev was clear that "people" had opposed him coming, and that his speech at the airport was a collective statement; he conceded at once that the final Declaration on the visit could be based on the Yugoslav draft. He then spoke less about Yugoslav relations than about the Soviet Union's recent history under Stalin, "the loss of many honest people", the need "to free thousands of people and take them back into the party". As the talks developed, so too did Khrushchev's reflections on Stalin. There was a lot of disagreement "amongst us" about how to relate to him and the unpleasant side of his life, but it was wrong to judge him on that phase of his life where he showed himself to be weak. The Yugoslavs, of course, had suffered, but Khrushchev was clear that he and his colleagues had had to put up with far greater insults from Stalin than the Yugoslavs had ever experienced.[42]

When the Declaration on the visit was signed on 2 June it still did not restore party relations as Khrushchev had wanted, but Tito had agreed to Khrushchev's proposal that letters could be exchanged on party matters to take things further, and that this correspondence would start even before the Soviet delegation left for home. Thus when the Presidium met on 6 June to discuss the visit, Khrushchev's verdict was that only limited success on party contacts could be reported, so "determination and patience" would be required. Molotov had still not given up. Two days later he used another Presidium meeting to challenge the notion that the talks in Belgrade had taken place "on the basis of Marxism–Leninism" and asserted once again that the problem in 1948 had been Yugoslav "bourgeois nationalism", which Beria had merely exacerbated. It was only on 20 June that the Presidium agreed to endorse Khrushchev's visit, with the proviso that Molotov's criticisms would be brought to the next plenum.[43]

The plenum of 4–12 July 1955, therefore, saw a direct clash between Khrushchev and Molotov. Khrushchev explained to members that in 1948, although the letter to the Yugoslavs had been written in the name of the Politburo, he for one had not even been consulted about it. He suggested that if Stalin had been properly informed about the situation in Yugoslavia, "I am convinced he would have looked into the matter more deeply and not allowed a break with Yugoslavia". It was Beria and Abakumov who fabricated the Rajk Trial in Hungary, and that trial had led to the 1949 Cominform resolution describing Tito as a fascist. Khrushchev accepted Molotov's point that at the 6th Congress of the Yugoslav League of Communists in November 1952 the Soviet Union had been categorised as "an aggressive state intent on world hegemony, representing a threat to peace in the whole world", but added that this had been an assessment made at the height of the Korean War, a war which the Soviet Union had started – "and who needed that war?", he asked rhetorically. Care would have to be taken, Khrushchev suggested, for much of the Yugoslav press and diplomatic service were indeed hostile to the Soviet Union, but it was the party's duty to "return to positions of Marxism–Leninism".[44]

Molotov repeated the views he had been enunciating for some time, but broadened his attack to Khrushchev himself by pointing out that he had entered into foreign policy matters without consulting the Ministry of Foreign Affairs. None of the other Presidium members, however, supported Molotov, indeed Bulganin recalled how in 1948 Molotov and Stalin had sat together huddled in a corner and, "to Stalin's dictation", Molotov had written the letter denouncing Tito, using material he thought up on the spot. Molotov's case was further weakened by a statement from Pavel Yudin, the former Soviet ambassador to Belgrade from the years 1947 to 1948. He informed members of the Central Committee that his actions had not always been helpful, and that recruiting Yugoslav Politburo member Sreten Žujović as an intelligence agent had inevitably irritated the Yugoslav leadership. In his concluding remarks to the plenum, Khrushchev, clearly tired of the long run-in with Molotov, referred darkly to the need "to rejuvenate" the Presidium.[45]

Towards the Secret Speech

The July 1955 Plenum culminated with the decision to hold the 20th Party Congress in February 1956. Khrushchev recalled how, on his return from Yugoslavia, he "first felt the falseness of the position" that Beria could be blamed for Stalin's crimes. "It was precisely from the Yugoslavs", he noted, "that I first heard a candid characterisation of Stalin; it grated on me at the time, and I got into an argument." However, as he thought things over he realised that Stalin *had* been responsible, "inwardly, subconsciously, a duality of consciousness" existed within Stalin.[46] On the first day of his talks with Tito he had said "I think it would be stupid to talk about this", referring to Stalin's crimes. He was no longer so sure. Shortly after his return from Yugoslavia, on 25 June, Khrushchev held a meeting with procuracy workers and raised the issue of Stalin's purges. "With troikas and the like, the same person arrested, investigated, judged – criminal! And how many cases were there like this?" Vigilance was necessary, enemies were sent against us, extreme measures were, of course, needed to "preserve the gains of the working class, to preserve our state", but, he insisted, "that was not the situation".[47]

After the July 1955 Plenum, Khrushchev determinedly pushed ahead with de-Stalinisation. Indeed, after Malenkov's dismissal the number of rehabilitations brought before the Presidium continued to rise steadily. Among the most prominent of Stalin's victims to be rehabilitated at this time were Nikolai Krylenko and Pavel Postyshev. On 11 May 1955, Rudenko informed the leadership that Krylenko, a former Commissar for Justice, had been condemned unjustly since the protocols of his interrogation did not include the fact that he had subsequently rejected the statements that he had initially been forced to make. A week later, Rudenko reported that there was no evidence, as had been alleged, to link Postyshev to Kosior, putting a question mark over the initial purge of the Ukrainian Communist Party in 1937.[48]

Addressing a factory cell on 11 August 1955 on the events at the plenum, Khrushchev was still haunted by the issue of what he now knew and what the party deserved to know. He told those present that Stalin had done a lot for the country, but he went on "there is a bad side, which we know and should not have been allowed and cannot be praised". He explained his long-standing position that "when it comes to Ezhov and Beria, the party should have been above them and not them above the party". However, Khrushchev was clearly still very uncertain about his verdict and how to proceed. "Stalin must be given justice, he loved his state, he did it in the interests of his state. He arrested the doctors, these innocent people, but he believed that they poisoned people, enemies put false documents in front of him." He had talked about Stalin to cadres in Leningrad, he had come near to telling the truth to the party members of this factory cell, but should the party as a whole be told?[49]

All the while, more and more cases of rehabilitation were being completed. On 1 October 1955 it was decided to rehabilitate all those concerned with the trial of members of the Jewish Anti-Fascist

Committee. In this trial it was clear not only that the evidence heard had been false but that the evidence had been obtained under torture. Thereafter, throughout October, more and more rehabilitations of leading communists from the past were announced. In this climate, the Presidium was understandably uncertain about how to mark the anniversary of Stalin's birth on 21 December. Meeting on 5 November it decided that the anniversary would be marked in the press but would be low key, without any marches, meetings or demonstrations. This was a compromise decision, reached after heated exchanges, with both Kaganovich and Voroshilov objecting and arguing that the Soviet people would not understand what was going on if there were no factory meetings. That Khrushchev was driving through the anti-Stalin policy was clear from Kaganovich's statement on 5 November: "I have no disagreement with you, Comrade Khrushchev ... I do not intend to undertake a struggle against you." Kaganovich was keen to stress in these exchanges that although he had always been loyal to Stalin, Stalin had frequently fallen out with him. Khrushchev's response was short but bitter: "cadres were killed, the military as well".[50]

On 24 December 1955, the decision was taken to rehabilitate the former leading Latvian communist Jan Rudzutak. The implications of this case were potentially shocking. As with other cases, the proceedings had ignored the fact that at his trial Rudzutak had rejected earlier statements on the grounds that they had been obtained through the use of torture. As with other cases, it was clear that the trial protocols had been doctored by the NKVD. However, the rewriting of the trial protocols in this particular case had been used to establish a link between Rudzutak and both Bukharin and Rykov. Clearly the Rudzutak case raised a question mark over the reliability of the show trials of Bukharin and Rykov.[51] Equally shocking were the results of an investigation Mikoyan had privately commissioned into the fate of the delegates elected to the 17th Party Congress in February 1934. During summer 1955 Mikoyan had contacted Lev Shaumian and asked him to undertake some research into the fate of delegates to the 17th Party Congress of February 1934. He also asked Shatunovskaya to put in writing a story she had heard in prison about irregularities during the investigation into Kirov's assassination in December 1934.

Mikoyan received both reports at the end of December 1955 and communicated the results to Khrushchev. When the Presidium met on 31 December, Mikoyan's material was discussed and Shatunovskaya's letter about Kirov's assassination was read out. Even before the reading was complete, Voroshilov had denounced it as "a lie". Khrushchev, on the other hand, felt that something "smelled fishy" about the assassination and the letter's reference to the mysterious death of Kirov's bodyguard, and he called for an investigation to be mounted into the role played by the NKVD both before the assassination and during its investigation. As to the fate of the delegates to the 17th Party Congress, the Presidium decided to establish a commission headed by Petr Pospelov to investigate just why so many delegates to the 17th Party Congress had not survived to attend the 18th Party Congress four years later. Khrushchev was soon heavily involved in the work of that commission.[52]

As the opening of the 20th Party Congress approached, so more and more details about the purges came to light. Khrushchev maintained in his memoirs that, for him and his Presidium colleagues, with the exception of Molotov, Kaganovich, Voroshilov and to a degree Mikoyan, the materials unearthed at this time came as a "complete surprise". This was clearly a bit of an exaggeration. He had long known about incidents of malpractice by the NKVD and he had never accepted the legitimacy of the Doctors' Plot and other conspiracies of Stalin's last years. However, it is possible that the sheer scale of the miscarriages of justice under Stalin might indeed have surprised him. On 22 January 1956, a report was produced on the progress made in working through the 25,368 cases of arrest between 1937 and 1938 in the provincial town of Chelyabinsk; work on some 943 cases had been completed and in all but two of these, the accused had been shown to be innocent.[53]

Khrushchev was determined to confront all members of the Presidium with the material that was coming to light. No longer satisfied with the individual rehabilitation cases coming before the Presidium for endorsement, he decided to involve the whole Presidium in the work of the Pospelov Commission and so, on 1 February 1956, the whole Presidium interviewed one of the leading interrogators of the Ezhov years, Boris Rodos, the man who had questioned the Ukrainian leaders Kosior and Postyshev, for Khrushchev two of the most significant delegates to the 17th Party Congress who did not survive to see the 18th Party Congress. To Khrushchev's question about how Rodos had "unmasked" Kosior and Postyshev, Rodos replied that no unmasking had been necessary, he had simply been told "from on high" that they were guilty. On the back of this revelation, Khrushchev got the Presidium to agree that the military trials of 1937 should also be investigated. Rudenko was now instructed to turn his attention to the cases of General Tukhachevskii and General Yakir, the latter Khrushchev's good friend.

There was no consensus in the Presidium on 1 February about what to do with all this new-found information. Averkii Aristov, a Central Committee secretary involved in the Pospelov Commission, asked Khrushchev "do we have the strength to tell the truth"? But for Molotov and Kaganovich the truth meant recognising Stalin as "the continuer of Lenin's cause". In these heated discussions, Mikoyan and Bulganin supported Khrushchev: Mikoyan insisted that history had to be confronted, while Bulganin insisted that "the party must be told the whole truth" or the leadership would look like fools; "Stalin liquidated the Central Committee elected at the 17th Party Congress" and as such could not be "the continuer" of Lenin's cause. Suslov also backed Khrushchev up, stressing that in the last few months terrible things had come to light, things which could not be forgiven.[54]

Molotov, Kaganovich and Malenkov categorically rejected the idea that Stalin's abuse of power be discussed at the 20th Party Congress. Khrushchev accepted Aristov's view that something had to be said at the congress, but he was still not sure precisely what. He was still wrestling with issues of responsibility, and against all the evidence that he had done so much to help assemble, he could still state during these debates that "Yagoda was probably clean, as was Ezhov". However, he was equally clear: "Stalin was committed to the socialist cause, but used barbaric methods; he destroyed the party; he was no Marxist; he wiped out everything that was holy in a person; everyone was subjected to his capricious temper." Still confused as to the best way forward, he concluded that "at the congress we will not talk about the terror, we must put forward the line of putting Stalin in his place". It was only after the Pospelov Report was presented to the Presidium on 9 February that Khrushchev changed his mind and decided that he had no choice but to talk about the terror at the congress.[55]

The Pospelov Report recorded that 1,980,635 people had been arrested between 1935 and 1940 and that of these 688,503 had been executed. It then went into grim detail about the butchering of the Central Committee elected at the 17th Party Congress. In particular, it noted that during the investigation of the Postyshev case, one investigator complained to Ezhov about the procedures being followed, but this complaint was ignored; in fact all the material about Postyshev's alleged spying had been written by an interrogator in the absence of Postyshev. Stalin's role in the Postyshev case, and in the use of torture against Kosior, was made equally clear. The report also suggested that the real reason for the arrest of Postyshev was the fact that he had begun to express doubts in public about whether some of those arrested, with whom he was acquainted, really had become Trotskyists. The report also outlined the key moments in the evolution of the purges: Stalin's order immediately following on from Kirov's assassination introducing emergency measures; his statement to Ezhov in September 1936 that the secret police was four years behind in its work; his call at the February–March Plenum in 1937 for "shift changes" in the make up of the Central Committee; and his coded telegram of 10 January 1939 defending the use of torture.[56]

Thus, it was only on the very eve of the congress, when the Presidium met on 13 February, that it was agreed that Khrushchev would make a speech about Stalin to a closed session at the end of the congress. At the same meeting it was agreed that copies of Lenin's Testament, in which Lenin had called for Stalin's dismissal as general secretary of the party, and his last essays on the national question, which had criticised Stalin's views on the degree of autonomy to be given to the constituent republics of the Soviet Union, would be circulated to congress delegates. Once again, Molotov, Kaganovich and Malenkov made clear their reservations about confronting these issues, while Khrushchev's supporters, such as Mikoyan, argued that it was now clear that Stalin had usurped power after 1934 and that if those people executed by him had been allowed to live, the triumphs of the Soviet Union would have been all the greater. Suslov even suggested that Stalin had been wrong on many issues before 1934.[57] It was a tense and angry meeting. Molotov and Kaganovich reportedly said at one point to Khrushchev: "What will you say about yourself, Nikita? Surely we were all mixed up in it." In the end Khrushchev had to make clear that if the Presidium did not present the issue of Stalin's crimes to the congress, then he would raise the matter from the floor as a simple delegate. It was only then, Khrushchev stated later, that "they agreed that the question of the personality cult be put before the 20th Party Congress".[58]

The congress took place from 14 to 25 February 1956. It was only on 18 February that Khrushchev was presented with the first draft of his speech, largely written by Pospelov and Aristov; on 19 February he adapted that text to make it his own, a task in which he was joined by *Pravda* editor and Central Committee Secretary Dmitrii Shepilov, thus revisions of the speech continued throughout the first week of the congress proceedings.[59] The agreed text was prepared for delegates on 23 February, but when Khrushchev actually delivered the speech in the early hours of 24–25 February, he made many extempore additions drawing more on anecdotes than Pospelov's statistics;

these were recorded in a version of the speech issued on 25 February. Khrushchev's speech lasted some four hours. His line was this: that in Lenin's day Stalin's failings had been embryonic, but that by his final years they "represented a serious abuse of power". Serious repression began, he said, "when socialism was basically constructed in our country, when the exploiting classes were basically liquidated, when the social structure of Soviet society had been so thoroughly changed that the social base for enemy parties, political tendencies and groups had shrunk away and the ideological enemies of the party had been politically routed long before". So why, he argued, had so many of the delegates to the 17th Party Congress, the Congress of Victors, been decimated? The assassination of Kirov, which provided the justification for the argument that Trotskyist and other enemies had penetrated the party, now seemed suspect and was quite possibly the work of the NKVD. The victims of the purges were Central Committee members like Postyshev, who at the time refused to accept the anti-Trotsky hysteria of the February–March 1937 Plenum and raised a common sense objection to Stalin's thirst for revenge: "how is it possible for a party member to go through those terrible years [1929–1933] loyal to the party and then in 1934 [when things got better] to go over to the Trotskyists?"[60]

Khrushchev was equally keen to point out that the Politburo had been kept in the dark about many crucial aspects of Stalin's rule. It had regularly been issued with the transcripts of confessions, but had never been subsequently informed of the frequent occasions on which the accused later withdrew their confessions on the grounds that they had been made under torture. The purges of the 1930s had harmed the country's progress to socialism and its defence preparedness. After the war things had got significantly worse; those working close to Stalin "learnt all about his maniacal suspicion". He alone was responsible for the break with Yugoslavia, thinking he could destroy Tito with a flick of his finger. By the time of the Doctors' Plot, when Stalin accused his intimates of being "blind kittens, [incapable] of discerning enemies", "we" began to feel that something was wrong, Khrushchev said. His concluding message was clear: "Stalin did all this in the interests of the working class ... that was the tragedy of it." After the speech had been delivered, Kaganovich criticised Khrushchev from departing from the agreed text. Khrushchev's response was angry, he had indeed expressed his own opinion in a number of places, but, he added, "nobody can stop me, I have that right, just like any other person!"[61]

Chapter 5:   Ousting Stalinists, 1956–58

Keeping De-Stalinisation on Course

Whatever might have been said about the need to keep the Secret Speech secret, the Presidium nevertheless decided just a week after it had been made, that it should be discussed at all levels within the party and Komsomol organisations, and also among those falling under the umbrella term of "non-party activists". Although on some occasions the speech was simply read out, and no discussion held, in most cases the reading of the speech was followed by question and answer sessions, with the most senior figure present agreeing to respond to written questions. Khrushchev attended such meetings himself in Moscow and Leningrad, and many later recalled the shock of attending such a gathering. Between 20 and 23 March the Central Committee member and leading historian Anna Pankratova made nine such presentations in Leningrad to a total audience of 6,000, and the audience questions she brought back with her to Moscow caused serious concern. At a meeting in Saratov a former district secretary recently rehabilitated expressed gratitude for being found work again, but could not understand why her former accusers remained in post. In Bălţi, Soviet Moldavia, the meeting raised the question of whether, given the revelations in the Secret Speech, Stalin's body could remain in Lenin's mausoleum.[1] The Komsomol leader at Moscow University's Journalism Faculty was even more forthright, making a speech claiming that the party was no longer acting in the name of the proletariat but had seized power from the proletariat. No wonder officials in the Central Committee complained that party instructions about holding these meetings were being ignored throughout the country.[2]

The impact of the speech was as dramatic abroad as it was at home. On 12 March 1956 the Polish communist leader, Bierut, died. Khrushchev went to the funeral, and then stayed on for the Sixth Plenum of the Polish United Workers' Party; he addressed the plenum on 20 March and returned to Moscow on the 21st. While in Poland he spoke at length about Stalin, repeating much of the Secret Speech, urging the Poles to do as the Soviet Communist Party had done and discuss the speech at every level of the party hierarchy; thus, unlike elsewhere in Eastern Europe, the Secret Speech was discussed in detail by the party membership as a whole and not just by the ruling elite. When Khrushchev returned to Moscow and reported to the Presidium on 22 March about his time in Warsaw, most members seemed content with what they heard, but Kaganovich expressed concern that the new climate meant that some of those Polish communists who had previously been members of the Polish Socialist Party were "lifting their heads".[3] Certainly the meetings held in Poland to discuss the Secret Speech raised potentially dangerous issues, like the arrests of Poles in the late 1930s, the impact of the Rajk Trial on Poland and Eastern Europe generally, and the possibility of countries within the Soviet Bloc adopting national roads to socialism as Yugoslavia had done.

Mikoyan later recalled that a "bitter battle" had begun immediately after the speech, and by the first half of April 1956 it was clear that the Presidium was making decisions which suggested that Khrushchev was being forced to backtrack. On 5 April *Pravda* published an article attacking those who used the criticism of the cult of personality "for every sort of dreamt-up insult or anti-party statement". A Komsomol plenum at this time was told that the term "Stalinist" was not one of abuse, "Stalinist", like Stalin himself, was inseparable from the term "communist". On 7 April *Pravda* reprinted an editorial from the Chinese party newspaper calling on communists to treasure Stalin's works and his "historical inheritance". The Presidium meeting on 13 April also took a number of key decisions, which did not fit with the spirit of the 20th Party Congress: when it discussed the greetings to be sent to "brother parties" on 1 May, it was decided there was no need to send greetings to Tito; the same meeting decided that whether portraits of Stalin continued to be displayed was something for the localities to decide.[4]

The Presidium meeting of 13 April also put a stop to further investigations into Stalin's crimes. Although it was agreed to establish, as promised, a commission on the Bukharin and Rykov show trials, by deciding that this commission should be convened by Molotov, with Voroshilov and Kaganovich as members, it was hardly surprising that it made little progress. On 26 April, the Presidium discussed the planned new history of the party, and again the divisions within the Presidium were clear to see: Mikoyan took the radical line, criticising the proposed account of 1917 in Petrograd since it scarcely mentioned the Petrograd Soviet, apparently on the grounds that Trotsky was involved in the soviet and chaired several of its sessions, which simply meant the crucial role the Petrograd Soviet played in preparing the October Revolution was never explained; Molotov focused on a very different issue, complaining that Stalin was denigrated in the text, and Kaganovich agreed with him, saying the new book was "not a history but a commentary on the 20th Party Congress".[5] Khrushchev visited Great Britain from 18 to 27 April and so did not take part in this ideological spat.

On his return to Moscow he was determined to continue pushing for de-Stalinisation in the realm of international relations, and in particular to capitalise on improved relations with Yugoslavia by restoring unity to the communist world. Khrushchev could not forget that in May 1945, at Stalin's urging, he had organised in Kiev "a good reception for Tito" and that even then he "took a liking to him".[6] The Cominform was dissolved on 18 April 1956 and not only did that open the way for Tito to visit the Soviet Union, but reopened the prospect of an agreement between the Soviet and Yugoslav Communist Parties. Yet opposition from Molotov was as intransigent as ever. When Yugoslavia was discussed by the Presidium on 25 May, he protested that Tito had once compared Stalin's actions to those of the Tsar. As in 1955, however, Molotov was on his own when it came to Yugoslavia; Kaganovich and Malenkov, usually his allies, argued that a flexible approach was now needed towards Yugoslavia. At first Khrushchev simply expressed disappointment that Molotov had not changed his views, but the following day he decided that enough was enough and proposed dismissing Molotov as Foreign Minister. Discussion of Molotov's future resumed on 28 May when it was decided he should go, but no agreement was reached over who should replace him. It was only on the day of Tito's arrival in Moscow, 2 June, that Shepilov took over as Foreign Minister.[7]

Tito travelled slowly, by train, and at every stop was greeted in the traditional way with bread and salt; in Moscow "hundreds of thousands" turned out to meet him. His visit lasted three weeks and this time he was fulsome in his praise for Khrushchev. "We believed that the time would come when everything that kept us apart would be transformed and that our friendship would acquire new and firm foundations. That time has now come, thanks to the Leninist policy of the government and the Soviet Party [and] the courageous and far-sighted policy of the collective leadership of the USSR." On 20 June 1956 the Moscow Declaration was signed, restoring relations between the communist parties of the two countries. There was just one small hiccough. When Tito signed the Moscow Declaration, he took the opportunity to denounce the Hungarian communist leader Rákosi. Tito still felt personally affronted by the Rajk Trial – after the verdict was announced in 1949 he had gone in person to the Hungarian embassy in Belgrade to hand in a protest note. Now he explicitly attacked Rákosi: "These men have their hands soaked in blood; they have staged trials, given false information, sentenced innocent men to death. They have dragged Yugoslavia into all these trials, as in the case of the Rajk Trial, and they now find it difficult to admit their mistakes before their own people."[8]

Khrushchev had promised Tito he would act against Rákosi, but was not at first able to do so. Disagreements within the Presidium about the pace of de-Stalinisation were ongoing and were restricting his freedom of manoeuvre. On 1 June, the eve of Tito's visit, Khrushchev decided that it was best to postpone until the autumn a Central Committee Plenum which would have assessed the results of the 20th Party Congress. That plenum would have been a stormy affair and its outcome by no means inevitably in Khrushchev's favour. Defence Minister Zhukov was determined to extend the case against Stalin and wanted to deliver a speech which outlined all Stalin's failings during the war. The draft of this speech not only gave chapter and verse about the Soviet Union's military unpreparedness in 1941, but argued that the cult of personality had harmed "military ideological work in the army". The Presidium discussions of 7 June on the entry under "Stalin" in the *Great Soviet Encyclopaedia* showed how sensitive the question of Stalin still was. Kaganovich protested that there was not enough discussion of Stalin's pre-revolutionary activity, his work on the national question, his role in 1917, his role during the civil war and his role in defeating the Nazis during the Great Patriotic War; nor was there enough about his theoretical writings.[9]

At the conclusion of the 20th Party Congress in February, the Presidium had established a commission of Suslov, Pospelov and Nuritdin Mukhitdinov to prepare a resolution on the cult of personality. The resolution was supposed to be ready within a month, but wrangling led to delays and it was only ready on 19 June.[10] However, before the agreed text was published on 30 June, the political climate had changed dramatically. In Poznan, Poland, there had been a long-standing disagreement about working conditions at the Cegielskii Metal Industries Works. On 23 June a delegation of workers had gone to Warsaw and apparently negotiated a resolution of the dispute, only to discover on their return to Poznan that the Ministry of Machine Industry had reneged on the deal. On 28 June mass crowds took to the streets, demonstrating, demanding bread, and shouting "down with the red bourgeoisie!" Some of the slogans were even more overtly political, such as "free elections supervised by the United Nations". As demonstrators marched from the factory to the city centre, some broke away, headed for the security police headquarters and seized weapons from the police. Once the operation to restore order had begun, fighting developed and ended only on 30 June. By then, 73 people had been killed as 10,000 soldiers and 400 tanks confronted the workers. These events were discussed in the Presidium as they occurred, on the night of 28 June, and inevitably coloured the resolution on the cult of personality.[11]

The resolution of 30 June took note of the Poznan events, and the supposed role of "imperialists" in fomenting them, and devoted a lot of space to criticising how "enemies" were making use of Khrushchev's revelations; indeed the revelations themselves, and their implications for the party, were not discussed in the resolution at all. Khrushchev's attack on Stalin was repackaged in an orthodox Stalinist framework, making "enemies" not Stalin the essence of the problem. Unlike the Secret Speech, the resolution was an attempt to balance Stalin's achievements in a way that Molotov and Kaganovich could accept: it noted how "self-criticism", which kept the party close to the people, had broken down under Stalin; it accepted that the vigilance campaign of the 1930s had led to limitations on democratic processes; it accepted that Stalin's ideological formulation of 1937 that the class struggle got more acute as the victory of socialism neared was "mistaken"; and it accepted that the party's loss of control over the security apparatus gradually turned into Stalin's personal control of that apparatus. However, the resolution was equally clear that the cult of personality had not been absolute and that there were times, such as during the war, when Stalin had ruled collegially. The resolution gave no figures for Stalin's repressions and gave no examples of how they had taken place. And it made clear that, while mistakes had been made, those mistakes had not had their origins in the nature of Soviet society. In the same spirit, on 16 July 1956, the Presidium sent a letter to party organisations making clear that no "anti-party" speech or demonstration should be ignored; the party should respond to any and every such incident; "liberalism" was impossible when the US was spending millions of dollars on anti-Soviet propaganda.[12]

The Poznan events, the resolution of 30 June, and the consequences of Tito's visit all had an impact on events in Hungary. Back

in June 1953, before the removal of Beria, the Hungarian communist leadership had been summoned to Moscow and instructed to
make Imre Nagy prime minister, while keeping Rákosi as head of the
party. When Beria was arrested, within days, Rákosi began a whisper-
ing campaign against Nagy, suggesting that he was "Beria's man".
At first Rákosi had little success and Nagy was able to start a dramatic
reform programme which by autumn 1954 had not only revived the
Hungarian economy but established a new Patriotic People's Front
as a respected democratic forum and organiser of local elections in
which the Communist Party no longer pre-selected the successful
candidates. When Malenkov was dismissed as Soviet prime minister
in February 1955, however, Rákosi took the opportunity to sack Nagy
and condemn his reform programme as a "Right Deviation". By
April 1955 Nagy had been expelled from the Politburo and Central
Committee, and at the end of the year he was expelled from the party.
Thus by the start of 1956 Rákosi had triumphantly returned to domi-
nate Hungarian politics.

When the Moscow Declaration had been signed between the
Soviet Union and Yugoslavia on 20 June, Khrushchev had given Tito
to understand that despite Rákosi's trouncing of Nagy, his days of
triumph were numbered; he sent Suslov to visit Hungary to prepare
for Rákosi's demise. Then came the events in Poznan and the resolution on the cult of personality. On 12 July, the Presidium considered
the situation in both Poland and Hungary and the hard line was
still clearly in the ascendancy. The Presidium decided in the case
of Poland that *Pravda* should publish an article which put events in
Poland down to the work of "imperialists" who "under the flag of
talk of independent roads to socialism" were trying to pick off the
socialist countries one by one. On Hungary, the Presidium concluded
that "the situation for Rákosi should be eased", in other words his
dismissal could be put on hold.[13]

The *Pravda* article duly appeared on 16 July and, as well as condemning the work of "enemies" in Poland, it turned its attention
to the emergence of an "enemy" in Hungary, the Petőfi Circle. The
Petőfi Circle was a group established within Hungary's communist
youth organisation which consciously tried to keep alive the reform
legacy of Nagy, despite his expulsion from the party. The circle was
soon the stomping ground for the radical Marxist philosopher Georg
Lukács, a veteran of the Hungarian Soviet of 1919. On 27 June 1956
the circle organised its biggest public event thus far, a meeting to
discuss press freedom. Attended by over 6,000 people, it caused a
sensation: Lukács attended and was photographed talking to Árpád

Szakasits, the former leader of the Hungarian Social Democratic Party and one-time President of Hungary in the 1940s, who had been arrested by Rákosi but released from prison in the aftermath of the Secret Speech. The meeting also heard from Géza Losonczy, one of Nagy's closest supporters, and he demanded that Nagy be restored to the party leadership. Not surprisingly, Rákosi responded to this public show of strength on the part of Nagy's supporters by summoning the Hungarian Central Committee to an extraordinary plenum, banning the Petőfi Circle and drawing up a list of some four hundred opposition activists, with Nagy at their head, to be arrested.[14]

This knee-jerk Stalinist response on Rákosi's part gave Khrushchev the opening he was looking for. The Presidium meeting of 12 July had decided to send Mikoyan "on holiday" to Lake Balaton in Hungary to monitor Hungarian affairs. On 18 July he attended the extraordinary plenum summoned by Rákosi and made clear to him that he would have to go since the days when the mass arrest of opponents was acceptable to Moscow were long past. Clearly Rákosi's overreaction had enabled Khrushchev to re-assert his authority. However, when it came to the choice of a replacement for Rákosi, Khrushchev had to bow to Molotov. Tito had been pressing for János Kádár to be appointed in Rákosi's place, a fresh face and someone briefly imprisoned under Rákosi. Khrushchev toyed with this proposal, but in the end backed Molotov's insistence that, if Rákosi had to go, he should be replaced by his deputy, Ernő Gerő. To rub in the significance of the message to the Hungarians, Mikoyan went straight from Hungary to Belgrade for further consultations with the Yugoslavs, before returning to Budapest on 21 July where he had a meeting with Nagy. Less than three weeks later, on 9 August 1956, Tito invited Khrushchev to pay a private visit to Yugoslavia in September.[15]

The Hungarian Setback

On 19 September 1956 Khrushchev paid his "private visit" to Yugoslavia. Tito then returned with him to Crimea on 27 September, where the two stayed until 5 October. In the course of these two holidays, Khrushchev held 10 days of talks with Tito, without intermediaries, interspersed with swimming and hunting. Together they seemed to be planning the renewal of communism. Hungary was high on their agenda, and Khrushchev summoned Gerő to join them on 2 October. Tito was initially cautious about endorsing the new Hungarian leader, but after he learned that Gerő had already held a preliminary meeting with Nagy at which it was agreed that Nagy could rejoin the party, Tito agreed to invite Gerő for an official visit to Yugoslavia; on 13 October, Nagy was duly accepted back into the party and on 15 October Gerő set off on a state visit to Belgrade.

Unfortunately for Khrushchev, more was involved in the renewal of communism than holidaying with Tito. He returned from Crimea to find the situation in Poland reaching crisis point, and that the contagion was spreading to Hungary. When the Polish party held its Seventh Plenum from 18 to 28 July, clear divisions had emerged on how to respond to the Poznan events. The Soviet representative at the plenum continued to blame "imperialist agents" and a "lack of vigilance" for what had happened, but the plenum also heard the view that the "clumsy attempt to present the painful Poznan tragedy as the work of imperialist agents and provocateurs" was "naïve". The author of these remarks was Wladisław Gomułka. Khrushchev had met Gomułka in 1945 when Stalin had sent him to help reconstruct Warsaw and the two had worked well together. However Gomułka had then emerged as a sort of Polish Tito opposing both the formation of the Cominform in 1947 and the programme of collectivisation launched in 1948–9. After periods of prison and house arrest he was freed in spring 1956 and at the Seventh Plenum he was readmitted to the party. It was under his influence that the plenum not only rejected "imperialism" as an explanation for the Poznan events but also passed a series of reforming measures to strengthen the democratic process by reviving parliament and local councils, and restoring the authority of workers' councils in the factories. Over the summer, Polish communists quickly polarised between those loyal to Moscow's version of events, and more radical elements, often based in the workers' councils, who backed Gomułka.[16]

While Khrushchev was entertaining Tito, the Presidium had become increasingly concerned about developments in Poland, especially the critical "anti-Soviet" tone emerging in the Polish press. However, the Presidium decided on a cautious approach and resolved on 4 October to do nothing, since commenting on what was happening with the Polish press might actually make the situation worse. At the same meeting it acceded to a Polish request that KGB advisers be withdrawn from the country. Disagreements in Poland focused on the figure of Gomułka. On 27 September, just before heading for Crimea with Tito, Khrushchev had raised the question of Gomułka, proposing that he be allowed to take a holiday in Crimea. Khrushchev rightly believed that Gomułka would eventually be brought back into Polish political life, and he was concerned that there was a danger of it happening "under the banner of anti-Sovietism" rather than through a controlled process of agreement.[17]

On 15 October, the Polish Politburo met, with Gomułka in attendance, and it was decided that the forthcoming Eighth Plenum would reappoint him leader. At once the opponents of Gomułka contacted the Soviet ambassador, who instructed Gomułka and the entire membership of the Polish Politburo to travel to Moscow for talks. The Poles refused the summons and instead called the Eighth Plenum for 19–21 October. With the Red Army organising "manoeuvres" around strategic sites in Poland and workers' councils organising mass rallies in the factories to resist any Russian occupation, confrontation seemed inevitable. The Eighth Plenum opened on schedule on 19 October, but then immediately adjourned because Khrushchev had arrived in Warsaw at the head of a Soviet delegation. Khrushchev and Gomułka had a stormy confrontation at the airport. Khrushchev accused the Polish Ministry of the Interior of using its military formations to restrict the freedom of action of the Polish Minister of Defence, a Russian of Polish descent Konstantin Rokossovski. Gomułka demanded that all Red Army movements cease.[18]

Khrushchev recalled later how, at the plenum, Gomułka angrily called on him to stop the Red Army's tank division then heading for Warsaw; Khrushchev "began by denying everything" pretending he had not ordered Soviet forces to move towards Warsaw, but after Gomuka make clear his loyalty to the Warsaw Pact and his willingness to defer to the Soviet Union in terms of foreign policy, by 1 am on 20 October, Khrushchev was sufficiently mollified to agree that the Eighth Plenum could continue its work. However, Khrushchev was equally clear that Soviet military intervention remained an option, since Gomułka had refused to allow any of Khrushchev's delegation to address the Eighth Plenum. Later on the 20th, the Presidium drew up contingency plans for more military operations and a "provisional revolutionary committee" to replace Gomułka should that prove necessary, but when the Presidium met the next day it dropped all such talk. The Eighth Plenum had completed its work; it had elected Gomułka the new Polish leader by secret ballot, but no specifically anti-Soviet decisions had been taken. As the Presidium debated the issue of armed intervention or continuing to monitor events, Khrushchev stated clearly that there should be no intervention; it was time "to show patience".[19]

At the height of the Polish crisis, events in Hungary also crowded onto the Presidium's agenda. Following on from the talks which

Tito and Khrushchev held with Gerő in Crimea, on 13 October, just prior to Gerő leaving for his official visit to Yugoslavia, Nagy was re-admitted to the party. However, this careful political choreography was running behind the tide of public opinion. This had become clear a week earlier. One of the slightly macabre terms put down by Tito for reconciliation with the Hungarian communists was for the reinterment of Rajk's body. This ceremony held on 6 October was rapidly transformed into a massive demonstration organised by the officially banned Petőfi Circle. Over 200,000 people took part, with a smaller group breaking away to demonstrate outside the Yugoslav embassy, cheering Tito and praising Yugoslav communism. As Gerő and his comrades started to grapple with the new post-Stalin world, they began to assert themselves a little. Like the Poles, the Hungarian leadership also raised the question of the future of KGB advisers in their country, and at the same time they raised concerns about the highly visible presence of Red Army forces in Hungary; on 20 October the Presidium decided to send Mikoyan to Budapest to discuss both these issues.[20]

Mikoyan was therefore in Budapest when students at Budapest Technical University issued a call on 22 October for a mass demonstration on the 23rd in support of Gomułka and the Poles' very public decision to stand up to Soviet pressure – that the Soviet leadership had just decided not to intervene militarily in Poland was, of course, known to no-one and Soviet military action still seemed very possible. The Hungarian leadership handled the demonstration of 23 October ineptly, making clear how little had changed under Gerő's leadership. The demonstration was at first banned, but then the ban was lifted when the demonstration went ahead anyway. Gerő, literally just back from his visit to Yugoslavia, first denounced the demonstrators as "counter-revolutionaries" and then decided to call on Nagy to address the crowds, even though at that point Nagy was officially just a rank-and-file party member, not a member of the leadership. Nagy's opening appeal to the crowd as "comrades" might have worked in 1953 but in 1956 it mistook the popular mood and far from the crowds dispersing as he had requested, they surged to the radio station to demand the right to state their case. As the first armed clashes began, Gerő called for Soviet support. Thus by the morning of 24 October, demonstrators were in control of the radio building, but Soviet tanks controlled the streets.

For the next week, Khrushchev was uncertain how to proceed, veering between hard-line and compromise solutions. The Presidium first discussed the situation in Hungary on the evening of 23 October, when Defence Minister Zhukov reported that some 100,000 people had taken part in the demonstration that day, which had ended with the radio station being set on fire. Khrushchev and the majority of the Presidium backed the proposal to deploy troops, but Mikoyan, initially a lone voice, proposed that the Hungarians restore order themselves. A political initiative was the only starting point for a solution to the crisis, he said. Deploying troops at once, he suggested, would "spoil our cause". Mikoyan had been closely involved in Hungarian affairs and so Khrushchev was persuaded, and changed his mind to back Mikoyan's view that an attempt should be made to work with Nagy. Mikoyan was sent back to Budapest to negotiate, but the more hard-line Suslov was sent with him, reflecting the delicate balance of views within the Presidium.[21]

By 26 October, the divisions within the Presidium were clear: Bulganin, Molotov, Kaganovich, Malenkov and Zhukov all felt that Mikoyan was "taking the wrong line" in working with Nagy. Nagy's initial actions on 24 and 25 October had been relatively easy to accept; he had formed a new government based on the People's Patriotic Front rather than the party and replaced Gerő as party leader with János Kádár. However, by 26 October it was clear that calling the new government a government of the People's Patriotic Front was not the usual communist sleight of hand, but the start of a genuine coalition government that would include representatives of the Smallholder Party, which in 1945–7 had dominated Hungarian politics and whose leaders had emerged from prison earlier in 1956. Khrushchev tried to sum things up, "we are not agreed with the government" but Mikoyan was only doing what he had been asked to try and do, work with Nagy.[22]

Things were scarcely any clearer on 28 October when the Presidium again discussed the situation in Hungary. By then a ceasefire had been declared between the Red Army and the insurgents, but not all the insurgents had agreed to abide by it. Khrushchev reported to the Presidium that this made the situation even more difficult. Kádár was suggesting holding talks with the hotbeds of opposition and, to facilitate this, was keen that the propaganda line should change: since workers throughout Hungary were supporting the insurgency, it no longer made sense to describe it as a "counter-revolutionary uprising". Implementing such a change, Kádár suggested, would only be possible if Suslov were recalled. Bulganin, Molotov, Kaganovich and Malenkov all still wanted immediate Soviet intervention, but Zhukov had changed his mind and now backed Mikoyan, arguing that since the initial decision to deploy troops on 23 October the situation had moved on, and a much more flexible response was now needed. He suggested organising an armed workers' militia to confront the insurgents, retaining Red Army troops in reserve.

Khrushchev himself was still uncertain. The key issue for him was whether the government which was emerging under Nagy was going to be "with us or against us", if it was "with us" it should surely be ready to request the deployment of Soviet troops. There was, he suggested, no firmness in either the party or the government, while the uprising seemed to be spreading to the provinces and the loyalty of the army was open to question. He was still hopeful that the government would act firmly, and "we will support it", but if Nagy turned against the Soviet Union and demanded the withdrawal of troops, then "we create a committee to take power", something he clearly felt was for now the "worst option". The Presidium reconvened later that night to hear a report from Suslov, and then somewhat later still a report from Kádár. After more bitter exchanges, Khrushchev supported Suslov's view that, for all his reservations, contact with Nagy should still be maintained and to facilitate this it was agreed to go ahead and publish the Declaration of Friendship and Co-operation between the Soviet Union and Socialist States. This declaration, which had emerged from Khrushchev's talks with Tito, recognised that each socialist country had a right to follow its own road to socialism, and that Soviet troops were stationed in Eastern Europe by agreement and could be withdrawn. The notes recording this momentous Presidium decision read: "Khrushchev summed up: we support this government, we talk to Nagy and Kádár. We issue the Declaration. If the hotbeds of opposition do cease firing we are ready for a cease fire and the withdrawal of troops from Budapest. Yugoslavia to be informed."[23]

When the Presidium reconvened on 30 October, Khrushchev had the impression things were working well. Although Zhukov had picked up reports that Nagy was playing "a double game", Khrushchev had talked to Mikoyan who was relatively upbeat. That session of the Presidium was attended by the head of a visiting Chinese delegation, Liu Shaoxi, and Khrushchev impressed upon him that the key to the way forward lay in the Declaration, which made clear that Soviet troops could be withdrawn from the People's Democracies if that is what they wished. Khrushchev reminded Liu that the Chinese Politburo had already endorsed the Declaration, a necessary reminder since at an earlier Presidium session he attended on 24 October, Liu had implied Chinese support for a hard line on Hungary by stressing that "the USSR is the centre of the socialist camp and there cannot be several centres". The situation in Hungary seemed to be righting itself, even if, as Shepilov noted, it would be necessary "for a long time to carry out a struggle against national communism".[24]

Less than 24 hours later, Khrushchev had completely reversed his position. As he explained to the Chinese delegation, "that very morning we received a report from Budapest that the counter-revolution had literally begun a pogrom: communists were being hanged by their feet, especially security police and party leaders". He had always reserved the right to attack Nagy if "he turned against us". On 31 October he told the Presidium that it was time to think again, that troops should not be withdrawn from Budapest but used to restore order. The imperialists, he said, would see the Soviet Union's weakness and walk in: "to Egypt they would add Hungary, we have no choice". The Presidium backed this abrupt turnaround and moved on to consider how to form a new loyal government, using that "worst option" of "a committee". In the original plan the veteran communist Ferenc Műnnich, whom Khrushchev had known since 1930 when the two men did reserve military training together, was identified as the head of this new administration, with Kádár as his deputy; if Nagy were willing, he might be offered a deputy premier post in the new administration. It was time, the Presidium resolved, "to talk to Tito".[25]

On 1 November, Mikoyan, who had rushed back from Budapest, was given the opportunity to make one last appeal to the Presidium that it revoke the decision to intervene. Force would be of no help, Mikoyan suggested, and supporting Nagy for just a further fortnight would enable him to stabilise the situation; later he suggested that supporting Nagy for just a further three days might be enough. The Presidium would not be swayed, Suslov would no longer defend working with Nagy, for him there was a real danger of "bourgeois restoration" and things were developing completely outside the control of the party – "only through occupation will we have a government which supports us", he said. Nor would Khrushchev be dissuaded, even when Mikoyan called at Khrushchev's home on the morning of 2 November and urged him once again not to use troops. "Mikoyan became extremely upset and even threatened that he could not vouch for the consequences and as a sign of protest might even do something to himself", Khrushchev recalled.[26]

From the moment the Hungarian crisis began, Khrushchev had been determined to involve Yugoslavia in its resolution. He received the Yugoslav ambassador on 25 October and warned him even then that it might be necessary "to answer force with force" if a political solution proved impossible. Thus, later on 2 November, Khrushchev flew to Tito's holiday island retreat of Brioni and from seven in the evening until five the following morning discussed the situation in Hungary and the preparations which were being made; Khrushchev made clear that at simultaneous meetings being held in Brest and Bucharest the other Eastern European leaders were all being brought on board, although in Gomuka's case this was not in fact true. Informed en route to Brioni that Kádár and Münnich had arrived in the Soviet Union, Khrushchev sought and got Tito's endorsement for military intervention to establish a new "revolutionary" government. For most of 1956, Tito had been working for Nagy's restoration to power and initially welcomed the government he formed, but, like Khrushchev, he was soon alarmed by what he saw as the resurgence in Hungary of the violent counter-revolutionary Right. Tito advised that the new "revolutionary" government should appeal to and work with the workers' councils which had been established throughout Hungary; to facilitate this, he suggested, the new government should be led by Kádár rather than Münnich and although Kádár's candidacy had been rejected by the Presidium on 31 October, Khrushchev readily agreed to it now.[27]

Khrushchev's choice of Kádár as the new Hungarian leader accentuated divisions within the Soviet leadership about policy towards Hungary, upsetting Molotov in particular. On 3 November, when the Presidium heard Kádár outline his plans for restoring communist power in Hungary, Khrushchev was ready to take some of the blame for what had happened. He focused on Rákosi, and concluded that the first mistake had been to delay so long in getting rid of him; the second mistake had been not to realise that Kádár would have been a far better choice than Gerő as Rákosi's replacement. Although Khrushchev was clear "we cannot consider Nagy a communist", he was equally clear that "some of the insurgents are not enemies". Molotov, on the other hand, "spoke sharply against Kádár", since Kádár initially "continued to regard himself as a member of the leadership headed by Nagy". On 4 November, Molotov opposed Khrushchev in the Presidium over the wording of Kádár's Declaration to the Hungarian People. It was too critical of Rákosi, Molotov said, and appeared to imply that Kádár was moving closer to Tito; Khrushchev, on the other hand, praised the wording of the declaration. Similar issues came up on 6 November about other programmatic statements issued by Kádár; Molotov always protested when criticisms were made about Rákosi.[28]

Retreating to Better Advance

Khrushchev's understanding with Tito about how the intervention in Hungary should develop did not last long. As the Soviet intervention began on 4 November, Nagy sought sanctuary in the Yugoslav embassy. This immediately persuaded Khrushchev's opponents in the Presidium that Tito was up to no good and pursuing his own agenda. In fact, the Yugoslavs had agreed to Nagy taking shelter in the embassy as part of the strategy they had reached jointly with Khrushchev, that Nagy should be isolated from "reactionaries" and persuaded to make a statement in favour of Kádár's new government; after all, the Presidium was of the view that he could be allocated a deputy premier post. Later on 4 November the Yugoslavs asked Moscow if a statement from Nagy was still needed. There was no immediate answer and when a Soviet response did come it was to the effect that a statement by Nagy, even if it could be obtained, was not now needed and Nagy should be handed over to the Soviet authorities. Khrushchev seems to have been genuinely surprised when, instead, Tito stated on 5 November that this was impossible now that sanctuary had been granted and proposed that Nagy be given free passage to Yugoslavia.

Khrushchev was furious, Tito really did seem to be playing a double game as his critics suggested. He told the Yugoslav ambassador that he had struggled in the Presidium to get Rákosi condemned, and now it looked as if the Yugoslavs were protecting Nagy in order to establish a new government opposed to that of Kádár. On 7 November, Khrushchev sent Tito an angry message making clear that "now that Nagy and his cohorts have found refuge in the Yugoslav embassy our assessment of the causes of the developments in Hungary requires a revision"; Molotov had consistently argued that the Yugoslavs had been inflaming the situation over the summer by their determined support for Nagy, and Khrushchev seemed to be moving towards such a view himself. Significantly, however, Khrushchev now called for Nagy to be transferred to the custody of Kádár's government, not the Soviet military; subsequent exchanges between 9 and 10 November calmed the situation considerably, as Tito wrote on 8 November it was "only as a result of the speed of events [that] matters were not clarified and problems were created".[29]

Misguidedly hoping to influence the power struggle so clearly taking place in Moscow, Tito decided to make a speech outlining the problem of de-Stalinisation as he saw it. Addressing an audience in Pula on 11 November, Tito explained that it had become clear to him when with Khrushchev in Crimea, that the Soviet leadership had not understood the true significance of the events taking place in Poland and Hungary. This failing arose because Khrushchev still approached the problem of Stalin from the question of his personality, and had not yet appreciated that Stalinism was more than an issue of personality, it was "a question of a system". Tito deliberately divided the Soviet leadership into "Stalinists" and reformers, hoping, he imagined, to help those "who are thinking in a new way". Unsurprisingly, the speech had the very opposite effect, since the Presidium was never going to tolerate foreign "advice" of this kind. Khrushchev told the Yugoslav ambassador that the Pula speech had hardened attitudes in the Presidium towards Yugoslavia considerably.

On 23 November *Pravda* made clear that the cult of personality was just that, the failings of an individual. There were no deficiencies in the Soviet system as such and it was wrong for the Yugoslavs to seek to impose their system on other states by constantly writing about a "Yugoslav road to socialism" that others should follow. The *Pravda* article appeared the day after Nagy left the Yugoslav embassy in Budapest. After the Yugoslavs had received a written understanding that Nagy was free to return home, he left the embassy and was promptly arrested by the Soviet military as he boarded the bus waiting for him. Understandably, the Yugoslavs were furious. That the Presidium were not all in agreement with this move is clear from Khrushchev's statement in the Presidium on 27 November that it was a mistake for "our officer to get on the bus".[30]

Since Tito's visit in June 1956, Molotov had not held any ministerial post, but on 21 November he was appointed Minister of State Control, the department for ensuring that government decrees were implemented. This was no great promotion, but nor was it the retirement Khrushchev had recently hinted at. Molotov's renewed authority was in evidence when on 6 December the Presidium discussed "strengthening the political work of party organisations among the masses and nipping in the bud any sally by anti-Soviet enemy elements". Discussion ranged over purging the party, changing the law and empowering the KGB to investigate and take cases through the court. Even Khrushchev conceded that some of those released from prison "had not deserved it", and later explained that if those released from prison "blathered all sorts of nonsense" then the party could not simply fold its hands and remain neutral. And there were some very public signs that the "contagion" from Hungary might be spreading to Moscow.[31]

On 22 October, at the height of the Polish and Hungarian crises, the Writers' Union organised a public discussion at Moscow's Central

House of Writers of the novel by Vladimir Dudintsev *Not by Bread Alone*, which had been appearing in the journal *Novyi Mir* since August. The tale of an inventor whose initiatives were frustrated by bureaucrats, and who experienced a Kafka-esque trial before his ideas were eventually taken seriously, was praised at the Writers' Union discussion by Konstantin Paustovskii, one of the Soviet Union's most respected writers. The event was reminiscent of the Petőfi Circle's debate on free speech. Dudintsev attended himself, joined by many authors and literary critics and literally hundreds of Soviet citizens including many university students, some reportedly clinging on to drainpipes to get access to the second floor Oak Hall where the meeting took place. The press had been running a campaign on the "technical creative work of the masses" which echoed the theme of the novel; *Pravda* on 17 October actually attacked the way the authorities dealt with inventors. As Paustovskii denounced bureaucracy and bureaucrats, and described the emergence of "a new tribe of plunderers and owners having nothing in common with our revolution" his words were met with continual applause and shouts of agreement.[32] Paustovskii's speech was widely but unofficially circulated, even though it was deemed "anti-Soviet". The official verdict on Dudintsev's novel was that the events he described were "not typical", although the hero's conclusion that he would spend the whole of his life struggling against bureaucracy suggested the very opposite. On 6 December 1956 the leadership of the Writers' Union was summoned to the Central Committee and told that *Not by Bread Alone* was "a call to arms Hungarian style" and should not have been published.[33]

When the Presidium met on 6 December it decided to send a "secret letter" to all party organisations on the dangers posed by the penetration of alien ideas into the country. Composing the right form of words took some time, however, and when the agreed text was issued on 19 December, Khrushchev had been able to modify it slightly, adding the phrase "those influenced by foreign propaganda should not automatically be considered enemy elements". However, the overall tone of the letter was clear, "we cannot have two views on how to struggle against them [ideological enemies], the dictatorship of the proletariat on this matter must be merciless"; what had happened in Hungary had nothing to do with democracy and was simply an attempt at "Horthyite restoration". The secret letter identified students and intellectuals as "most at risk" and during 1957 there were almost 2,000 arrests for anti-Soviet activity, though somewhat ironically, most of those arrested were disgruntled workers rather than intellectuals.[34]

Whatever the impact of the events in Poland and Hungary on his position, Khrushchev was already working on one of his most radical domestic reforms. On 20 November he had called for the plan for 1957, and indeed the whole of the current Five-Year Plan, to be reconsidered; more funds had to be found for housing construction and improved supplies for the population. Speaking in 1964, he recalled that at the 20th Party Congress "we adopted the most stupid Five-Year Plan" and immediately were forced to correct it. Khrushchev clearly struggled to get his Presidium colleagues to agree. On 29 November it was accepted that the next plenum would discuss the plan, but on 13 December the Presidium was still discussing the target figures and the plenum was postponed until 20–24 December; on 18 December the Presidium established a commission "to finalise the details" of the Five-Year Plan. According to Khrushchev's son, what lay behind this evident disagreement among the leadership was Khrushchev's fury that the published figures for plan fulfilment were going to be massaged so that it appeared that targets had been met when in fact they had not. Khrushchev would not go along with such blatant deceit and it was left to Bulganin to speak at the plenum on "questions of improving the economy".[35]

During this discussion of the 1957 plan, Khrushchev had stated in the Presidium on 29 November that it was time "to irritate *Gosplan*", the state planning agency. This was the opening shot in a campaign to radically restructure the operation of the economy, a precursor to the proposal he put to the Presidium on 28 January 1957 with the title "improving the leadership of industry". Behind this bland title lay the start of the so-called *Sovnarkhoz* Reform, but at this stage all Khrushchev claimed he wanted was support in principle for the idea of decentralising economic decision-making, because in Khrushchev's view "we overestimate the leadership of the Moscow ministries". Seven members of the Presidium supported Khrushchev's proposal, two hesitated and three, led by Molotov, opposed it; Malenkov was not present. When candidate members of the Presidium were excluded, the vote was closer, only five for and three against.[36]

Khrushchev was not deterred. A working party was set up to debate the reform at length on 4 February and its report was duly presented to the next Central Committee Plenum on 13–14 February. On the very eve of the plenum, "at three in the morning", Molotov sent Presidium members a note outlining his objections to what was proposed. Nevertheless, the plenum endorsed Khrushchev's proposal that 10 All-Union and 15 Union–Republican ministries should be abolished and replaced by 70 "Councils of the National Economy" or *Sovnarkhozy* operating at a regional level. These were envisaged as powerful organisations, with a staff of between 300 and 500, often composed of people transferred from the liquidated ministries. It was anticipated that the reform would not only make planning more regionally based and thus more responsive to local needs, but that significant administrative savings could be made: establishing the *sovnarkhoz* in Krasnoyarsk, for example, involved liquidating 12 trusts and other organisations, thus removing 1,600 posts and producing salary savings of 31 million roubles; a further 2,400 administrative jobs would go as the reform continued.[37]

Aware that his backing in the Presidium was uncertain, Khrushchev proposed that the *sovnarkhoz* proposal be put before the country for discussion and the plenum agreed that a countrywide discussion should take place from 31 March to 4 May. The "theses" for this discussion were hotly debated at a series of Presidium meetings between 22 March and the end of the month. Molotov led the criticism, but he was not alone, Bulganin, initially a supporter of Khrushchev, was worried about the change of role proposed for *Gosplan*: it was to lose its responsibility for longer-term perspective planning and concentrate entirely on yearly plans. Shepilov also voiced concerns: he favoured the principle of decentralisation, but felt Khrushchev's plan was poorly thought through. In fact, Khrushchev himself had criticisms of his first version of the proposal, which had included the establishment of an overarching Supreme *Sovnarkhoz* with a coordinating role: Khrushchev later commented "I do not think we need to have such a body".[38]

It was this absence of an overarching co-ordinating body which concerned Molotov the most, however. On 24 March 1957, he sent a note to the Central Committee outlining his view that the proposed decentralisation of the economy went to an impossible extreme: there were not even committees which might ensure some central co-ordination of economic affairs. Khrushchev responded to Molotov's note on 26 March but on 27 March, when the Presidium was back in session, Molotov opened up a new front in his attack by insisting that the "theses" Khrushchev was now proposing to use as the basis for a countrywide discussion went beyond his original proposals. In an extraordinary breach of protocol, Molotov had raised this concern at a meeting of the Council of Ministers on 26 March, making clear that disagreements within the Presidium were making normal work impossible. This lapse of party discipline on Molotov's part was duly condemned by the Presidium on 27 March, but that did not prevent Molotov from continuing his campaign.

Molotov argued that he had accepted the principle of more decentralisation adopted at the February Plenum, but maintained that Khrushchev was now interpreting those decisions one-sidedly. As the Presidium discussions of 27 March continued, so tempers frayed. Khrushchev denounced Molotov as "cut off from life": he did not like the Virgin Lands Campaign, he opposed foreign policy initiatives and now he wanted another commission to be set up before the economic reform could go ahead. Letting his anger get the better of him, Khrushchev added: "Molotov was not always so unhurried, he hurried at the time of collectivisation, he hurried when a group of generals were repressed". Khrushchev got his way. His reform "theses" were published on 30 March, were debated in the press as planned until 4 May, and at its session of 7–11 May the Supreme Soviet endorsed the abolition of the ministries and the formation of the *sovnarkhozy*.[39]

Khrushchev's outburst about Molotov and the repression of generals was not accidental. On 25 April 1957, the Presidium formally rehabilitated Generals Tukhachevskii and Yakir. Khrushchev used the occasion to take another swipe at those who had been closest to Stalin. "Let the old members of the Politburo tell us how they decided the question of bringing Yakir before the responsible authorities, how this first step was prepared", he said. Kaganovich rose to the bait saying glibly: "it was like this, there was a report, we took a decision". This same Presidium meeting also rehabilitated one of those on the fringes of the Leningrad Affair, prompting Khrushchev to comment that "in this matter my friend Georgii Malenkov played an unfortunate role, the accused was a victim of palace intrigue". At this meeting Khrushchev also suggested that, given the work of the Party Control Committee and the steady flow of rehabilitations, it might be time to return to the question of guilt, or "would we continue to remain silent about it towards the party?" From Khrushchev's perspective, de-Stalinisation was back on the agenda, but Kaganovich in particular seemed always ready to defend himself. At a Presidium meeting about this time Khrushchev proposed investigating the cases of Zinoviev, Kamenev "and others, that is the Trotskyites". This prompted Kaganovich to remind the Presidium about Khrushchev's own Trotskyist past.[40]

However, if Khrushchev was still clearly determined to confront Stalinism within the higher echelons of the party, he was equally concerned that confronting Stalin should not result in undermining the position of the party as had so clearly happened in Hungary. His understanding of events in Hungary was that the rot had set in with the emergence of the Petőfi Circle, and the danger of a Moscow

Petőfi Circle still seemed to be there. In spring 1957 he received a surveillance report from the Central Committee's Department of Culture which suggested that the Moscow section of the Writers' Union was still wedded to an "incorrect line"; the discovery at about this time of a "true Leninist" underground cell within the Komsomol organisation at Moscow University suggested that this was not pure fantasy. So in May Khrushchev decided to address the situation particularly among Moscow writers where a group led by the poet Margarita Aliger had effectively gained influence and, from his perspective at least, seemed intent on forming some sort of club like the Petőfi Circle; as Khrushchev commented later, "if we had not intervened, then it is not certain how it might have ended". Aliger had been one of those who had founded a new journal, *Literaturnaya Moskva,* in 1956, an initiative which had also involved Paustovskii. So with the Writers' Union due to gather on 14–17 May 1957, Khrushchev was determined to pre-empt matters.[41]

The day before the Writers' Union assembled, on 13 May, he organised a meeting with writers to remind them that criticising the cult of personality did not mean denying the positive role Stalin had played in the development of the country and the victory of socialism. Repeating the earlier attack on Dudintsev, he claimed to detect a certain "hesitation" among intellectuals towards the regime. He insisted that the political struggles of the late 1920s and early 1930s had been "correct", since these "enemy" groups had opposed the socialist transformation of the country. The leadership had "wept sincerely" when Stalin died, but condemned those crimes which led to the loss of "many honest and dedicated people". Khrushchev then moved on to criticise the actions of Malenkov, "who fell entirely under Beria's influence" and "skilfully made use of Stalin's weaknesses", thus "in many cases he pushed him towards those actions which deserve firm condemnation". A couple of days later, on 19 May, at a meeting with leaders from the arts, he linked the events of Poland and Hungary to current developments and asserted that it was essential to oppose "those who try to use those mistakes of the past to push leadership in literature and the arts away from the party and state". Again he extended his criticism to Aliger, who was present at the meeting and dared to challenge him. This exchange seems to have caused Khrushchev to drop his guard and he began talking not only about Malenkov's past but the current difficulties he was having in the Presidium, particularly the rows with Molotov. As had been the case with Molotov's comments at the Council of Ministers not long before, the whole Presidium later criticised Khrushchev for such a flagrant breach of both discipline and etiquette.[42]

Khrushchev's exasperation with Molotov was prompted by the fact that he was still trying to subvert the *Sovnarkhoz* reform. With Molotov in the lead his opponents tried to frustrate the introduction of the *Sovnarkhoz* Reform by constantly challenging the names of those people proposed to head the *sovnarkhozy*, and routinely tabling amendment after amendment at Presidium meetings. Then, on 27 April 1957, as Minister of State Control, Molotov proposed a reorganisation of his own ministry: once the details had been considered, the Presidium decided on 31 May to send the proposals back for reworking; in Khrushchev's view they were "unacceptable", and those present at the meeting were agreed that Molotov's proposals were aimed at giving his ministry the right to exert centralised executive authority over the new *sovnarkhozy*. Kaganovich and Malenkov supported Molotov's proposals, even though the majority in the Presidium was of the view that the proposals needed to be changed root and branch.[43]

The Anti-Party Group Affair

From 6 to 13 June 1957, Khrushchev was in Finland, accompanied by Bulganin. On 18 June, mimicking the manoeuvre used when Beria was arrested, Bulganin called on Khrushchev to attend a meeting of the Council of Ministers, which was then transformed into a meeting of the Presidium with only one agenda item, the removal of Khrushchev. As it later emerged, although Molotov was the ideological driving force behind this move, it was Malenkov who had taken the lead in "running from office to office" whipping up support. Ostensibly, the case against Khrushchev was this. In his clash with Aliger on 19 May, Khrushchev had broken the cardinal rule of party discipline when he referred to the difficulties Molotov was causing him in the Presidium. There were, it was suggested, other occasions on which Khrushchev's loquaciousness or his rudeness had led to embarrassment. As Malenkov put it, it had been a mistake to resurrect the post of First Secretary in September 1953 and it was now time to reconsider the whole relationship between the Presidium and the Secretariat. Once this reorganisation had been completed, Khrushchev would be allocated a new role in the Secretariat, probably with responsibility for agriculture. Although the *sovnarkhoz* Reform was not specifically listed in the indictment, both Malenkov and Molotov argued that the *Sovnarkhoz* reform showed how under Khrushchev the party was getting sucked into "narrow pragmatism", obsessing about economic detail rather than grand political tasks.[44]

Within the voting members of the Presidium, Khrushchev was in a minority on 18 June, but he, supported by Mikoyan, argued persistently that this was not a decision that could be made by the Presidium alone, but needed to involve both full and candidate members of the Presidium plus the Central Committee secretaries. As it was, not even all the Presidium members were present: three full members were not there, nor were three candidate members and three Central Committee secretaries. At first the unrepresentative nature of the proceedings was ignored and the charges against Khrushchev continued to be set out. Kaganovich described the "atmosphere of fear" which supposedly existed in the Presidium and the way Khrushchev had abused his position as First Secretary. Molotov asserted that Khrushchev had moved towards "right opportunism and adventurism". Malenkov added that Khrushchev had equated the dictatorship of the proletariat with the dictatorship of the party "in the manner of Zinoviev". As this list of ideological sins continued, Kaganovich reminded his colleagues once again that Khrushchev had supported Trotsky in the early 1920s, referring to him as a "Trotskyist recidivist".[45]

This language of a Stalinist witch-hunt did not impress the man who would ultimately decide how the days' events turned out, Defence Minister Zhukov. Shepilov believed from previous conversations with Zhukov that he was on the side of the Anti-Party Group. Bulganin also recalled that Zhukov had been one of those to speak to him about the need to abolish the post of First Secretary and change the relationship between the Presidium and the Secretariat. When Zhukov arrived at the Presidium meeting – after a terrifying drive to the Kremlin at over 70 miles an hour – he passed Bulganin a note which read: "I propose that we bring the discussion to an end, issue a stern reprimand to Khrushchev for violating the principle of collective leadership and leave everything as it is for the time being, and look again at the situation later." He then made absolutely clear that the army would not support a change of leadership in the Central Committee. His exact words were later subject to dispute, but both recorded versions are equally clear: "I will appeal to the army and the people and they will follow me" or "tanks can move only on my order".[46] Khrushchev's supporters were also starting to rally. The new security chief, head of the KGB Ivan Serov, with whom Khrushchev had clashed in Western Ukraine in 1939, played a key role, as did Nikolai Ignatov, then the Gorky party secretary, who worked the phones; the two men organised a delegation of some 15 to 20 Central Committee members who quite literally banged on the door of the room where the Presidium was meeting, as it resumed for a second day of discussions on 19 June, and demanded to know what was going on. They insisted that a full Central Committee Plenum was essential if the party leadership were being discussed.[47]

Eventually, as head of state, Voroshilov agreed to go into the anteroom and talk to the delegation, and Khrushchev insisted on accompanying him. Serov spoke for the delegation, repeating the argument that a decision of such magnitude could only be made at a plenum and was beyond the competence of the Presidium. According to some accounts Voroshilov responded with a curse and Serov grabbed him by the throat. After an hour's delay, Voroshilov and Khrushchev returned to the Presidium meeting and Khrushchev stated that Voroshilov had been forced to concede that the Presidium was not acting according to the rules and that a plenum should take place. By the afternoon of 20 June some 57 Central Committee members had arrived in Moscow and these, when added to those members employed in Moscow, meant that 107 of the 130 full members of the Central Committee were on hand, a clear quorum. The leadership now had no choice but to accede to the petition presented by the 57 arguing that a plenum be held at once. It took place from 22 to 28 June.[48]

Suslov spoke first, conceding that Khrushchev was sometimes "sharp and hot-tempered", and that some of his speeches had been given "without the due agreement of the Presidium"; Khrushchev was aware of these issues, however, and had confirmed that he would correct them. Zhukov was quick not only to take up Khrushchev's defence but to focus at once on the role Malenkov, Molotov and Kaganovich had played under Stalin. Surely, he mused, after the revelations of the 20th Party Congress they should have said something about their guilt. Here, Zhukov developed a distinction which all Khrushchev's supporters felt was important: Malenkov, Molotov and Kaganovich had not only implemented Stalin's orders during the purges but they had also acted as instigators. They had not only acted to implement Stalin's will "but had also on their own initiative" encouraged the purging process. Zhukov gave figures for the executions sanctioned by Stalin, Molotov and Kaganovich between 27 February 1937 and 12 November 1938: 38,679 executions were sanctioned, 3,167 on 12 November 1938 alone. Kaganovich in particular had written to Ezhov demanding more arrests, and had scrawled insults on Yakir's death sentence. Malenkov, with his responsibility for cadre policy at this time, was even more responsible than Kaganovich, Zhukov insisted; instead of ensuring the party controlled the NKVD, he helped the reverse happen. Zhukov also raised an issue which would reverberate throughout the plenum, the allegation that at the time of the Leningrad Affair, Malenkov had been involved in planning the construction of a special prison to house arrested party members.[49]

Zhukov's intervention opened up a bitter series of exchanges about who had done what during Stalin's purges. As had been the case in the past, Malenkov denied any responsibility for the Leningrad Affair: he accepted that he had visited Leningrad with Beria, but it was Abakumov who had directed the Leningrad Affair acting "under the personal direction of Comrade Stalin". Aleksei Kosygin, a former mayor of Leningrad, one time Minister of Finance under Stalin and now deputy chairman of *Gosplan*, begged to differ. According to Khrushchev, Kosygin's life had "hung by a thread" at the time of the Leningrad Affair and Kosygin now made clear that at that time he had been interrogated on two occasions, once by Beria but the second time by both Beria and Malenkov. At one point in these acrimonious exchanges, Malenkov commented sarcastically "and you of all of us are completely clean, comrade Khrushchev".[50]

Kaganovich made a similar point in another heated exchange with Khrushchev during the plenum. He urged members of the Central Committee to keep in mind that 1957 was not 1937: the atmosphere had been very different then, there had been enemies, there had been a bitter class struggle, "the situation was bitter, we acted very quickly" and so troikas were established, on which every regional party secretary sat. As tempers rose, Khrushchev interrupted Kaganovich to say that everyone who appeared in front of a troika was shot. When Kaganovich denied this Khrushchev countered that "the absolute majority were shot". It was at this point that Kaganovich shouted: "and you really did not sign any execution papers for Ukraine!" Khrushchev's response was crystal clear: "we all approved such things". He conceded that on many occasions he had "voted and slagged people off as traitors", even his old friend Yakir; but this was before he had joined the Politburo. Those outside the Politburo carried out orders, but more was expected of those on the Politburo. "I believed you, I considered you had uncovered that Yakir was an enemy and had betrayed our trust – you were a member of the Politburo and should have found out."[51]

Molotov tried to put a stop to this trading of insults by stressing that the resolution on the cult of personality of 30 June 1956 had been adopted unanimously and this document also talked of Stalin's positive achievements. Khrushchev immediately cut in and demanded to know if Stalin's positive achievements included the use of torture to obtain confessions. Molotov replied that he had certainly signed papers endorsing the use of torture, but stressed that "taking physical measures was a general decision of the Politburo". When Khrushchev suggested that, as "second person" after Stalin, he bore more responsibility than most for the crimes committed, Molotov insisted that he had stood up to Stalin more than anyone else, "more than you, comrade Khrushchev". Because of those confrontations with Stalin, he had experienced "much unpleasantness", he said, an oblique reference to the fact that Stalin had had his wife arrested. One of Khrushchev's supporters would not allow Molotov to gain the moral high ground in this way and demanded to know whether it was true that Molotov had added in his own hand on one case file "kill him, kill him, kill him".[52]

As the plenum heard charge and counter-charge being traded, Khrushchev revived the argument he had made before delivering the Secret Speech. He suggested that Molotov, Malenkov and Kaganovich had not only ingratiated themselves with Stalin by actively engaging with the purges, but that they had helped to create the climate in which the purges could flourish. As Nikolai Shvernik, the chairman of the Party Control Committee, commented, it was Malenkov, working alongside Beria, who "formed Stalin's consciousness in questions concerning the mass repression". Another Khrushchev supporter went even further: "they created the cult of personality, they pushed Stalin and isolated him from the people". Khrushchev himself said something rather similar: "I think that if around Stalin there had not been these evil geniuses Beria and Malenkov, then much could have been prevented. It was possible to talk to Stalin. When Beria was far from Stalin, I agreed many things with him". In further exchanges about the Leningrad Affair, Khrushchev said to Malenkov: "you whispered to Stalin, when in those last years he was an ill man". Malenkov's response was one of utter disbelief, "what, I guided Stalin, as they say, it makes you laugh".[53]

Ultimately, however, Khrushchev recognised that Stalin had chosen those who surrounded him. His basic case was that he had signed death warrants himself, but he had not been as close to the centre of power as Molotov, Malenkov and Kaganovich and he had not encouraged Stalin in the purging process, nor had he been involved in the fabrication of evidence. His concluding message at the plenum was clear: Malenkov, Kaganovich and Molotov "even without pressure on Stalin's part" had ordered the arrest of honest party workers. During the previous year the Party Control Committee had reviewed the cases of 4,730 people expelled from the party during the purges and had restored 4,620 people to party membership. Central Committee

Secretary Aristov told the plenum what Khrushchev wanted to be heard: after reminding Central Committee members that Khrushchev had personally defended him on one occasion from Stalin's wrath in 1952, he stated unequivocally that there was no evidence that Khrushchev had proposed the arrest or execution of anyone.[54]

The day after the plenum ended Molotov, Malenkov and Kaganovich were expelled from the Presidium and from the Central Committee; all were then allocated junior posts designed to keep them out of the limelight. Molotov was made ambassador to Mongolia, Kaganovich was sent to run an asbestos plant in Sverdlovsk, and Malenkov was made director of the Ust-Kamenogorsk hydroelectric power station. Having defeated the Stalinists at home, Khrushchev turned his attention again to de-Stalinisation abroad. On 31 May 1957, not long before the Anti-Party Group crisis had flared up, Khrushchev informed the Presidium that, as part of the preparations for the 40th anniversary of the October Revolution later in the year, he had invited members of the Yugoslav leadership to holiday in Crimea. After the defeat of the Anti-Party Group it was quickly agreed to go further than this and arrange a meeting between Khrushchev and Tito. This took place on 1–2 August in Snagov, near Bucharest in Romania. Although the final resolution on the meeting noted that "friendly personal relations were re-established between Tito and Khrushchev", this second honeymoon proved very unstable. A Yugoslav delegation agreed to attend the 40th anniversary on 7 November, but at the very last minute the Yugoslavs decided not to adhere to the Declaration of the World's Communist and Workers' Parties signed on that occasion; Tito was unhappy with the final wording.[55]

Removing Zhukov

On 5 July 1957, Zhukov made a speech in Leningrad where he called for Stalin's role in the repression of army officers to be brought into the open. However, when this speech was reported in *Pravda* some 10 days later, the anti-Stalin tone had been glossed over. This was not the first time Zhukov's anti-Stalin zeal had been seen as uncomfortable. Zhukov and the head of the Political Directorate of the Red Army, Aleksei Zheltov, had clashed over the April 1956 issue of the military journal *Voennyi Vestnik*. The journal had published an article describing the Soviet Union's lack of military preparedness in June 1941 on the eve of the invasion by Nazi Germany. In response, in May 1956 the party's military newspaper *Krasnaya Zvezda* had used its Victory Day issue of 9 May to criticise the *Voennyi Vestnik* article. On 12 May Zhukov protested that both the Central Committee and

Political Directorate had quite unjustifiably criticised *Voennyi Vestnik*, and had done so without discussing the matter first in the Presidium.

In response, *Krasnaya Zvezda*'s editor was willing to concede that military unpreparedness was a reality in 1941, but argued that it was not an issue for the public press. It was in the context of this row that, on 15 May 1956, Zhukov proposed dissolving the Military Council of the Soviet Council of Defence on the grounds that it had never met since being established on 9 February 1955. At the same time Zhukov also proposed making the military soviets of the army districts purely advisory, and issued an order "On the state of military discipline in the army" which would have ended the right of party conferences to criticise military commanders. Zhukov was known to be concerned about excessive party interference in the affairs of the army. As early as April 1953 when he was brought into political life as Deputy Minister of Defence, Zhukov had proposed to Beria that the time had come to abolish the political departments in the army, to which Beria had supposedly responded "be a little patient, we cannot do everything at once".[56]

After the defeat of the Anti-Party Group, Khrushchev was presented with a report issued by the Central Committee but drafted by Zheltov. In the past, relations between Khrushchev and Zheltov had not been particularly good: prior to the 20th Party Congress, Zhukov had told Khrushchev that Zheltov was inactive, worked badly and ought to be transferred to other work since political work in the army was suffering, and Khrushchev had seemed to agree. Zheltov's Central Committee report was discussed in the Presidium on 17 October and it showed that in all sorts of ways, the activities of his Political Directorate were being circumscribed: he needed permission to visit troops, and reports on military preparedness were redacted before being provided to the Political Directorate. In addition, Zhukov had proposed establishing a Military Council of the Chief of the General Staff, something confirmed by the Soviet Council of Defence on 29 April 1957, but this Military Council of the Chief of the General Staff concentrated power in the hands of generals, rather than the Presidium members who could attend the Military Council of the Soviet Council of Defence, which Zhukov wanted abolished.

A further source of tension had been over who should command Soviet troops in Hungary: Kádár, and therefore the Presidium, wanted the existing commander to stay in post, but Zhukov insisted on having him transferred. On a personal level, Zheltov stated that Zhukov believed that he, Zheltov, had opposed Zhukov's appointment and was therefore hostile to the concerns he raised. In the Presidium's subsequent discussion, it was accepted that, at best, Zhukov regularly dismissed political workers in the Red Army as "chatterers", which was to misunderstand the correct relationship between the party and the army and, at worst, Zhukov had started to believe that his own position as Minister of Defence was inviolable, or as Khrushchev put it, "there is me and me alone".[57]

After more discussion in the Secretariat, Khrushchev informed the Presidium that it had been decided to act against Zhukov who "was thinking about taking power in the country and has been undertaking serious efforts in this direction". When Zhukov next attended the Presidium on 26 October, he was confronted with his behaviour. He stated that he was ready to admit errors and correct them, although he did not agree that he had reduced the importance of political work in the army although it was true, he conceded, that he believed Zheltov was not up to the job. Despite such self-criticism, the Presidium was of the view that Zhukov had been distancing the army from the party, especially in the localities. Khrushchev summed things up: in this "heavy drama", the threads which bound the army to the party were being cut. He explained in a speech to party activists in the Ministry of Defence shortly afterwards that the party had acted because it feared that a drop could become a stream, a stream a river, and a river a flood; there was a problem with political education in the army and it had to be nipped in the bud. Those who tried to downplay the role of political workers, or the reverse, undermine commanders, were both wrong; both commanders and political workers needed educated soldiers and without collaboration between commanders and political workers there would be no army. After the removal of Zhukov, the number of party cells in the army more than doubled, as did party recruitment within the army; by 1961 90% of officers were party members.[58]

With the Anti-Party Group defeated, with the threat, real or imagined, posed by Zhukov removed, Khrushchev appeared for the first time as the unchallenged leader of the Soviet Union. In recognition of this, on 25 March 1958 the Presidium proposed that Khrushchev be made both Party First Secretary and Prime Minister, replacing Bulganin. Khrushchev was cautious, initially stating that "it would be better for me to remain Central Committee Secretary". However, his colleagues insisted, with only Mikoyan saying that the two roles really should be kept separate. When he wrote his memoirs Khrushchev was clear not only that it had been a mistake to take on both posts, but that ultimately his pride and self-belief had got the better of him. "I sincerely say that they had to persuade me. I was reluctant ... [but] weakness on my part was displayed here, and perhaps something was gnawing at me inwardly weakening my resistance ... It was with difficulty that I arrived at this decision, but there was no alternative."[59]

Chapter 6: Constructing Communism at Home, 1958–62

Social Reform

Back in August 1953 Khrushchev had told a meeting of agricultural activists that the Soviet Union was gradually moving from socialism towards communism. He then added a little anecdote. He had said the same to a group of peasants, and one had commented: well, under socialism we have no pancakes, will there or won't there be pancakes under communism? Khrushchev was determined that as the move towards communism accelerated under his watch, there would indeed be pancakes. The agricultural situation in 1958 was good. The grain harvest was 30% above the previous year, which was in turn almost 70% above the average harvest for 1949–53. The Virgin Lands Campaign seemed to have paid off, and the growing of wheat in the Virgin Lands enabled other parts of the country to move over to maize production, which could both feed the population and be used as animal fodder.[1] Khrushchev saw this as rationalising Soviet agricultural production: growing grain had once been the concern of the whole country, but now areas like the Baltic States, Northwest Russia and even parts of Ukraine could concentrate on things like dairying, pig breeding or industrial crops. Of course, more could have been done. In the Soviet Union as a whole there was only one tractor per 190 hectares of ploughed land, and even in intensively farmed areas like Kazakhstan the figure only rose to 281. As late as 1960, Kazakhstan only had storage facilities for half the projected harvest. It was partly to address the efficient use of farm equipment that in March 1958 Khrushchev decided to dissolve the old Machine Tractor Stations, which under the Stalin system had hired out tractors and other equipment to collective farms, and allow the collective farms to

113

buy agricultural equipment; by 1 January 1959 only 385 of the former 8,000 Machine Tractor Stations remained.[2]

The Soviet people not only needed to be fed, they needed to be housed. Large-scale housing construction began in 1957, focusing on the development of new dormitory "micro districts" of anywhere between 5,000 and 20,000 inhabitants. The policy envisaged each micro district providing crèches, schools, libraries, health facilities, a social club, a canteen and a shop offering semi-prepared food. The decree of 31 July 1957, which made it the duty of local soviets to provide accommodation for local inhabitants and increased the planned volume of construction from the 84 million m^2 agreed at the 20th Party Congress to 113 million m^2, promised to resolve the housing shortage within 10 years. Spending on housing between 1956 and 1960 was double that from 1951 to 1955. These ambitious targets were increasingly met by the use of modular prefabricated building techniques, thus the percentage of new flats built from 4 m^2 concrete panels rose from 1.5% in 1959 to 28.5% in 1965.[3] The 1957 decree made clear that soviets were to build blocks of flats of either four or five stories.

Khrushchev was very clear about the benefits of this approach; it meant that there was no need to provide a lift and no danger that water would have to be pumped to the upper storeys. Although the ambition was that each family "including young couples" would have "a well-appointed flat corresponding to the demands of hygiene and the cultural way of life", Khrushchev understood that quantity was more important than quality. As he later recalled, "we limited ourselves to the task of creating minimally acceptable conditions in the lives of residents, we made this decision consciously". After Khrushchev's removal from power, the nine-storey block of flats became the norm, and so Khrushchev's five-storey blocks became readily distinguishable and were universally referred to as "Khrushchevki", for most, but not all, a term of endearment.

It was an astonishing achievement. In the last years of his rule, between 1961 and 1964, 8.2 million people annually moved into new accommodation. This meant that by 1960 the average living space per person was 8.8 m^2, very nearly the 9 m^2 "sanitary norm" established by the Soviet Government back in 1926.[4] Of course, micro districts frequently failed to provide the promised crèches and the housing programme was inherently inflexible: the two or three different apartment designs could hardly accommodate the reality of multi-generational families, and the new refrigerators which began to come off the production line protruded 7 cm above the standard height of the kitchen units provided; this was despite a US fitted kitchen being transported to Moscow for analysis in 1955. However, the housing programme gave many the privacy of their own family home for the first time and the press was understandably full of images of construction and of people moving into new homes.[5]

Back in October 1955, Khrushchev had sent the Presidium a note in which he outlined the most pressing social problems which demanded an immediate response: these were the low level of pay, the low level of pensions and the pitiful state of old people's homes and homes for the disabled. He proposed addressing these issues by ending the policy of annual price cuts which had developed under Stalin. These issues, the Presidium agreed, should all be included in the speech Khrushchev made to the 20th Party Congress, his lesser-known public speech as opposed to the well-known Secret Speech. Of these, pension reform was the most controversial. While Malenkov was prime minister, proposals for pension reform had been discussed in the Presidium in March, May and August 1954, but no agreement had been reached; a final proposal from him was discussed in March 1955, after his dismissal, but again it did not find favour. Malenkov had proposed a pension funded through contributions to an insurance fund, but once Malenkov was out of the way, Khrushchev brought forward his own scheme for state-funded pensions. This was backed by the Presidium, presented to the 20th Party Congress and, after further discussion in the Presidium and then the Supreme Soviet, came into force on 1 October 1956. Its impact was dramatic: by 1957 pensions were more than double their 1955 value. The pension scheme meant men retired at 60 and women at 55, with lower retirement ages for those working underground or in extreme conditions. Because the scheme was not contribution based, early retirement did not have an impact on the level of benefit.[6]

The Sixth Five-Year Plan, 1956–60, was supposed to tackle low wages by raising salaries by 30%. To supplement this on 8 September 1956 it was agreed to introduce a minimum wage, taking effect from 1 January 1957. This legislation had a noticeable effect; in June 1953 42.6% of workers earned under 50 roubles per month, whereas by 1958 this figure had fallen to 35%. A social survey carried out by the newspaper *Komsomol'skaya Pravda* in autumn 1960 revealed that 72.2% of the population felt that their standard of living had gone up in recent years and statistics bore that out: during the years 1959–61, the annual growth in income was 6.6% while for the years 1962–5, it had risen to 7.25%; in 1958 the salary income of the entire Soviet population was 79.5 billion roubles, and by 1965 this had risen to

127.5 billion roubles. The planned improvement in the standard of living was even greater: between 1959 and 1965 average salaries were supposed to rise by 27% but actually rose by 18%, while real income was supposed to rise by 40% but only rose by 33.7%; however, the standard of living improved markedly under Khrushchev.[7]

State social spending was one and a half times the official state spending on defence in 1956 and had risen to two and a half times the official state spending on defence in 1965. The official figures for defence spending were always an underestimate, but a consistent underestimate, so as a yardstick for the overall growth in social spending under Khrushchev the figure holds good. Some social spending was the direct concern of the state, such as the decision of 26 March 1956 to increase maternity leave from 77 days to 112 days; other spending was the concern of public bodies like the trade unions. In March 1960 most health sanatoria were transferred to the care of the trade unions: 20% of stays in sanatoria were entirely free, while the remaining 80% were charged at 30% of the real cost. In this context it is also worth mentioning a negative spend, the decision of 19 March 1957 to end the "voluntary" raising of loans from the population; pressurising those on low salaries to take out state loans was one of the most unpleasant duties party and Komsomol activists had to perform.[8]

Education reform was part of this overall modernising package. Fees for secondary and higher education were dropped on 6 June 1956, and Khrushchev wanted secondary schools to adapt to the comprehensive range of students who now stayed on to study. Addressing the 13th Komsomol Congress in April 1958, Khrushchev criticised the way schools only prepared students for higher education, something that, by definition, the majority of children would not achieve; secondary schools needed to be closer to the world of work and initially it was proposed that students could only enter higher education after having worked in industry or agriculture for two years. The Presidium began to discuss the reform in June and in September Khrushchev's memorandum was published and put out for nationwide discussion. When the Central Committee theses were published in November 1958, it had already been agreed to drop the idea that students had to work for two years before entering higher education. After widespread consultation with bodies such as the Academy of Sciences, the final law proposal, which was published on 24 December 1958, lost much of its anti-elitist tenor while formally retaining its commitment to strengthening links between education and working life. In line with Khrushchev's concern to decentralise power as much as possible, one key element of his education reform was that it would be the

Supreme Soviets of the Union Republics which would enact the law, adapting Khrushchev's proposals in a way "which would respond to national traditions and peculiarities".[9]

A further reform introduced at this time was that of the trade unions. Discussed in spring 1957 and debated by a Trade Union Plenum in June, the final proposals were published on 21 August. The number of unions was reduced by half and trade union councils, rather than central management boards, were to become the main focus of activity. They would conclude collective agreements with the *Sovnarkhozy* and ensure that those agreements were carried out; in the past these rights had been vested in individual trade unions and their central apparatuses, which now also ceded their finance and budgetary powers to the trade union councils. At the December 1957 Party Plenum it was decided to institute a more radical change, allowing workers to take much more of a role in influencing factory affairs. It was agreed "to transform production conferences in enterprises and construction sites into permanent structures", something ultimately formalised in December 1961 in a new trade union statute. Alongside the right to influence management decisions through the production conferences, workers, through the trade unions, also gained the right in July 1958 to become involved in drafting factory plans and to receive regular reports from managers. Worker representatives also had to be consulted by management whenever workers were to be dismissed.[10]

The All-People's State

For Khrushchev, these initiatives were not part of a programme of piecemeal modernisation. He believed he was developing a coherent programme for a new type of state, a communist society which would be at the same time an "all-people's state". On 18 April 1958, in the address to the 13th Komsomol Congress, Khrushchev raised for the first time the concept of how such an all-people's state would operate. Perhaps Khrushchev had been stung by the charge of the Anti-Party Group that he avoided big political issues and was obsessed with purely administrative reforms, perhaps the 40th anniversary of the October Revolution and the Conference of Communist and Workers' Parties had reminded him of the purpose of their common endeavour, whatever the reason, Khrushchev was determined to engage with a key point of Marxist theory, that as socialism moved towards communism, so the state would begin to "wither away". Khrushchev brought a practical slant to this question, not a philosophical one. He told the Komsomol: "We say that under communism the state will die away. What bodies then will be preserved? Social ones! Whether they will be called trade unions, the Komsomol or something else, but there will be social organisations through which society will regulate its relationships. We must think about the way forward to this, to teach people, so they learn the new skills of this sort of activity."[11]

Some elements of self-activity really did take off with the encouragement of the party. Perhaps the most successful were the "women's soviets". Bringing life to the new micro districts was no easy matter and the women's soviet movement was soon encouraging women to take ownership of the new housing complexes, particularly where it came to the running of crèches and other aspects of childcare. Making sure that such facilities were properly equipped, and making sure that the needs of working mothers were adequately recognised at the workplace were constant themes in the activities of the women's soviets. Two other initiatives which lasted were the volunteer workers' militia and the comrade courts. It was on 2 March 1959 that a law was passed "On the participation of workers in the maintenance of order". This established a volunteer workers' militia tasked with aiding the police to keep order on the streets; armed with nothing more than red arm bands, their main concern was rowdies returning home from the beer bars. The comrade courts dealt with low-level disputes between neighbours and the like; they were mediated by a volunteer judge who had been given a very modest level of legal training. The way they operated was not that dissimilar to the English system of justices of the peace.[12]

On 19 July 1958, Khrushchev invited Boris Ponomarev, considered an expert on the international communist movement, to discuss the withering away of the state and the development of an all-people's state at a private meeting held at his dacha: there Khrushchev raised the issue of incorporating the concept of the withering away of the state into a new party programme. He asked Ponomarev to start work on such a programme at once, but recognised that this would not be easy. One of Khrushchev's advisers later recalled how the idea "caused a scandal" when it was presented to the Presidium, and only Khrushchev's determined perseverance got it through. The problem for Khrushchev was that the Central Committee he was dealing with had been elected in 1956, before the Secret Speech had been read and before the Anti-Party Group had thoroughly discredited the hard-liners. What is more, those quietly sympathetic to the Anti-Party Group might well have challenged the starting point for Khrushchev's analysis. The Anti-Party Group had been accused of being fanatical enthusiasts for seeking out enemies of the people because they accepted Stalin's argument, advanced most forcefully at the February–March Plenum of 1937, that the closer a society got to socialism, the more acute the class struggle became. The 30 April 1956 resolution on the cult of personality had classed this theory as mistaken, and Khrushchev's starting point in developing the theory of the all-people's state was that Stalin's thesis of the 1930s was completely wrong.[13] Of course, back in 1934 Khrushchev had himself backed Stalin and ridiculed the notion that the class struggle might be over, but that was before the class struggle impacted on the party itself in 1937–8.

Khrushchev now argued forcefully that the class struggle was a thing of the past as far as the Soviet Union was concerned. The workers, allied with the majority of the peasants, had seized power in 1917, carried out a socialist revolution, successfully combated rich peasant (kulak) resistance to that revolution during the collectivisation campaign, and thus established a socialist state of workers and peasants by the mid 1930s. Two decades later, the distinction between worker and peasant had virtually disappeared, and the old predominantly blue collar working class had steadily evolved as the country modernised to include a huge white collar work force. Such changes reflected the fact that the old class antagonisms had disappeared, and the Soviet Union really had become an all-people's state. Khrushchev was determined to discuss these ideas, even if his comrades on the Presidium and Central Committee were not yet convinced. On 23 October 1958 Khrushchev persuaded the Presidium to call an extraordinary 21st Party Congress. The ostensible purpose of the congress was to debate "the target figures for the economic development of the Soviet Union from 1959–65". Khrushchev had succeeded in persuading his colleagues to abandon the Sixth Five-Year Plan after three years and adopt a Seven-Year Plan, a plan which included an increase in the funds assigned for consumer goods of 100 billion roubles; it was, after all, pointless to increase salaries dramatically if there was nothing for the population to buy. However, when the congress opened on 27 January 1959 the actual subject matter was rather different. Behind the very bland title of his speech on "the target figures for the economic development of the Soviet Union from 1959–65", Khrushchev developed his ideas for a communist future.[14]

He began by outlining the tasks of the new Seven-Year Plan: this was the "period of the developed construction of a communist society", which meant creating an economic base which could compete with capitalism and, through the constant raising of labour productivity, lead to significant improvements in the standard of living; in the political sphere it meant "the development of socialist democracy, participation and self-initiative of the broad popular masses in the construction of a communist society, developing the role played by social organisations in resolving matters of state". The scale of the plan was immense, capital investment during those 7 years would be as great as for the preceding 40 years of Soviet power. An increase in labour productivity of 45–50% during the same period would allow for higher pay, a shorter working week and "a considerable improvement in the social and cultural services offered to the population". Khrushchev spoke of his commitment to a 7-hour day from 1960 and a 40-hour week by 1962. The task, in Khrushchev's view, was to overtake the most developed capitalist countries in terms of labour productivity and thus outstrip the economy of the US. "Target figures" was for Khrushchev a simple code for constructing the economic base of communism.[15]

The superstructure of the communist future was articulated in section four of Khrushchev's speech. Here the narrow subject of the economic targets' control figures was left to one side and a "new stage in communist construction and certain questions of Marxist–Leninist theory" were addressed. Khrushchev argued that, as the development of the Soviet Union from a socialist to a communist society approached, it was clear that this divide offered no huge barrier. The economic prerequisites for communism would soon be in place and communism would "grow out of socialism", it would be its "direct continuation", and it would be quite wrong to think of communism as something "that appears all of a sudden". The key was to develop the productive forces of society, and then, the closer the country moved towards communism, the greater the level of social spending as society took care of "every person from birth to deep old age". A key teaching of Marxism–Leninism, he said, was that "the state would gradually wither away, that social administration would lose its political character and turn into direct popular administration", in other words "the development of socialist statehood into communist self-administration"; this in turn would mean developing democracy and "attracting the broadest possible groups within the population into the administration of the country's affairs". For Khrushchev, this was real rather than "bourgeois" democracy, "fully developed self-activity, the self-activity of the labouring masses in their self-administration". As he had already told the 13th Komsomol Congress, many state functions could readily be transferred to social organisations.[16]

Khrushchev stressed he was not being utopian, there were clear limits on the withering away process. While the threat from the capitalist West existed, the army and security services were still needed: "Leninism teaches", he argued, "that the withering of the state will only occur with the full victory of communism, in present circumstances weakening the socialist state means to help our enemies." However, things had moved on since the 1930s. The Soviet Union was not any longer surrounded by capitalist states as it had been under Stalin; there existed two competing social systems in the world, the dying forces of capitalism and the growing forces of socialism. This had important consequences for the Soviet people: it meant that "the danger of capitalist restoration in the Soviet Union was excluded, socialism had conquered not simply fully but finally". The implications of this statement were enormous. The justification for all Stalin's purges had been the supposedly endless attempts by enemies and traitors, supported from abroad, to restore the capitalist system in the Soviet Union. If socialism had triumphed for good and all, no new purge could be justified, no limitations in judicial process could be tolerated. At the end of his speech, Khrushchev suggested that this new era the Soviet Union was entering into required a new constitution, one that would reflect an essential element of the communist future– the greater activity it implied for soviets, soviets as the organs for self-administration and for cutting through bureaucratic obstruction.[17]

Those close to Khrushchev were quick to back him on these programmatic issues. Kirichenko, now a Central Committee secretary, and Pospelov spoke of a "grand programme for the developed construction of communism in our country"; Aristov elaborated on the ramifications of the notion that socialism had triumphed "fully and finally"; and Mikoyan commented that far from being a "dry" speech as its title suggested, Khrushchev had given "a symphony on communist construction" and suggested that Khrushchev's speech should be the basis for a new party programme. Opponents were not so sure. Suslov was concerned that, despite what Khrushchev had said about the "full and final victory of socialism", more still needed to be done to combat "survivals of capitalism" and "the influence of bourgeois ideology". He was careful to avoid using the term "withering away of the state" and stressed that even as social organisations played a greater role in society, "this would not lead to a lessening of the role of state and economic organs". When Suslov had opened the congress, he had explained that this was an extraordinary rather than a regular congress, and so there would not be a report from the Central Committee. The implication was clear, Khrushchev was speaking for himself, not on behalf of the Central Committee.[18]

When he was not reflecting on the nature of the communist future, always, surely, a legitimate topic for a communist leader, Khrushchev was careful to keep within agreed positions. He stuck strictly to the assessment of Stalin agreed in the June 1956 resolution on the cult of personality: Stalin oversaw great social and economic transformation and defeated opposition from various class enemies on the way. The tone of Shvernik's report from the Party Control Committee was very similar: all violations of socialist legality had been addressed, and all those communists unjustly condemned had been rehabilitated; the Stalin issue was in the past. Equally, when it came to Yugoslavia, Khrushchev's line was fully orthodox: "they deny the Leninist teaching of the party as the leading force in the struggle for socialism"; while each country had its own individualities, it was not possible "to get to socialism by some path lying outside the general path shown by Marxism–Leninism". Khrushchev made only the briefest of references to the Anti-Party Group, and left it to his closest supporters to be less restrained. Thus it was Ivan Spiridonov from Leningrad who called them "traitorous", while Serdyuk, Kirichenko, Aristov and Kozlov denounced them with similar force. Such attacks were not the agreed purpose of the congress and not all the speeches condemning the Anti-Party Group were given in full in *Pravda* reports, although they did appear in the Italian communist daily *Unità*.[19]

Where the prospect of the transition from socialism to communism had a distinctly negative impact was on the church and other religious communities. There had been a short-lived campaign against religious belief in summer 1954, but Khrushchev had called it off that November because believers had been "insulted". There was no such hesitancy in 1959. The continuance of religious activity was felt to be incompatible with communist life and after 18 April 1959, when the KGB presented the Presidium with a note on progress in the "campaign against religious survivals", a systematic assault on the church began. The head of the Council for Russian Orthodox Affairs advised the Patriarch that roughly half the convents and hermitages which still operated were to be closed, and tax changes were introduced which would significantly cut church income. Those bishops who resisted were transferred to other duties, and bishops' residences were seized for non-payment of taxes; financial pressures forced the closure of 361 churches in 1959. If anything the attack on the church intensified in 1960, when a new head of the Council of Russian Orthodox Affairs was appointed. Under his watch, Perm Cathedral was closed as a supposed traffic hazard, the theological seminary in Kiev was also forced to close, and the Archbishop of Kazan was put on trial for embezzlement, although in reality he had refused to implement the programme of church closures. In 1961 the Archbishop of Chernigov was sentenced to eight years' imprisonment because he too had refused to close churches when so instructed; by the end of 1962 a total of 12 cathedrals had been closed, along with 4,500 parish churches.[20]

A Consumer Economy

The importance of the economy in providing an economic basis for the communist future, and the dramatic increases in productivity called for at the 21st Party Congress, meant that economic planning was at the centre of Khrushchev's attention. Back in October 1957, when the Presidium was discussing plan implementation, Khrushchev had called for failings in consumer goods production to be addressed, angrily dismissing the work of the planners – "in *Gosplan*, they approach planning like illiterates", he said. In March 1959 he appointed Kosygin as chairman of *Gosplan* with a clear remit of improving the situation. Nine months later, Kosygin had focused in on the need to better distinguish between the work drafting annual plans and the work developing longer-term perspective plans; Kosygin made clear that, as things stood, the situation was not working. Then, on 7 April 1960, the Central Committee and Council of Ministers issued a decree on "further improving planning and the management of the economy" which clarified that Kosygin and *Gosplan* were to be in charge of current planning, while a State Economic Council (*Gosekonomsovet*) would be in charge of long-range planning.[21]

However, Kosygin's powers were accumulating: one of *Gosplan*'s key roles would be "to harmonise the development plans of different economic regions", in other words to give more central direction to the regional initiatives taken by the *Sovnarkhozy*; then on 4 May 1960 Kosygin was appointed Deputy Premier and his role was defined as overseeing both *Gosplan* and the *Gosekonomsovet*. Kosygin's increasing powers over the economy were reinforced over the summer. On 18 June 1960 a new *Gosplan* was established for the Russian Federation, and when on 13–16 July a Central Committee Plenum met to discuss the economy, only 11 of the 25 speakers referred positively to the *Sovnarkhozy*. The net effect of these changes was to turn *Gosplan* into a sort of super-*Sovnarkhoz* for the entire Soviet Union, even though it had no right to control the overall activities of the *Sovnarkhozy*, which still notionally came under the Council of Ministers. As Kosygin's star rose, so did the centralising features of economic management.[22]

If, in terms of annual plans, the July 1960 Plenum reinforced Kosygin's centralising instincts and his aversion to experimentation, in terms of perspective planning it suggested the opposite; moves towards experimentation were being encouraged. The *Gosekonomsovet* was instructed to work on pricing and establish "real prices" which would enable "self-regulation rather than command", in other words, moves away from traditional planning in terms of targets for volume of production and towards some version of a socialist market. The plenum also established a Commission of the Academy of Sciences under Vasilii Nemchinov which would work together with Aleksandr Zasyadko, the head of the *Gosekonomsovet*. Under Zasyadko, the *Gosekonomsovet* acquired, according to one of its members, its own "distinct physiognomy" and began to aspire "to the role of pace-setter in working out a strategy for the scientific and technological development of the country". Tension between Kosygin and Zasyadko about the future direction of planning would be a regular feature of the next couple of years.[23]

By autumn 1960, however, it was not planning but agriculture which seemed to be undermining the economic bases of communism. For the next five months agriculture topped Khrushchev's agenda, with Central Committee Plenums in December 1960 and January 1961, and trips to every corner of the Soviet Union in February and March. On 29 October 1960, Khrushchev informed the Presidium that the Virgin Lands were no longer delivering what they had initially promised and that meat, milk and butter were in short supply; there was a danger that the country could "slide back to where we were in 1953". At the resulting Plenum on 16 December 1960, Khrushchev talked knowledgeably and at length about the agricultural situation and stressed what would become one of his themes, the need to facilitate contacts between research and technology, and the collective farms. Discussion of agriculture continued at the January 1961 Plenum, when a post-mortem was held into the disastrous Ryazan Affair; a model programme for increasing livestock production was discovered during October and November 1960 to have been a complete scam, and a scam that had resulted in the unnecessary slaughter of peasants' cattle.[24]

The ambition of the Seven-Year Plan adopted at the 21st Party Congress was that meat production should double by 1965, from

8 million to 16 million tons per annum; meat production in the Soviet Union was only 38 kg per head of population in 1958, compared to 94 kg in the US. The idea was to pressurise peasants into transferring the cattle they currently raised on private plots to common ownership, making them part of ever larger herds of collectively owned cattle, herds that then would be intensively reared and slaughtered. In the initial phase of this campaign, the Ryazan region seemed to have been particularly successful, and soon the Ryazan method was being trumpeted as the model for others to follow. One aspect of the scheme worked: the compulsory purchase of cattle from peasants reduced the number of cattle in private ownership in the Ryazan region by 15.5% between January 1959 and January 1960. However, it gradually became clear that the claimed tripling of meat production in Ryazan was all a game of smoke and mirrors and cattle were double counted: they were held on the farm "to be fattened", but at the same time in reality transferred to the slaughter house; thus the same cows could be counted first as belonging to a farm and second as having been delivered for slaughter. When the scheme unravelled, the Ryazan regional party secretary decided he had no choice but to commit suicide. The total number of cows in the Soviet Union fell from 2.4 million in 1957 to 0.9 million in 1960, a disastrous policy which left many rural households without the cow which had until then provided their milk supplies.[25]

Disagreements about planning and concerns about the state of agriculture were part and parcel of a more fundamental concern about economic priorities which had characterised the leadership ever since the defeat of the Anti-Party Group. Kosygin had written in *Pravda* on 4 July 1957: "Everyone is well-aware that successes in agriculture do not at all mean that heavy industry should develop more slowly in this connection. The party always has been and always will be concerned for the preponderant development of heavy industry. It will never deviate from this line." However, in the edition of *Pravda* which commemorated the 40th anniversary of the Bolshevik Revolution on 7 November 1957, Khrushchev had stressed that "without detriment to the further development of heavy industry and machine building, we can develop light industry at a considerably higher speed". As part of this, in May 1958 Khrushchev introduced a programme for developing the chemical industry, which he asserted was "a decisive branch" of heavy industry.[26] That the traditional "steel eaters" could see through this sleight of hand is clear from the way the chemical industry struggled to find investment funds; Kosygin told the Supreme Soviet, in a speech reported by *Pravda* on 28 October

1959, that the only area where the Seven-Year Plan was falling behind was the chemical industry. When Khrushchev addressed the Supreme Soviet on 5 May 1960, he noted how "some comrades" had criticised his pro-consumer moves, fearing a loss of status for heavy industry. After his detailed investigation into the state of agriculture after the Ryazan Affair scandal broke, Khrushchev became aware of the regular downgrading of agricultural investments, for example the way the Zaporozhe works stopped producing combine harvesters and went over to producing the much sought after Zaporozhets mini car.[27]

Khrushchev, like Malenkov before him, realised that the issue of improving the standard of living of the Soviet people could not constantly be ignored. At the 17 January 1961 Plenum, Khrushchev addressed the balance between industry and agriculture, the old debate of guns or butter. He spoke out against what he saw as the "steel eaters" and, echoing Malenkov, suggested that "agriculture must keep in step with industry", adding that "the building of communism today calls for a different and swifter rate of agricultural development", which meant spending more on both agriculture and those industries which served agriculture. Khrushchev stated: "Today our country has such a powerful industry and such a powerful defence, that it can, without jeopardising the development of industry and the strengthening of its defence, devote more funds to the development of agriculture as well as increasing the production of consumer goods." Metal production was not the only index of success, but "the amount of goods a man receives or eats". The results of the plenum were discussed by the Presidium on 20 January 1961, when the decision was taken "to reconsider the plan for machine construction" and "to work up a plan for the production of agricultural machinery". On 21 February 1961 *Pravda* reproduced a speech in which Khrushchev criticised "some comrades" whose "appetite for metals" unbalanced the economy; he also referred to "dangerous consequences" if consumer demand were not met.[28]

When Khrushchev reported to the Presidium on 16 February, Aristov, one of Khrushchev's most loyal supporters, was removed from his post as secretary responsible for the Russian Federation; he was, Khrushchev felt, "too calm a person" to enforce policy in the difficult area of agriculture and Ryazan had occurred on his watch. Disciplining those not up to the job was one thing, persuading "steel eaters" to re-orientate the economy towards agriculture was more difficult. On 13 March 1961, Khrushchev informed the Presidium: "Leading officials, including some in *Gosplan* ... have erroneously concluded that the equipment now used in agriculture is adequate."

During a visit to the British Trade Fair on 20 May, in comments not reported in the Soviet media, Khrushchev said that "the primacy of heavy industry would in time be replaced by equal rates of development for the consumer and light industrial sector". And so the agenda returned again to planning.[29]

At the Presidium meeting of 17 June 1961, Khrushchev suggested that if the "steel eaters" needed their big projects, those projects should at least be cost effective. So he addressed the need for some sort of better financial control over capital investments. Khrushchev challenged those who suggested that project overspend was a result of the *Sovnarkhoz* reform; in Khrushchev's view that was not the case, although he accepted that "the lack of discipline" in financial matters did coincide chronologically with the *Sovnarkhoz* Reform, it was not the reform that was the problem but a lack of determination: "I think we lead industry badly. *Gosplan* leads badly and the Council of Ministers leads badly." Khrushchev then took a swipe at Kosygin: he was "first deputy" in this area; a lot depended on him; more co-ordination was essential; the Council of Ministers needed instructions; and yet bureaucracy was everywhere – the party should act, "time is passing", he concluded, "and nothing changes".[30]

The New Party Programme

The Presidium meeting of 17 June 1961 not only discussed the economy, the base of a future communist society, but also witnessed key discussions on what Marx suggested would be the superstructure of a communist society. The June Plenum finalised work on a new party programme. The 21st Party Congress had hinted at the need for a new programme, and from autumn 1959 onwards Khrushchev had been arguing for a more democratically functioning party as the key to a communist future. On 15 October 1959, he told the Presidium that whereas under Stalin it had been felt that opposition was impossible and when it had occurred, it had to be destroyed, today further democratisation was the task: "our cadres have grown up", he said. On 14 December 1959, the Presidium discussed the work Ponomarev had done so far on drafting the new party programme, in particular it discussed the section on democratisation. Khrushchev insisted that the main task was to democratise the party's structure and bring new people forward, including new people to the Central Committee and Presidium. To this end, the party rules needed to be adapted to make sure that at least one-third of all Central Committee delegates were regularly renewed. Khrushchev insisted that Soviet society had entered a new, democratic phase and that this had to be clearly sig-nalled. In general, officials should only serve one, possibly two terms. Khrushchev summed it up thus: "if everyone knew he was elected for one term, two at a maximum, then our apparatus would not be bureaucratised. It would mean that bold people would come forward, it would promote democratisation in the party, the people and the country".[31]

In autumn 1959, Khrushchev had made clear that he was simply thinking out loud when talking about the need for a regular rotation of cadres, but that proposal remained central to his thoughts as a drafting commission worked throughout 1960. At the January 1961 Plenum, dominated by the issue of agriculture, it was also resolved to summon the 22nd Party Congress, and this meant Khrushchev push-ing ahead with work on the new party programme. One troubling issue for the communist future was whether or not nations would survive under communism. Dogmatic Marxist–Leninists suggested that as communism developed, so nations would effectively "merge together", but Khrushchev was not convinced. On 29 March 1961 he sided with those who favoured "the brotherly coming together of nations" rather than their "merging". In a letter to one of those on the commission drafting the new party programme, he made clear that part of his thinking was purely pragmatic: if the new programme talked of "brotherly coming together" that would have more reso-nance for those peoples in Asia, Africa and Latin America struggling against imperialism and for their national cause. Throughout April, Khrushchev continued to work intensively on the new party pro-gramme, chairing the drafting commission at this time.[32]

The programme was presented to the Presidium in draft form on 6 May and approved in outline on 24 May. The Presidium returned to discussions on 17 June, when Khrushchev agreed to some com-promises and accepted that more discussion was needed on certain proposals. Two matters stood out. First, perhaps not surprisingly since it affected the futures of all present, what should be done about the proposals for the regular rotation of cadres? Khrushchev had to accept that his proposal that no party leader should serve for more than two terms would have to be modified: it was decided that col-leagues could serve a maximum of two terms of office in posts below republican level, but that at republic level and above, they could serve three terms. Second, on ideology, he accepted Suslov's point that "the leading role of the working class for the whole period of the construction of communism" should not be "hidden" by phrases such as "the whole Soviet people". Suslov was adamant that the leading role of the working class should still be referred to, even in a document which was based on the proposal that the class struggle was over and the Soviet Union was an all-people's state.[33] On 19 June 1961 a Central Committee Plenum "ratified" the draft programme, but sharp-eyed journalists noted that it only accepted "in principle" the proposed new party statute, which was to introduce the rotation of cadres. In the end, Khrushchev had to accept that although in the republics and regions one third of the leadership was to be replaced at every election, in the Presidium and Central Committee the rotation would affect only one quarter of members. On 30 July *Pravda* launched a public discussion of the new party programme: officially 44 million people attended meetings of various kinds, at which some 3.5 million spoke. [34]

Endorsing the new programme was the task of the 22nd Party Congress, which took place on 17–31 October 1961. The message of Khrushchev's report was essentially the same as his message to the 21st Party Congress: the economic basis for communism was falling into place since capital investment between 1956 and 1961 had been greater than for the whole period 1917–56. This dramatic economic advance, he suggested, reflected a fundamental change in the class make-up of the Soviet Union: "proletarian democracy was turning into all-people's socialist democracy" and this meant that "each Soviet person would become an active participant in administering the affairs of society", that, Khrushchev stressed, was "our slogan and our task". Khrushchev was clear, if in Lenin's day white collar administrative staff had been the sons and daughters of the possessing classes, now they were the descendants of workers and peasants, and this meant that class differences were disappearing and "everyone was a labourer for a communist society".[35] Developing this theme towards the associated concept of the withering away of the state, he stated: "we are going towards communism, where people themselves, without any special apparatus, will administer the concerns of society ... socialist statehood is becoming social self-administration". Thinking through the implications of all this, Khrushchev continued: "in practice this could mean that, let's say, the apparatus of party administration could be reduced in size, while the ranks of party activists are increased". A further implication was that trade unions could once more broaden their functions; production assemblies in particular, he noted, "should become more influential bodies, enabling improvements in the work of enterprises".[36]

Turning to the party programme itself, Khrushchev stressed that it was the 20th Party Congress which had called for a new programme and that its starting point was the recognition "of the full and final victory of socialism in the USSR". Since the material basis for communism now existed, and a classless society had been created, one in which all citizens were able to take part in the administration of social affairs, "the broadest development of socialist democracy" meant that society was preparing for the full realisation of the principles of communist self-administration", for even "the development of the communist economy" was impossible without "the active participation of the whole people in the administration of production". Socialist democracy was possible because of the development of the Soviet Union into a classless society, because that meant that the need for the dictatorship of the proletariat had vanished: "unique among the classes of history", Khrushchev said, "the working class did not seek to perpetuate its rule", On the contrary, "the state, from being a weapon of class rule, becomes an organ expressing the general people's will".[37] It was because of the radical implications of this change that the congress decided that the Soviet Union needed a new constitution.

As at the 21st Party Congress, unless all this sounded too utopian, Khrushchev stressed that this transition to communism would be a very gradual process. There was, he suggested, no great wall between the dictatorship of the proletariat and the all-people's state; even at the birth of the dictatorship of the proletariat elements of the all-people's state had existed, and even in the all-people's state, the state apparatus would continue to play a role for many years, "long after the victory of the first stage of communism". Khrushchev was equally clear: "the process of the withering away of the state will be a long one, it will take a whole historic epoch and will be complete only when society is fully ready for self-administration". He did not specify when that moment would come, but he did indentify the agents of democratic change. The key to developing self-administration would be broadening the rights and responsibilities of the soviets. As to the future of nations in a communist utopia, Khrushchev stated that the Russian language would increasingly become an essential language of communication as the nations of the Soviet Union grew closer together, but all children had, and would always have, the right to education in their mother tongue; even as communism in its basics was being constructed, it was "too early to talk of the merging of nations".[38]

The proceedings of the 22nd Party Congress make clear that not all delegates endorsed Khrushchev's radical instincts. Suslov again chose his words very carefully, repeating the concession he had wrung out of Khrushchev. He spoke of "an all-people's government in which the working class, as the most advanced and organised force of Soviet society, would continue to carry out its leading role until classes disappeared". And Khrushchev noted in his own speech that "other comrades" had gone further and suggested that the dictatorship of the proletariat should be preserved until the full victory of communism. "Such comrades", he said "completely leave out of account the objective conditions evolving in our country and rely on arbitrary snatches of quotation, leaving aside the essence of the teachings of Marx, Engels and Lenin on the dictatorship of the proletariat as a state, a state of the transition period from capitalism to socialism and the first phase of communism; they do not take into consideration that in our socialist society there are now only labouring classes." Khrushchev's critics had also sought to link the idea of an "all-people's state" to the proposal of the German utopian socialist Ferdinand Lassalle to establish a "people's government", a proposal much criticised by Marx in the 1860s. One such critic was Molotov, who, while the programme was still in its discussion stage, had criticised its "anti-revolutionary spirit" and had tried to get his criticisms published in an article submitted to the theoretical journal *Kommunist* to mark the 90th anniversary of Lenin's birth in April 1960.[39]

De-Stalinisation Resumed

At the 22nd Party Congress, Khrushchev decided to discredit the critics of his new vision of communism by linking them to the Stalinists expelled at the time of the Anti-Party Group crisis. Since Shvernik's report to the 21st Party Congress, the process of de-Stalinisation had effectively stalled. However, in November 1960 Shatunovskaya had been asked to explore more fully the question of whether Stalin had played a role in the assassination of Kirov. Thus, at the end of January 1961 the Party Control Committee had sent Khrushchev a report which suggested that Stalin had ordered the assassination because over a hundred votes had been cast against him as party leader at the 17th Party Congress. That report caused a stir. In April two members of the Party Control Committee were removed because they refused to accept the decisions of the 20th Party Congress on the cult of personality. In May, the Presidium ordered a new investigation, which was ready by the end of September. This report rejected Shatunovskaya's more sensational claims about

Stalin's role in the assassination and the size of the opposition to him in February 1934, and concentrated instead on the major public show trials of Bukharin, Rykov and others.[40]

Unlike in his speech to the 21st Party Congress, Khrushchev used his speech to the 22nd Party Congress to elaborate on this material and confront the view expressed by Molotov, Malenkov, Kaganovich and Voroshilov that it had been wrong to address Stalin's crimes. It had not been wrong, Khrushchev said, it had been essential, essential for two reasons: first, because not confronting those crimes meant supporting those forces which were "chained to the past and unable to think creatively", and second, because as the full facts became clear, the moral case was overwhelming. The party "risked being cut off from the masses", he said, if it continued to be silent about Stalin's crimes. The Anti-Party Group had turned on the leadership in 1957, Khrushchev stressed, because "they bore personal responsibility for many of the mass repressions". Khrushchev's supporters then gave chapter and verse, with Ukrainian Secretary Nikolai Podgornyi recalling Kaganovich's actions in Ukraine in 1947 and Spiridonov, secretary of the Leningrad region, reminding delegates of Malenkov's role in the Leningrad Affair.[41]

The line adopted at the congress was the same as the line adopted at the June 1957 Plenum: there was a legitimate distinction which could be made between those, like Khrushchev, caught up in implementing the purges, and those who helped instigate the purges and even revelled in them. The editor of *Pravda*, Pavel Satyukov, stressed that Molotov's speech to the February–March Plenum in 1937 had provided "the theoretical basis for repression" by developing the notion that wreckers were disguising themselves as fervent supporters of communism. Shvernik, reporting for the Party Control Committee and its work with rehabilitations, repeated his view that Molotov, Kaganovich and Malenkov had been "initiators in creating circumstances of suspicion and mistrust"; for example, Kaganovich had written at least 32 personal letters demanding the arrest of some 83 people. Aleksandr Shelepin, who had replaced Serov as KGB head, gave even more details of recent discoveries. He revealed that Kaganovich had been involved in drafting the resolutions to establish extra-judicial bodies like the troikas which implemented the mass purges, and that, together with Stalin and Molotov, he worked jointly on bringing the case against Postyshev and Kosior; Kaganovich had also scrawled abuse on Yakir's final plea to Stalin for clemency. As for Malenkov and Molotov, Shelepin insisted that Malenkov's role in the Leningrad Affair had been established beyond doubt, while Molotov's vindictiveness was clear from an incident when Stalin asked for advice on the case of Georgii Lomov, and Molotov responded "arrest the bastard Lomov at once".[42]

In his speech winding up the discussion of the new party programme, Khrushchev returned to the importance of confronting Stalin's crimes "so that similar occurrences are not repeated". More and more evidence was coming to light, he said and the Kirov murder looked increasingly suspicious. Ignoring the concerns of the Party Control Committee about its reliability, Khrushchev drew on Shatunovskaya's report of January 1961 and explained how Kirov's assassin had been detained twice while visiting the Leningrad party headquarters, where the killing took place; on both occasions he had been carrying a gun, yet on both occasions he had been released without charge. At the time of the assassination, Kirov's senior bodyguard had been sent away for reasons that were not clear. Kirov's actual bodyguard on the day of the assassination was being taken in for questioning when he died in a mysterious and apparently staged traffic accident; none of those involved in the accident had survived, except the driver. It was in this context that Khrushchev took two momentous decisions: he endorsed a proposal from a group of Old Bolsheviks that there should be a permanent memorial to the victims of Stalin and, not long before the congress ended, he proposed to the Presidium that the time had come to remove Stalin's body from Lenin's mausoleum.[43]

Khrushchev wanted to take de-Stalinisation still further. In 1956 the protocols of the interrogations of Bukharin and Rykov had still not been traced, but by 1961 they had been. Once the 22nd Party Congress was over, on 19 January 1962, Shvernik was put in charge of yet another commission, this time to investigate the show trials; it produced a two-hundred-page report making clear that the trials were false, and this report was eventually submitted to the Presidium on 18 February 1963. The report suggested that the origins of the trials could be traced to Stalin's "incorrect" argument to the January 1933 Plenum that "with the growth in strength of the Soviet state, so would opposition grow on the part of the remnants of the dying classes". Shvernik therefore proposed to the Presidium that Bukharin be rehabilitated, and was supported by Shelepin, but Suslov and Kozlov were opposed and the issue was shelved.[44]

Reflecting on the early findings of the commission while in Bulgaria in May 1962, Khrushchev showed that he still fundamentally supported the arguments of Shatunovskaya, even though by then she had been removed from membership of the show trial commission. He explained that he was now convinced that after over one hundred delegates had voted against Stalin at the 17th Party Congress in 1934 and that "Stalin had invented the idea that the more thoroughly the revolution was winning, the more fiercely the class enemies were resisting, simply as a justification for the murders that were committed", the murders of those who had voted against him. Shvernik's commission had assembled "several volumes", Khrushchev said, but that was probably the end of the matter: "We assembled everything there, and assembled everyone who was left alive. It is hard for us to investigate, and after us it will be harder yet. We want to leave it and let others read it after us." He later told Shatunovskaya that he envisaged the volumes being published in 15 years' time.[45]

Deadlock on the Economy

On more than one occasion when addressing the 22nd Party Congress, Khrushchev had criticised the work of the planning bodies and the frequent mistakes they made in determining the volume of production. As he stressed repeatedly, over the coming 20 years the Soviet Union planned to invest six times as much as had been invested in the years 1917–61, and as far as he was concerned investments on this scale would require completely new levels of "progressive planning", planning aimed at ensuring that each annual plan really was an organic part of the longer-term perspective plan. Criticism of the current planning process was echoed by some of Khrushchev's more vociferous supporters, like Podgornyi and Spiridonov. For Khrushchev, a radical new approach was the way forward: "we need to raise the significance of profit ... give enterprises greater powers to allocate profits, making use of profit to incentivise good work within the collective".[46] In this spirit, on 20 November 1961 the authoritative *Ekonomicheskaya Gazeta* published an article by Leon Leontiev which questioned some of the fundamental economic laws formulated by Stalin, and sought to rehabilitate economic theories prevalent before the 1930s. Then, early in 1962, Zasyadko called a conference of one hundred reform-minded economists.[47]

Alongside planning reform, there was the more immediate demand for an increase in spending on agriculture and consumer goods. When the Presidium discussed the state of the economy on 3 December 1961, Khrushchev repeated his demand that agriculture needed increased industrial investment to produce more tractors, seeding machines and harvesters. He summoned yet another plenum on 5–9 March 1962 to debate the issue of agriculture, and opened proceedings by attacking "some leaders" who wanted to direct funds from agriculture to other areas; on the contrary, he suggested, three new factories needed to be established to provide essential agricultural machinery. Expressing himself as forcefully as ever, he declared: "You cannot call for high productivity and cut maize with hatchets." *Gosplan*, he asserted, was quite wrong to suggest that issues concerning the mechanisation of agriculture had been solved. Yet, for all his eloquence, Khrushchev failed to move the Central Committee from its gut instinct that heavy industry should always have priority. By the end of the March Plenum, Khrushchev was forced to eat his words, advising the Central Committee "to talk less about the shortage of machines". No additional funds for agriculture were forthcoming, and under pressure from heavy industry, he had had no choice but to backtrack.[48]

This defeat made Khrushchev even more determined to address the issue of planning. Effective planning meant more could be done by the efficient deployment of existing resources. On 22 March 1962, the Presidium discussed industry rather than agriculture, and Khrushchev insisted that spare capacity within the industrial sector opened up real opportunities, which the party should exploit, yet nothing seemed to happen and proposals from the *Sovnarkhozy* were ignored. A year passed, he said, things were not built, no one asked why, nobody checked up; innovation was opposed by both *Gosplan* and *Gosekonomsovet*, while lots of new initiatives in science and technology were not supported. Khrushchev offered no very clear solutions, but suggested the formation of co-ordinating committees for both the *Sovnarkhozy* and various branches of industry and agriculture. When the Presidium again discussed the economy on 31 May 1962, Khrushchev concentrated his fire on the failings of *Gosplan*: "there they think like adding machines", he commented. More oversight and intervention on the part of the party in industrial matters were needed since factory directors were not given enough encouragement to think about questions of investment. *Gosplan* officials, on the other hand, had no experience of factory life and just sat at a desk and counted figures. "Our *Gosplan* is now in such a state", he said, "that we need to think of some sort of body to control it; in *Gosplan* there are many people who 'were born' in *Gosplan*."[49]

Khrushchev was becoming extremely impatient. As he told the Presidium, he had been making similar points since the 21st Party Congress, but nothing of substance had changed. This frustration led him to start questioning the nature of the current economic system. It was, he thought, a problem of bureaucratic stability. If capitalists suffered from boom and bust, "our bureaucrats do not suffer, everything is guaranteed them". If the party did not exercise more control, did not intervene more, then the result would be "stagnation". New people were needed in *Gosplan*, Khrushchev suggested, or *Gosplan* staff needed to take work placements to see what factory life was really about. Neither Zasyadko, for *Gosekonomsovet*, nor Kosygin, for *Gosplan*, were listening, Khrushchev complained. He wanted Zasyadko to think of ways of developing production, addressing spare capacity, but Zasyadko, like Kosygin, had other matters on his mind. Building communism was proving expensive and the Soviet budget was no longer in balance. Both Zasyadko and Kosygin were more focused on that immediate priority than perfecting the planning system, yet their responses to the budget imbalance reflected their basic differences in approach: Zasyadko wanted to raise taxes and maintain expenditure, while Kosygin favoured cuts in investments and delays in salary increases. This was a debate which Khrushchev did not want to have but which could not be avoided.[50] It was decided in the end to balance the budget by introducing price rises. On 17 May, the Central Committee approved price rises of 35% for meat and poultry and 25% for milk and butter, to be introduced on 1 June 1962.

In February 1961, Khrushchev had hinted at "dangerous consequences" if consumer demand were not met. For many workers the wage reform of the 1950s had had unintended consequences. The plan had been to raise basic wages and reduce the extent to which wage levels depended on overfulfilling "norms". By 1961, on average, 73% of earnings came from the basic wage, leaving less than 30% to be linked to norms. Yet several anomalies had developed as the new arrangements spread out from Khrushchev's Donbas mines where they were first trialled. In its early stages, the reform led to a fall in earnings for many workers and machine operators in particular felt hard done by as the new pay system evolved, since they had been classified at the bottom of the skills grade. To counter this, individual enterprises began to exploit loopholes and pay bonuses as a matter of course, or simply to ignore instructions to revise norms downwards.[51] The decision to raise prices dramatically when many workers were still adjusting to new salary arrangements was almost bound to cause trouble. Leaflets appeared in Moscow, Leningrad, Kiev and elsewhere calling for protests, but the most serious outbreak of unrest occurred in Novocherkassk.

In the Novocherkassk Electric Locomotive Works workers had already experienced an effective pay cut of 30–35% on 1 January 1962 because of adjustments to norms; the management had seen no need to fudge these changes as had happened elsewhere. Therefore, on the evening of 1 June workers were in an angry mood when they assembled in the main factory courtyard and demanded "meat, milk and higher wages". No serious negotiations took place. The factory director commented crassly "never mind, you'll have to go over to pies with liver sausage", while the Rostov regional party secretary simply repeated the government's decree. The two officials spoke from the balcony overlooking the courtyard and soon bottles were being thrown at them. The crowd then invaded the administrative building and the officials were briefly trapped, until KGB operatives succeeded in rescuing them.

The next day the workers decided to march to the centre of town and a crowd of possibly 10,000 set off behind red banners and a large portrait of Lenin. They passed military roadblocks without trouble and arrived in Lenin Square outside party headquarters. A small group broke away from the main assembly to try to enter the police headquarters, in the same building, to free some workers already arrested the previous day. When they entered, troops fired in the air and after another warning shot, a worker grabbed a rifle and a soldier shot into the crowd. The workers fled back into a courtyard where more troops opened fire. Five died and 30 were arrested. Meanwhile, about noon, tanks and personnel carriers arrived and formed an arc in Lenin Square between the crowd and the party building. An officer called on the crowd to leave, and fired a warning volley in the air. Convinced that the troops only had blanks, some of the crowd tried to rush forward. Some reports say there was a second warning shot before the troops fired into the crowd; whether they fired with just one shot or in sustained shooting is also disputed by witnesses, but between 50 and 100 were killed. In the aftermath 300 were detained and 146 identified as ringleaders.[52]

The Presidium dispatched Kozlov and Mikoyan to try and resolve the situation, with Khrushchev placing great hope on Mikoyan's renowned negotiating skills. He at once talked with some of the striking workers, accepting that they had a clear case and later appealed for calm on the radio. Kozlov, meanwhile, telephoned Moscow to ask for permission to use force. Khrushchev agreed that force could be used "in case of extreme necessity" and, to Mikoyan's anger, Kozlov decided to abandon talks and use force at once. When the Presidium met on 10 June to review what had taken place, it accepted Kozlov's view that there had been no alternative to the use of force. Khrushchev was clear, however, that the whole episode had been unnecessary: at a Presidium meeting later in the summer, while talking once again about the need to increase industrial production, Khrushchev referred to "the idiot factory director" who had completely mishandled the question of increased norms and had cheerfully told the party organisation that if workers could not afford to eat meat they would have to eat more cabbage – "only an enemy could say something like that", Khrushchev said.[53]

The Novocherkassk tragedy only reinforced Khrushchev in his view that something radical had to be done with the economy. On 12 July 1962 he raised in the Presidium, almost in passing, the question of whether it might "be worth developing a ten-year plan", and at its meeting a fortnight later, he again suggested that some "overarching" body might be needed to oversee *Gosplan*. By the Presidium meeting of 20 August, Khrushchev was proposing that a plenum be held on the economy for the end of November or early December. He was clear about his starting point for this discussion: raising industrial productivity was the only way to avoid a future Novocherkassk and, as it stood, *Gosplan* was not up to the job. "*Gosplan* has us by the throat: everything stays the same", he said, and he went on: "we, members of the Presidium, are of the opinion that the *Sovnarkhozy* should be preserved and strengthened, and that *Gosplan* should be reconstructed". The problem was that everything had to go through Kosygin's hands, and that created an impossible bottleneck. "There were", he suggested, "failings in our structures: *Gosplan* is an organisation which cannot be directed, and the Council of Ministers is unable to supervise it." The *Sovnarkhozy* had justified themselves, he believed, with some pluses and minuses, so the de-centralised territorial principle needed to be retained, but "we need to build in something vertical". As Khrushchev saw things, these economic changes were urgent and could not wait.[54]

In this mood of growing determination to confront the economic planners, Khrushchev was introduced to the work of the Kharkov-based economist, Evsei Liberman. Liberman had first written about how to reconcile planning and profit in an article in the theoretical journal *Kommunist* in October 1956. After the events in Poland and Hungary that month, the party was not ready for such radical ideas. They resurfaced briefly at the time of the 21st Party Congress when a further article by Liberman appeared in *Kommunist*, but it was Zasyadko's decision to hold a conference of reform economists which prompted Liberman to try again. In April 1962 the Council on Scientific Principles of Planning of the Academy of Sciences asked him to give a report to its plenary session on some experiments he had carried out with the Kharkov *Sovnarkhoz*. In August 1962 the academic journal *Voprosy Ekonomiki* published an article by him, and so he decided to see if he could not reach a wider audience. He wrote a populist piece and sent it to *Izvestiya*, the daily paper of the Soviet administration which was edited by Khrushchev's son-in-law, Aleksei Adzhubei, and had established itself as a more liberal daily than the party paper *Pravda*. At the Khrushchev family dacha Adzhubei showed the article to Khrushchev, and somewhat to Adzhubei's chagrin, Khrushchev decided that it should be published in *Pravda* in order to start a public debate about economic policy.[55] Liberman's article "Plan, Profits and Bonuses" was published in *Pravda* on 9 September 1962, and on 21 September, Nemchinov of the Council on Scientific Principles of Planning came out in his support. Liberman's proposal was beguilingly simple: "what is profitable for society should be profitable for every enterprise".[56]

According to Liberman's 1962 proposals, *Gosplan* would still determine not only the volume and assortment of production, but also the quality of products and the deadlines for deliveries. However, labour productivity, employment levels, wages, costs, prices, investments and any proposed new technologies would all be determined at enterprise level. Maximisation of profits would be the only source of incentive funds and bonuses. The scheme would also revitalise the *Sovnarkhozy*. They would no longer be mere transmission belts for planning decisions, "but centres where all the threads of basic economic planning crossed", with information coming both down from the central planners and up from the enterprises. With the aim of more efficient and flexible plan fulfilment, profit would be the sole success indicator at enterprise level.[57]

When the Presidium again turned to the economy on 12 October 1962, Khrushchev's impatience with *Gosplan* was once more palpable. "*Gosplan* knows the economy of the country very badly", he said, it simply "juggled with figures". On paper the plan looked perfect, but once it left the *Gosplan* office there was "complete disorder". He attacked Kosygin in person over his evident hostility to the *Sovnarkhozy*. *Gosplan* always raised the issue of the local horizons of the *Sovnarkhozy*, and Khrushchev conceded that this "localism" could be a danger, but he was adamant that decentralisation was still essential; the role of the republics was important, in fact, he insisted, it was in the republics that most of the planning should be done, with just a small apparatus in Moscow to co-ordinate things. At present, the republics came up with ideas, but *Gosplan* quashed them. As Khrushchev became more heated, several swear words escaped his lips.[58]

Chapter 7:   Confronting Capitalism

The Future of Germany

The shootings in Novocherkassk, the price rises which preceded them, and Khrushchev's reluctant concession to the steel eaters only make sense if the international position of the Soviet Union under Khrushchev is kept clearly in mind.

As soon as he had consolidated his position as the post-Stalin leader, he pushed through a sustained programme of conventional weapon disarmament. Between 1955 and 1957 the Soviet Union unilaterally reduced its troop strength by more than two million men. In January 1958 a further 300,000 were cut, and in May 1958 the Soviet Union announced it was reducing its troop levels in Eastern Europe by 119,000. However, the purpose of these reductions was only partially to find the resources needed for agricultural development and improving the living standards of the Soviet people; their purpose was essentially to free resources for the development of new military technology. Khrushchev was convinced that the future of warfare lay in missiles and declared in his memoirs that by 1957 "our missiles had made the US tremble". However, he was equally aware that, for all his spending on new missile systems, the Soviet military was way behind the US in this new technology. If the US really was "trembling" at Khrushchev's achievement, it was all based on bluff. As Khrushchev admitted in retirement, the Americans argued that if disarmament proposals were to be real, there would have to be mutual aerial monitoring of missile sites, but "we could not agree to that at the time, because we were weaker than the United States and its allies in terms of armaments and did not want to reveal that".[1]

In the belief that he could negotiate with the "trembling" Americans from a position of strength, Khrushchev decided in autumn 1958 to try and resolve the future of Germany. It had long been apparent that the Potsdam Agreement of summer 1945 had fallen victim to the outbreak of the Cold War. It had been agreed at Potsdam that the temporary occupation of Germany at the end of the war would be brought to an end after a suitable period of time had elapsed; occupation forces would be withdrawn and a peace treaty would be signed with a united German state. The formation of two German states, the Federal Republic in the west and the Democratic Republic in the east, at the height of the Cold War division of Europe in 1948–9, was followed, after Stalin's death, by the failure of the reunification talks in 1954–5. With NATO being formed in 1949, the Warsaw Pact in 1955 and East Germany joining the Warsaw Pact in 1956, the division of Germany was complete.

Khrushchev felt this new reality had to be faced and a "Two Germanies" solution found. He had known the East German leader, Walter Ulbricht, for many years; Ulbricht had joined Khrushchev during the Battle of Stalingrad on a mission to persuade demoralised German soldiers to change sides, and Khrushchev had always stood firmly behind the project of building socialism in East Germany. He had condemned Beria's proposal in 1953 that German reunification should be given precedence over the construction of a socialist state, and during Molotov's long diplomatic negotiations in the summer and autumn of 1955, first at the Geneva summit of 18–23 July, which Khrushchev attended, and then the Foreign Ministers' Conference of 26 October to 16 November, Khrushchev opposed any concessions on the future of East Germany, telling a meeting in Berlin that July: the working people of East Germany would not accept "the liquidation of their democratic reforms". As he told the Presidium on 7 November 1955, "the question of European security ... can be resolved with two Germanies".[2]

It was to the concept of two Germanies that Khrushchev returned in 1958. Since spring 1957, the Soviet Union had been very concerned that the West Germans might adopt a programme of nuclear armament, and although this threat was reduced in summer 1958 when the French showed their disapproval, the rhetoric coming from West Germany was aggressive: not only did the West German Government demand the reunification of Germany on the West's terms, but it insisted on making "revanchist" demands for a reunited Germany to regain control of those territories gained by Poland, Czechoslovakia and the Soviet Union at the end of the Second World War. When, in September 1958, East Germany contacted all Western states and suggested negotiations which might lead to a resolution of the German issue, these met with no response. By October 1958 Soviet intelligence was convinced that West Germany was planning some sort of dramatic action against East Germany. Indeed, when the US journalist Walter Lippmann met Khrushchev on 24 October 1958, he found him comparing the West German Chancellor, Konrad Adenauer, to the last president of Weimar Germany, Paul von Hindenburg, and suggesting that the current situation was similar to that which had prevailed on the eve of the Second World War: the Americans were encouraging West German militarisation and seemed unaware of its consequences.[3]

It was in this context that Khrushchev decided to confront the West over Germany. On 6 November 1958 the Presidium backed Khrushchev's suggestion that the 1945 Potsdam Agreement on the future of Germany was now dead and buried, and that it was time to move on. On 27 November Khrushchev issued his ultimatum to the West: "within six months" there either had to be a start to negotiations for a peace treaty signed between Germany and the wartime alliance as anticipated at the Potsdam Conference, a procedure which would from a Soviet perspective involve turning West Berlin into a demilitarised free city, or the Soviet Union would sign a separate peace treaty with East Germany, and access to West Berlin would be transferred to the control of East Germany.[4] The West's response came on 16 February 1959 with a proposal to reconvene the Four Power Conference of Foreign Ministers, which had not met since 1948. When the Presidium met on 21 February 1959 to discuss the line to be taken as preparations for such a meeting got underway, there was no change of policy: for the Soviet Union there were now two Germanies, not four occupation zones; unity through confederation was the best option for the two Germanies, but the Soviet Union was ready to sign a peace treaty with East Germany if that failed. The ultimatum was still in force. Khrushchev had wanted the future of Germany to be discussed at a summit meeting in Geneva, not delegated down to a conference of foreign ministers, and he was irritated by the West's response. However, when the British prime minister, Harold Macmillan, visited Moscow on 23 February and hinted that the conference of foreign ministers could well lead to a summit, Khrushchev was mollified. He made clear that his six-month deadline, due to expire on 27 May, was not set in stone; on 30 March he agreed to participate in the conference of foreign ministers.[5]

The conference of foreign ministers got under way on 11 May 1959 and from a Soviet perspective useful progress was made at first. The future of Germany and Berlin was at last being discussed and, unlike at previous four power meetings, both the West and East Germans were allowed to attend as observers. With the West accepting that an interim agreement on West Berlin was a possible way forward, and with a committee of both the West and East German states being formed, small steps forward were being made. Reviewing the situation on 24 May, the Presidium discussed every eventuality, including how to phase out troop deployments in East Berlin in the run-up to a full peace treaty, as well as repeating the threat to sign a treaty with East Germany if progress on "concrete matters" did not continue. During the next fortnight, however, progress stalled, "concrete matters" failed to be addressed and on 10 June Khrushchev decided the time had come to re-issue his ultimatum. The conference recessed on 20 June and although it reconvened and continued meeting until 5 August, it had run its course.[6]

Khrushchev was not dismayed. He had taken the precaution of trying to open up a back channel to Washington which might reduce the level of international tension. Mikoyan arrived in Washington in January 1959, and it was clear from Khrushchev's comments at the 21st Party Congress in February that this visit had been a success: "this trip to a degree enabled an increase in the temperature of relations between our two countries from below zero to zero and even higher", he said. There was no immediate development from Mikoyan's visit, but after the Geneva conference of foreign ministers had gone into recess, on 23 June, Khrushchev received Averell Harriman, the veteran US diplomat and Democrat politician. Khrushchev told him forcefully, and in highly colourful language, that the Soviet Union was in no mood to back down. The Khrushchev–Harriman encounter was soon big news and was raised with President Eisenhower at a press conference on 8 July. Eisenhower, who had been arguing that only making progress in Geneva would result in a summit conference being held, suddenly decided that the way to break the log jam in Geneva was to invite Khrushchev to the US for talks; a last minute attempt to make that invitation dependent on a positive attitude from the Soviet side when the Geneva talks resumed came unstuck. The invitation was issued on 13 July and Khrushchev accepted on the 21st; the public announcement was made on 3 August, at the end of US Vice President Richard Nixon's visit to the Soviet Union.[7]

Khrushchev arrived in the US on 15 September, and after a tour of the country, including a much photographed meeting with the film star Marilyn Monroe in Los Angeles, he held talks at Camp David on 25–27 September. Khrushchev proposed that Eisenhower sign a peace treaty with West Germany and allow the Soviet Union to sign peace treaties with both Germanies. Eisenhower said he had no problem with a Soviet–East German treaty, so long as the US position in Berlin was not affected. Khrushchev dismissed this as "impossible": all he would guarantee was that West Berlin would be "peaceful and prosperous" as a "free city". Eisenhower then proposed some "permanent consultative machinery" to review the situation, based on a shared commitment to taking no unilateral action; Khrushchev dismissed this as simply institutionalising Geneva and delaying any resolution. Although on the next day the main topic of conversation was China, agreement on Germany was unexpectedly reached: it was accepted that Khrushchev would drop his ultimatum and, in return, Eisenhower would accept that the current situation in Berlin could not be seen as permanent and thus a four power summit would take place before the end of 1959. Eisenhower would then pay a return visit to the Soviet Union, pencilled in for 10–19 June 1960.[8]

Khrushchev returned to Moscow on 27 September in triumph. He had been welcomed in Washington with a red carpet and a 21-gun salute. During the 10 days that he had toured the US there had been endless photo opportunities and a variety of spats with US officials. News coverage of this type was quite unprecedented. Not only was this the first time a Soviet leader had toured the US, but Khrushchev could claim that it was mission accomplished; there would be a four power summit on Germany. No wonder he went straight from Moscow airport, past enthusiastic crowds, to the Luzhniki sports stadium for a rally. His speech on that occasion reflected the enthusiasm of the moment, rather than the underlying realities of the Cold War. He made clear that, while the Cold War could not end overnight and warmongers fought for the president's ear, Eisenhower "sincerely wished to see the end of the Cold War".

Chinese Dogmatism

No sooner was Khrushchev back from the US, than he set off for China to attend the celebrations of the 10th anniversary of the Chinese Communist Revolution, arriving in Beijing on 30 September. Exactly five years prior to this, Khrushchev had visited China for the first time and had used that occasion to bring to an end some of Stalin's more discriminatory policies towards his eastern ally. As had been the case in Eastern Europe immediately after the war, Stalin had established a number of joint Soviet–Chinese companies and their terms of trade had been such that China was effectively being exploited; in his memoirs, Khrushchev even claimed that he had opposed Stalin when the Soviet dictator had suggested instructing the Chinese to give the Soviet Union land on which to build a pineapple canning factory. Before setting off for China in 1954, Khrushchev had persuaded his rather reluctant colleagues that relations with China needed to be put on a more correct footing and an extensive package of aid was extended to Beijing. Khrushchev also settled the future of the two cities of Port Arthur and Dairen by transferring them to Chinese sovereignty in May 1955. However, despite all that was on offer to China, the talks were not a complete success. Outside the official talks, Mao asked that the Chinese be provided with atomic bomb production facilities and a submarine fleet. Khrushchev refused point blank, lecturing Mao "like an arrogant merchant".[9]

On his return from China in 1954, Khrushchev was understandably concerned that "Mao's thinking was permeated with nationalist notions" and as a result the matter was discussed within the Presidium. During 1956, Khrushchev bent over backwards to keep the Chinese informed of developments in Poland and Hungary, and this the Chinese seemed to welcome. When Mao came to Moscow in November 1957 for the 40th anniversary of the October Revolution, Khrushchev recalled that their conversations "were of the friendliest kind", even though Mao let it be known that he felt he should have been consulted on the dismissal of the Anti-Party Group. This, of course, was a preposterous idea since Khrushchev had not planned the Anti-Party Affair but had rather been hijacked by it. Perhaps to placate Mao, however, he did warn him when he planned to replace Bulganin as prime minister and take on the post himself.[10]

Relations with China took a sudden and dramatic turn for the worse in summer 1958. Under the existing military treaty between the Soviet Union and China, Soviet planes had refuelling rights at Chinese military air bases. As a logical extension of this, the Soviet side assumed that, once Soviet submarines were being deployed in the Pacific, the Chinese would not object to the Soviet Union having a radio station based in China to enable regular communication with those submarines, forgetting that four years earlier Khrushchev had categorically refused to allow the Chinese to purchase Soviet-produced submarines. At this point, Chinese sensibilities about their national sovereignty seem to have become entangled with a break down in the personal relationship between Mao and the then Soviet ambassador. On 22 July 1958 Mao summoned the Soviet ambassador and accused the Soviet Union of advancing proposals for China to "share a fleet" with the Soviet Union. Mao then went on to accuse the Soviet Union of "never having had faith in the Chinese people" and considering them as unreliable an ally as Tito and the Yugoslavs. During this and subsequent exchanges, Mao insisted that Khrushchev should come to China and explain exactly what was meant since his behaviour seemed no better than Stalin's.[11]

The Presidium discussed the letter from the Soviet ambassador to Beijing on 24 July 1958. What seemed to have happened was this. The Chinese prime minister, Zhou Enlai, had written to Khrushchev on 28 June requesting help in constructing a navy. The response sent on 15 July may have included the phrase "common fleet", but this was in the context of joint action for a specific purpose and not some permanent arrangement. Khrushchev felt the ambassador had got things wrong and the tone of the 15 July letter had been condescending. In his view there was no alternative but to visit Mao and try to put things right. Accompanied by his new Defence Minister Malinovskii, he set off for Beijing on 28 July, arriving on the 31st. In the talks, Khrushchev stated explicitly: "There is no thought of a joint fleet. You know my point of view, I was against joint companies during Stalin's lifetime." However, having made his point, Khrushchev was determined to resist the notion that he was behaving as Stalin had once behaved. He condemned Stalin's "senile foolishness about the canned pineapple concession" when "his sclerosis was at work" and his "semi-colonial" attitude to China, and he could not resist reminding Mao that it was the Chinese who had criticised him in 1956 for condemning Stalin. At this point in the discussion Mao said "of Stalin's ten fingers, three were rotten", to which Khrushchev replied "I think more", and Mao retorted "wrong, his life was mainly one of merit". Khrushchev did not push the point and accepted that Stalin was "a fighter who battled for the working class", but one who "committed many errors", and one of those errors had been to "incorrectly evaluate the revolutionary possibilities of the Communist Party of China".[12]

No sooner had Khrushchev returned to Moscow, than China's national sensitivities were again a matter of concern. On 23 August 1958, China began a military bombardment of two small islands in the Taiwan Straights, close to the shore of mainland China but part of Nationalist China. The US threatened the use of nuclear weapons if China persisted and, on 7 September, Khrushchev made clear to Eisenhower that an attack on China would be considered an attack on the Soviet Union; at the same time, however, he sent Andrei

Gromyko, who had taken over as Foreign Minister from Shepilov in February 1957, on a secret visit to China to make clear that any ideas about starting a Third World War in the Pacific had to be dropped. Khrushchev took the same line nine months later when on 20 June 1959 Moscow informed Beijing that it would not give China a prototype of an atomic bomb: the situation concerning the Geneva four power conference of foreign ministers was still at a delicate stage and the Soviet Union was also in talks with the West about banning the testing of nuclear missiles; the time, therefore, was not right for equipping China with a nuclear arsenal, and given the bellicose mood in China, this was a wise decision. On 28 August 1959 hostilities broke out between China and India. This was not a war the Soviet Union had any interest in supporting since it had long been working to improve relations with India. So, on 9 September, the Soviet telegraph agency put out a statement expressing "regret" at the fighting between the two states.[13]

Thus when Khrushchev, buoyed up by the success of his visit to the US, arrived in Beijing on 30 September 1959, he was no longer as pliant or apologetic as he had been the year before. When the talks started on 1 October, Khrushchev raised, as he had promised Eisenhower he would, the case of some US prisoners held by the Chinese. He was also at pains to explain to Mao that Eisenhower had hinted at Camp David that he might be amenable to the idea of two Germanies, and so two Chinas just might also be acceptable to the US. In this context, he subjected Mao to a short lecture on Soviet foreign policy. He reminded Mao that, in the 1920s, Lenin had made huge diplomatic concessions: he had agreed to cede the Armenian town of Kars to Turkey; he had agreed to the formation of the Far Eastern Republic which had existed in eastern Siberia from April 1920 to November 1922; and he had agreed to "the separation of the Baltic States" – all with the greater aim of winning international recognition for the Soviet Union. This appeared to cut little ice with Mao, who made clear he wanted nuclear weapons, if not a bomb. He also insisted, once again, that Stalin had been too large a figure within the world revolutionary movement for his fate to have been decided unilaterally by Khrushchev and the Soviet Communist Party; an assessment of him should have been the result of joint discussion.[14]

As the talks continued on 2 October, Khrushchev was not only critical of the Chinese war with India, of which he had been given no warning, but also of the oppressive situation in Tibet, which had provoked an uprising there in March 1959 and had prompted the flight of the Dalai Lama to India. When the Chinese started to draw historical comparisons between the Dalai Lama's role in Tibet and that of Alexander Kerensky during the Russian Revolution of 1917, and then to suggest parallels between the Soviet war with Nazi Germany and the current Chinese war with India, Khrushchev made crystal clear that such comparisons were utter nonsense. He was blunt: "we think the Tibetan events are the fault of the Chinese communists and not [India's prime minister Jawaharlal] Nehru". When Mao insisted that Nehru was to blame for fomenting unrest in Tibet, Khrushchev said that this was about as accurate as saying that the US was responsible for the events of 1956 in Hungary: "we supported that fool Rákosi, that was our mistake, not the USA". Khrushchev rejected the Chinese stance, insisting firmly: "we hold a principled, communist position ... we should support Nehru and keep him in power".[15]

Khrushchev's firmness seemed to pay dividends. When the talks ended on 4 October it was agreed to work for a common line. Mao reassured Khrushchev that he appreciated his lesson in history; since the Soviet Union had waited 22 years "to recover" the Baltic States, he considered the re-conquest of Taiwan to be a long-term issue also. In Mao's view there was only "one finger" of difference between China and the Soviet Union, and Khrushchev reported to the Presidium on 15 October that relations seemed to be on the mend. Such a conclusion proved far too optimistic. The final report on Khrushchev's visit was only produced in December 1959 and even by then things had begun to deteriorate; the report made clear that disagreements between the two countries were serious and were largely caused by Mao's growing cult of personality. Meanwhile, in China, Mao called a special meeting on foreign policy that December and informed his colleagues of his perception of Khrushchev's visit: there was something that was not good "about the style of the Soviet party and people"; Khrushchev and his group did not understand Marxism–Leninism and were "easily fooled by imperialism". Khrushchev, he felt, was "not a good Marxist", but equally he was "not a complete revisionist". Khrushchev's mistakes could be corrected, Mao felt and so he repeated his view that there was only "one finger" between the two leaders and unity was "of greater importance".[16]

The cause of unity was not helped by Khrushchev's blunt use of language. On 4 February 1960, in the cosy atmosphere of a Warsaw Pact meeting, Khrushchev, recalling his autumn visit to China and the row over India, referred to Mao disparagingly as being like "a pair of worn-out galoshes standing discarded in a corner". Early in March, the Chinese Communist Party decided the time had come to begin the process of "correcting" Khrushchev's mistakes by using the 90th anniversary of Lenin's birth, 22 April 1960, to launch a campaign against revisionism; by May, Mao had changed Khrushchev's classification from "not a complete revisionist" to "half-revisionist". When the communist world gathered to attend the Congress of the Romanian Communist Party, which opened on 18 June, outstanding issues between the two communist parties were supposed to have been resolved and the Chinese claimed they had been informed of this on 2 June. However, in what the Chinese saw as a pre-emptive strike, on 21 June Khrushchev distributed to all congress delegates a rebuttal of the Lenin anniversary articles written by the Chinese. The next day he received the Chinese delegation and gave them a piece of his mind. In response, throughout China from 5 July to 10 August, the Chinese organised party meetings at which Khrushchev was criticised. It was in this atmosphere that the 13–16 July Plenum decided to withdraw Soviet specialists from China.[17]

In the second half of 1960, Sino-Soviet relations improved a little. After mediation from Vietnam, a Chinese delegation visited Moscow on 15 September and a second delegation followed on 5 November. Despite some bitter exchanges, mutual compromises were made and, on 30 November 1960, agreement was reached; a Chinese delegation led by General Secretary Deng Xiaoping signed the common declaration issued in the name of 81 communist and workers' parties. However, that reconciliation was relatively short lived and did not survive the 22nd Party Congress a year later, with its twin decisions to adopt a new party programme establishing an all-people's state and to remove Stalin's body from Lenin's mausoleum. Zhou Enlai attended the 22nd Party Congress as head of the Chinese delegation, but his speech on 19 October challenged Khrushchev's interpretation of world events and his decision to lay a wreath at the mausoleum on Red Square dedicated to "J.V. Stalin, the great Marxist–Leninist" was scarcely in tune with the prevailing mood of the congress. When Khrushchev met Zhou for private talks on 22 October, Khrushchev was blunt and made no attempt at reconciliation, instead telling Zhou dismissively that "we used to be in great need of your support, but now it is different". In these circumstances, it was not surprising that an enlarged meeting of the Chinese party held on 11 January–7 February 1962 decided that Khrushchev was in fact "a quite comprehensive revisionist".[18]

The U2 Incident

As relations with China continued to deteriorate, so Khrushchev's new relationship with the US turned sour. At first there seemed no problem. The four power summit did not take place before the end of 1959 as Khrushchev had hoped, but the postponement was modest by diplomatic standards, only until 16 May 1960. Khrushchev felt confident enough in his belief that the Cold War was beginning to wind down to launch a new round of disarmament. Thus on 8 December 1959 he sent a note to the Presidium calling for more troop reductions in view of the new "conjuncture" produced by the success of his visit to the US. Justifying this move, he noted "we now have a rocket assortment to solve any military problem" and "maintaining such a large army means narrowing our economic potential". Thus when he addressed the Supreme Soviet on 15 January 1960, after referring again to the lessening in tension after his meeting with Eisenhower, he announced an arms cut of 1,200,000 men. Khrushchev linked the troop reduction to the growing importance of rockets: "The airforce and navy have lost their former importance ... almost the entire airforce is being replaced by rockets ...[while] in the navy the submarine fleet assumes great importance and surface ships no longer play the part they once did. In our country, the armed forces have to a considerable extent been transformed into rocket forces."[19]

This reduction in the size of the armed forces by a third caused serious discontent within the army, for few generals appreciated Khrushchev's obsession with rockets; in his address to the Supreme Soviet, Defence Minister Malinovskii recognised that rocket forces were "the main arm of our armed forces" but stressed as well that modern warfare was possible "only on the basis of the unified use of all means of armed struggle". On 23 March 1961 Khrushchev paid an official visit to Paris, but by the time of his return on 3 April the row about further arms reductions had become acute. When the Presidium met on 7 April, Khrushchev's colleagues were keen to remind him of what he had said so often before his visit to the US the only thing that Washington responded to was the threat of force. The most high-profile opponent of further troop reductions was Marshal Ivan Konev, the Supreme Commander of the Warsaw Pact; he was immediately sacked. To bring officers into line, writing in the army newspaper *Krasnaya Zvezda*, Malinovskii reminded the military of the fate of Zhukov and the need to keep the army firmly under party control; a conference of party secretaries in the army was called for mid May. On 28 April 1960, Voroshilov stated at a Presidium meeting that the reasoning behind the proposed defence cuts did not seem at all clear to him; at the next meeting on 4 May he was ordered to resign and Leonid Brezhnev took over as the new head of state.[20]

After Khrushchev's visit, the US had stopped its policy of high-level photographic reconnaissance using U2 spy planes. The cessation lasted for some seven months; however, with the personal authorisation of President Eisenhower, these flights resumed on 9 April 1960, just a month before the planned four power summit in Paris, and just as Khrushchev was in the middle of dealing with the opponents to his troop reduction programme. Khrushchev felt betrayed, and the warnings of his critics within the Presidium seemed fully justified. He retreated for a brief Crimean vacation, and then made a speech in which he repeated his ultimatum: if the four power summit made no progress, the Soviet Union would sign a peace treaty with East Germany and deprive the West of control of West Berlin. This hard line towards the West was strengthened on 1 May 1960, when a U2 spy plane was shot down by a Soviet fighter.[21]

The Soviet airforce had been ordered to intercept the U2 flights as soon as they had resumed, but doing so was at the limit of their technical capacity. However, on 1 May 1960 the Soviet airforce struck lucky. Not only did a Soviet airforce pilot succeed in downing a U2, but its pilot, Gary Powers, was captured alive and his plane was intact. When Khrushchev addressed the Supreme Soviet on 5 May, he gave Eisenhower what he saw as a test. He suggested that the Powers flight could have stemmed from the machinations of hardliners in the US administration; if that were the case, then President Eisenhower would surely be ready to issue an apology and, in the event that such an apology was forthcoming, he would have a card to play when arguing within the Presidium for further talks with the US. On 12 May, he told the Presidium that he still intended to go to the four power summit in Paris, but if no apology was received from Eisenhower then, the improved relations between the two countries would be put on hold.[22]

Khrushchev was as good as his word. He arrived in Paris on 14 May and explained to President de Gaulle of France, the summit host, that unless Eisenhower issued an apology, it would not be possible for him to take any further part. When the summit tried to begin its work on 16 May, Khrushchev insisted on making an opening statement which demanded an immediate apology from Eisenhower: once an apology was received, he suggested, it would be possible to call a recess in the summit proceedings and then resume the summit discussions after a brief period of time had elapsed; Eisenhower's visit to the Soviet Union, as a consequence, would have to be postponed by six months. Eisenhower responded by making clear that the U2 flights had stopped and would not resume, but he insisted that this was not a topic to be discussed by the four powers, but in separate bilateral talks between the US and the Soviet Union. There was no meeting of minds: Khrushchev repeated his demand for an apology, and again asked Eisenhower who had put him up to resuming the flights; Eisenhower stressed that there would be no more flights within his presidency, but he would not apologise.

So Khrushchev refused to attend the next round of summit talks, preferring instead to go off with Malinovskii and find the village where the Soviet Defence Minister had been billeted as a soldier in the Imperial Russian Army fighting on the Western Front during the First World War. At a final raucous press conference, Khrushchev reminded journalists of his working class youth and how he loved "coming to grips with the enemies of the working class".[23] Khrushchev's anger is easy to understand. He had taken a great domestic risk in entering negotiations with the West. His troop reductions had led to what he later referred to as "the silliest of inventions" of US propaganda, stories that "officers and generals who had lost their jobs owing to a cut back in the armed forces [were] opposed to him". These were not "silly inventions", of course, but the truth; there is no doubt that Khrushchev had been forced by unrest in the ranks to dismiss several senior generals and he had to deploy leading party figures such as Brezhnev, Suslov and Nikolai Ignatov to quell discontent in the army; all three addressed the 11–14 May 1960 conference of party cells in the army.[24]

Khrushchev's anger at the US over the U2 incident spilled over into his determination to take part in the United Nations session scheduled for that autumn at which he intended to embarrass the US as much as possible. He set sail for New York on 9 September, arrived 10 days later and at once sought a meeting with the new *enfant terrible* of the Western world, Fidel Castro, the revolutionary leader of Cuba. Not long after the overthrow of the Batista regime in Cuba on 1 January 1959, the Soviet Union had established relations with Castro's government and in February 1960 Mikoyan had visited Cuba, returning full of enthusiasm for the young revolutionary and his government; the atmosphere of revolutionary Cuba had reminded Mikoyan of his own youth among the revolutionaries of Baku. In July 1960 Fidel Castro's brother, Raul, had visited Moscow to discuss trade, and so when Khrushchev arrived in New York for the United Nations session on 19 September, one of his first visits was to Castro, who had taken up residence in a relatively cheap hotel in Harlem. The arrival of Khrushchev's motorcade caused quite a stir.[25]

When the United Nations session opened, Khrushchev was determined to make his mark: he heckled the British prime minister, Harold Macmillan, when he referred to the recent unfortunate failure of the Paris summit; he shouted at the Spanish delegation when it failed to applaud his speech; and then, on the last day of the session, he caused an uproar by banging his shoe on his desk. A delegate from the Philippines had dared to compare Soviet policy towards Eastern Europe to Western colonialism, stating that Eastern Europe had been "swallowed up" by the Soviet Union. One of the themes of the United Nations session was decolonisation, a process in which the Soviet Union saw itself as playing a positive role, and Khrushchev was furious at the way the Philippines delegate had cut the ground from under his feet. Although the official diplomatic advice given to Soviet representatives in such circumstances when the Soviet Union was "slandered" was to walk out, Khrushchev recalled his youth and the press reports he used to give his fellow labour militants from *Zvezda* and *Pravda* about the work of their local Social Democrat deputy, Petrovskii, within the Imperial Duma; Petrovskii had often whistled and catcalled to disrupt the debates of this hostile "bourgeois" assembly. Khrushchev decided to do the same. He banged his fist on his desk so hard that his watch fell off and, bending down to pick it up, suddenly thought that if he used his shoe to bang on the desk, he could cause even more consternation, so that is what he did, banging it on the desk repeatedly.[26]

The Berlin Wall

On 8 November 1960 John Kennedy was elected President of the US. Three weeks later Khrushchev met Ulbricht and told him that if the new Kennedy administration did not move to resolve the German issue then, as he had repeatedly threatened before, "we will sign a peace treaty with East Germany". However, the purpose of these talks was to prepare Ulbricht for a significant concession on Khrushchev's part. He made clear that, whatever he had said for Western consumption about ending the international status of West Berlin, that was effectively out of the question. Berlin would not come under East German sovereignty, some sort of international control over West Berlin would continue, but "we will work out with you a tactic for gradually crowding out the Western powers from West Berlin, but without war". A rather reluctant Ulbricht was told that he should take no unilateral action concerning Berlin. Four months later, still awaiting a clear assessment of the new Kennedy administration, on 10 April 1961, Khrushchev received the veteran US journalist Walter Lippmann and made clear to him that, as far as he was concerned, the issues of Germany and Berlin could be separated: "we are ready to take any actions that could guarantee the freedom and independence of West Berlin and the non-interference in its affairs", he said.[27]

The period of assessing Kennedy's intentions ended on 12 May 1961, when Kennedy made the first move and proposed a summit meeting with Khrushchev in Vienna. Khrushchev accepted. He was in confident mood. On 12 April 1961, the Soviet Union had sent the first man into space when Yurii Gagarin's *Vostok 1* spacecraft successfully made a full orbit of the earth. The Soviet Union might be behind the US in terms of standard of living, but it had won the first round of the space race. The massive crowds which turned out to greet Gagarin on his return to Moscow suggested genuine popular pride in Khrushchev's communist project. There was another reason why he was confident. He was coming to the conclusion that Kennedy was "weak". On 17 April 1961 anti-Castro exiles landed an expeditionary force at the Bay of Pigs on Cuba: this was an operation planned by Eisenhower which Kennedy decided not to cancel, but neither was he prepared to supply the air cover which was essential for an amphibious landing to succeed in such open territory. The Bay of Pigs was an operation which was bound to fail. To Khrushchev this was weakness, as was the conviction of some of his advisers that Kennedy was little more than the plaything of his advisers and backers, such as the millionaire J. D. Rockefeller.[28]

The summit on 3–4 June achieved little. Kennedy brought nothing to Vienna on the future of Berlin. Instead, he raised general issues, such as whether communism really was destined to replace capitalism, and other less pressing issues in dispute, the need for a ceasefire and neutral government in Laos and progress in the test ban treaty talks. For Khrushchev, this was a step backwards – after all, Eisenhower had at least acknowledged that the situation in Berlin was "abnormal" and could not continue. On Germany, Kennedy simply asserted that "he had not assumed office to accept arrangements totally inimical to US interests". In the final session of talks, when Khrushchev offered the possibility of an interim agreement on Berlin's future, Kennedy turned it down at once, ignoring Khrushchev's sniping comment that "if the United States wants war, that is its problem". So Khrushchev used the summit to re-issue his deadline of six months for a settlement of the Berlin question, although he saw little prospect of success. Reflecting this worsening in relations, the decision to reduce the size of the Soviet Army was cancelled on 8 July and the military budget increased by one third.[29]

Proof that Kennedy would be no easier to deal with than Eisenhower came when, on 25 July 1961, Kennedy effectively issued an ultimatum of his own. He made clear that any unilateral Soviet action against West Berlin would mean war with the US and, to make this threat look credible, he announced a panoply of military preparations. Khrushchev responded by changing his mind on nuclear testing. Although at the Vienna summit he had said that he would only resume the testing of nuclear missiles in response to the US doing the same, he now announced that the Soviet testing programme was being restored. Khrushchev decided that the hardening of Kennedy's stance meant that he was not in control of the hawks within his administration, indeed, he was scarcely in charge of his administration. He told the Italian prime minister that the US was "a barely governed state", it was like the *veche* (council) of the medieval city state of Novgorod where one party "defeated the other when it tore off half their beards", although in reality the same forces still continued to govern the city. Kennedy was young, inexperienced, no match for the military industrial complex of the US and terrified that if he backed down he would be called a coward. However, the open threat of war issued on 25 July persuaded Khrushchev that the Berlin issue had to be resolved with as little damage as possible.[30]

Before the Vienna summit, at a Warsaw Pact meeting on 28–29 March 1961, Ulbricht had proposed that a "barbed wire" border be constructed in Berlin. There was no Soviet support for the idea at the time, but after the failure of the Vienna summit, a border through Berlin seemed a possible way forward, one that avoided the diplomatic dangers of signing a separate peace with East Germany. For all its bellicosity, Kennedy's speech of 25 July had referred to the importance of Western access to West Berlin, but had made no mention of freedom of travel from West Berlin to East Berlin. East Germany was quick to spot this, and the very next day it formally proposed to the Soviet Ministry of Foreign Affairs that the border between West and East Berlin should be closed. The Soviet Government did not respond at once, but also noted signs that the US might accept such a move: on 30 July Senator William Fulbright, the chair of the Senate Committee on Foreign Relations, stated that he could not understand why the West–East border was not closed, and both Fulbright and Kennedy's adviser, Arthur Schlesinger, referred to "something like a wall" being a possible way forward. Ulbricht came to Moscow on 31 July and was told of Khrushchev's decision: there would be no peace treaty with East Germany, Khrushchev feared such a treaty would inevitably mean East Germany controlling access to West Berlin; however, the border between West and East Berlin would be closed. Ulbricht was back in Moscow on 5 August for detailed planning, and work on the wall began on 13 August.[31]

The lack of any response from the US side, despite what Kennedy had said on 25 July, persuaded Khrushchev that all would be well. That was put to the test on 26–27 October 1961 when, during the 22nd Party Congress, there was a stand-off between Soviet and US tanks in Berlin. Khrushchev had been informed by Soviet intelligence that an attempt was to be made to breach the wall by force, so when US tanks approached Checkpoint Charlie, one of the heavily guarded crossing points between West and East Berlin, Soviet tanks moved to bar their way. Once Khrushchev had ascertained that Kennedy was not personally involved ployment of these tanks, he ordered the Soviet tanks to leave the scene, prompting the US tanks to leave shortly afterwards. Khrushchev interpreted this incident as a victory, telling the Presidium: "we taught them a lesson". As if to explain what that lesson might be, on 30 October 1961, at the end of the 22nd Party Congress, the Soviet Union exploded a 50 megaton nuclear bomb, its biggest ever.[32]

The Cuban Missile Crisis

After the test of the 50 megaton bomb, to reassure public opinion in the US, Kennedy revealed publicly for the first time what the intelligence community had known all along, that the US had military superiority over the Soviet Union in terms of nuclear rockets; Kennedy's message was clear, there was plenty of spare capacity for the US to respond if there were ever a Soviet first strike with nuclear missiles. In fact, the US estimate that the Soviet Union possessed 75 operational intercontinental ballistic missiles was an overestimate; the real figure was only 20. If in 1957 Khrushchev could say that the US had been made "to tremble" at the thought of Soviet rockets, his bluff had now been called. This was unwelcome news when the Central Committee was preparing to debate the competing demands of agriculture and heavy industry, and in particular whether investments in agricultural machinery should be prioritised. Khrushchev put the dilemma to the Presidium at its meeting on 8 January 1962: in Germany a victory had been won; Kennedy was capable, but lacked authority among those who held the real power in the US, and China was engaging the Soviet Union in a stupid argument. All this meant additional expenditure on arms and the adoption of an expansion of military spending, certainly until 1965, after which time, he hoped, it would be possible to scale back military spending once again.[33]

Was there any way out of this dilemma? The solution came to Khrushchev during his visit to Bulgaria, which began on 10 May 1962. He was joined in Bulgaria by Malinovskii, who was keen to give him a report on the US Jupiter missiles which had just become operational in Turkey. As Khrushchev and Malinovskii walked along the beach near the Bulgarian port of Varna, Malinovskii pointed out that on the opposite shore of the Black Sea there were bases for the Jupiter missile, quite capable of attacking Moscow. Khrushchev had a eureka moment: "what if we throw a hedgehog down Uncle Sam's pants", he said. Rather than achieving missile parity through the expensive route of building intercontinental ballistic missiles, it could be done by placing much cheaper medium-range missiles in Cuba. As he recalled in his memoirs, "it was during my visit to Bulgaria that I had the idea of installing missiles with nuclear warheads in Cuba without letting the United States find out they were there until it was too late to do anything about them". Surprise, he believed was essential: "if we installed the missiles secretly and then if the United States discovered the missiles were there after they were already poised and ready to strike, the Americans would think twice before trying to liquidate our installations by military means".[34]

This moment of inspiration quickly became an obsession. At the March 1962 Plenum, Khrushchev had had to eat his words and drop the idea that not enough was being spent on agricultural investment; now there seemed a way to meet the country's defence needs and increase the well-being of the Soviet people. Khrushchev was unable to get the Cuba scheme out of his mind. "All these thoughts kept churning in my head the whole time I was in Bulgaria. I paced back and forth, brooding over what to do." He and Foreign Minister Gromyko discussed the missile deployment on their flight back to Moscow on 20 May. Gromyko was cautious, as was Mikoyan; however, the very next day the Presidium discussed aid to Cuba and agreed to reach agreement with Castro on a military treaty for mutual defence. Precisely what such a treaty meant was resolved at a combined meeting of the Defence Council and Presidium on 24 May: there the decision was taken to go ahead with Khrushchev's scheme and a delegation set off for Cuba on 27 May. Things then moved forward with great speed: the first supply vessel docked in Cuba on 26 July; the first medium-range missiles arrived in mid September; and the first warheads were delivered on 4 October. At the same time negotiations between the Soviet Union and the Cubans were taking place in Moscow for the formal defence treaty which would justify the missile deployment; the Cubans asked repeatedly and rather nervously why the deployment had to be secret and what would happen if it were discovered. The agreement on the treaty was signed in September, but initially kept secret; the plan was to make it public during Khrushchev's proposed visit to Cuba, after the mid-term elections in the US that November and after the missile deployment was a fait accompli.[35]

US intelligence monitored reports of some sort of military build-up on Cuba early in July and by August the CIA believed it was possible that medium-range missiles were being deployed. However, they had no definitive proof and Kennedy did not believe it was likely. Privately convinced that no such weapons were being deployed, he made a fairly blunt statement on 4 September in which he made clear that "the gravest issues would arise" if weapons of "significant offensive capacity" were deployed in Cuba. Khrushchev's response to this warning was rash. Instead of drawing back in realisation that the US had discovered something, he not only accelerated the deployment programme but added new weaponry, while in public issuing a flood of false reassurances that nothing remotely threatening was taking place; the Soviet ambassador in Washington repeatedly told the White House that no missiles were being deployed.[36]

The Soviet side took every precaution to disguise what was happening as the missiles and related equipment were transported to Cuba, but once on Cuban soil, the construction protocols used for the missile sites were initially the normal ones, giving no instructions to disguise what was taking place. With U2 flights crossing Cuba regularly, it was only a matter of time before things went wrong, indeed, to quote William Taubman, the most informed scholar on US–Soviet relations, "the surprise is not that Soviet rockets were discovered before they were ready but that it took so long for Khrushchev's scheme to unravel". A U2 flight over Cuba on 14 October revealed what was happening and Kennedy was informed on 16 October. He had a long-planned meeting with Soviet Foreign Minister Gromyko on 18 October and decided to use that meeting as a test of Khrushchev's sincerity. Gromyko was given every opportunity to come clean and explain what was happening in Cuba, but he did not. He talked about a possible visit to the US by Khrushchev; he warned that, once the US mid-term elections were out of the way, the Soviet Union would find itself with no choice but to return to the issue of Germany and sign a peace treaty with East Germany, and he condemned US intimidation of Cuba. Once it was clear that Gromyko had no intention of mentioning the missile deployment, Kennedy repeated his threat of 4 September.[37]

In his memoirs Khrushchev wrote the following: "I want to make one thing absolutely clear, when we put our ballistic missiles in Cuba, we had no desire to start a war." That explains why, in the end, he was prepared to back down. His aim was always twofold, to reach nuclear parity with the US on the cheap by deploying medium-range missiles in Cuba rather than the much more expensive intercontinental ballistic missiles, and to deter the Americans from invading Cuba. When, at seven in the evening on 22 October, Khrushchev learned that Kennedy was about to make a television address to the nation, he called the Presidium together immediately. He assumed, correctly, that the missiles had been discovered and told his Presidium colleagues what he later stated in his memoirs: "the thing is, we were not going to unleash war, we just wanted to intimidate them, to deter the anti-Cuban forces". Thus, even before he had heard Kennedy's television address, he ordered that in the event of a US invasion of Cuba, no nuclear weapons should be involved in any Soviet response.[38]

When Khrushchev read the text of Kennedy's television address, which called for "quarantining" Cuba through a US naval blockade, he realised that Kennedy had backed away from what seemed the most likely response, an immediate invasion of Cuba. Thinking that Kennedy had "blinked", he composed a blustering response when on 23 October he received Kennedy's formal letter repeating what he had said in the television address and making clear that the "quarantining" of Cuba through a naval blockade would continue until the Soviet Union's "offensive weapons systems" were removed from Cuba. "You wish to compel us to renounce the rights that every sovereign state enjoys", he fumed. "You are trying to legislate in questions of international law." The Soviet Union strictly observed "the norms which regulate navigation on the high seas" and to recognise the naval blockade would mean "submitting to arbitrariness". US policy in Cuba was "the folly of degenerate imperialism" and had been got up simply to garner votes in the forthcoming mid-term elections. In such circumstances, the Soviet Union could not fail "to reject the arbitrary demands of the United States". In the meantime, to suggest all was calm in Moscow, on the evening of 23 October, Khrushchev and key Presidium colleagues went to the opera to see a US production of *Boris Godunov* and socialised with the singers afterwards. When the Presidium met on the morning of the 24th to endorse Khrushchev's letter, despite the orders given the previous day that all Soviet ships should keep on course for Cuba, it was decided to order those approaching the naval blockade to change course.[39]

Kennedy's response on 25 October was short and to the point: you lied repeatedly about the deployment, and on that basis "I urged restraint upon those in this country who were urging action in this matter at that time". In his first letter, Khrushchev had asked rhetorically "who asked you to do this?" Kennedy's response made clear implicitly that there were "hawks" in his administration pushing for an invasion of Cuba, to whom Kennedy had stood up and might stand up to again if Khrushchev's lying ceased. Khrushchev picked up the hint, and in his letter to Kennedy of 26 October he began by suggesting an end to "exchanges of opinion" and adopting a new focus of avoiding the calamity of war: "you threaten us with war, but you well know that the very least you would get in response would be what you had given us; you would suffer the same consequences". Khrushchev assured Kennedy that the missile deployment was not "offensive", merely designed for the defence of Cuba and to prevent another Bay of Pigs. There was no need for "piracy", any Soviet ships now intercepted would show that all the missiles needed for the defence of Cuba were already in place. It was time to negotiate a settlement, and if there were an assurance "that the United States would itself not take part in an attack on Cuba ... that would change everything", for then "the necessity for the presence of our military specialists in Cuba will be obviated".[40]

The outline of a settlement was there, but Khrushchev wondered if more could be salvaged from the situation. The US journalist Walter Lippmann, whom Khrushchev had received in October 1958, had suggested that a solution to the crisis might be for the withdrawal of Soviet missiles from Cuba to be linked to the withdrawal of US missiles from Turkey. So Khrushchev reconvened the Presidium on 27 October and persuaded them that, since the United States had not yet invaded Cuba, it probably would not invade and that meant he would write to Kennedy again and try to link the withdrawal of the missiles from Cuba to the removal of missiles from Turkey. His letter to Kennedy of 27 October proposed linking the removal from Cuba of weapons "which you regard as offensive", if the US would "remove its analogous means from Turkey". However, by 27 October, there was a real danger the situation in Cuba was getting out of control. That day a U2 plane was shot down over Cuba and its pilot killed; the Soviet missile controllers felt obliged to honour a Cuban order to shoot down any plane entering Cuba's airspace and acted without getting final clearance from Moscow. Later on the 27th, Castro, convinced that a US invasion of his country was just hours away, wrote to Khrushchev urging him to make a pre-emptive nuclear strike; this request arrived in Moscow in the early hours of 28 October. Waiting before agreeing to back down was clearly only making the situation worse, and Kennedy's response on the question of Turkey did state that a quick settlement of the Cuban situation could "enable us to work toward a more general arrangement regarding 'other armaments'".[41]

Thus, on 28 October, a Sunday, the Presidium met once more. Khrushchev made a brief reference to the forced retreat Lenin had made in March 1918 when he signed the Treaty of Brest-Litovsk, and then dictated a letter to Kennedy which made clear that the missiles would be returned to the Soviet Union. In subsequent discussions in Washington, the Soviet ambassador was reassured that, while nothing would be said in public, the missiles in Turkey would also be withdrawn at an appropriate moment, as indeed they were. When Khrushchev addressed the Supreme Soviet on 12 December, he referred briefly to the Cuban events, calling them "a victory for common sense": the US had dropped its plan to invade Cuba and the Soviet Union had agreed to withdraw its missiles. Khrushchev did not, of course, explain that until his deployment of Soviet missiles there had been no imminent danger of the US invading Cuba. Khrushchev had created a crisis and then had been forced to back down. He was more honest with his Presidium colleagues at their meeting on 27 October. He stated simply: "Did we make a mistake or not? It will only be possible to determine that later." Only history would decide.[42]

Khrushchev's assessment of Kennedy had been confused and contradictory. He saw him as "weak" and therefore believed that he would back down; but he also believed, that, since he was "weak", he was the plaything of hawkish warmonger reactionaries operating behind th scenes who were determined to invade Cuba. Weakness could not work both ways, and as the Cuban crisis showed, Kennedy was quite able to stand up to "hawks". The result was that Khrushchev "improvised madly" as he sought a solution to a problem that was entirely of his own making, for he had insisted on the secrecy of the operation against the advice of Gromyko and Mikoyan. The Cuban fiasco put an end to his hopes of finding a quick, inexpensive way to establish Soviet strategic parity with the US. US nuclear superiority could neither be disguised by bluff and deception, as had been the case with Eisenhower, nor overcome by a single gamble, like the Cuban deployment; nuclear equality was for the long haul and would require time and money. As William Tompson put it succinctly: "Khrushchev could realise his ambition to be treated by the Americans as an equal only at the expense of his plans for domestic prosperity."[43]

Chapter 8:   The Reformer Ousted

The November 1962 Plenum

There is no doubt that the outcome of the Cuban Missile Crisis weakened Khrushchev's position. This was most clearly evident in the fate of talk about radical economic reform. Before the crisis developed, Liberman had written his famous article in *Pravda* on 9 September 1962, and *Izvestiya* continued to publish articles by reform economists supporting Liberman's ideas until 29 October. Liberman was even interviewed on the radio early in November. However, his ideas were firmly rejected by the Soviet leadership at the Central Committee Plenum of 19–23 November. On the eve of that plenum, an article in the party's theoretical journal *Kommunist* condemned Liberman's proposals, and the November issue of the economics journal *Voprosy Ekonomiki* carried three articles on Liberman, two attacking him and only one supporting him: a former finance minister set the tone by criticising "oversimplification in solving complex questions" and insisting that the planning agencies were quite capable of accurately assessing the production capacities of enterprises; the Director of the Institute of Economics in the Academy of Sciences simply condemned Liberman's ideas as unsound; it was only Nemchinov who once again defended Liberman, pointing out that critics of "reviving the capitalist category of the price of production" had completely misunderstood Liberman's proposals and were essentially raising a red herring.[1]

When the Presidium met to prepare for the plenum on 5 November, Khrushchev was still denouncing the conservatism of *Gosplan*, with the events in Novocherkassk very clearly on his mind. He blamed *Gosplan* for overproducing metal and other essentials for heavy industry and failing to provide sufficient funds for consumer goods and pay increases. Workers could not endlessly be told that there were problems and they would have to wait, that was the road to "forgetting the needs of the workers and tearing us away from the masses". If the party cut itself off from the workers, Khrushchev said, the workers would express their discontent, and the trade unions, and "we as members of the trade unions", really should be resisting "the bureaucrats sitting in *Gosplan* and the Council of Ministers". "In a word," he said, "we are bad at making use of the new, despite our revolutionary nature, we have grown old, and I increasingly have the impression that what turned us sour was the work of *Gosplan*." He then asked: "how many times, comrades, have we, the members of the Presidium, taken a decision, that *Gosplan*, when we suggested it, endorsed it, but later, when the annual plan was developed, threw it out". He then went on to link current economic woes to the failure to complete the defeat of Stalinism: "We changed some things for the better after Stalin's death, but not everything to the very end. That is understandable, for we all worked with Stalin, and vices which were laid down in Stalin's leadership, well, of course, we are not free of these vices because we lived with them." Today the economy had been transferred to the republics, "but we still plan in the old way, one plan is developed in the republic and another plan is developed by the centre" and this "parallelism" meant that old forms of practice continued.[2]

As Tito had suggested he should do in 1956, Khrushchev was edging towards arguing that it was not just Stalin's cult of personality that had been at fault, but that there had been problems with the entire Stalinist system. The radicalism of this agenda was clear, even if, as he explained to his colleagues, his ideas were still not fully formulated. He had in mind, he said, a system whereby plans would be finalised by the republics and then co-ordinated by a "small, qualified *Gosplan*"; but the centre of gravity would stay with the regions since the *Sovnarkhozy* needed more rights. And workers too, Khrushchev continued, needed more rights: "not now, but I would like to say that in the future we need to somehow democratise the administration of factories". The Leninist principle of one-man management would remain, but in "the youth of the revolution" production norms would never have been changed without involving the trade unions and in those early revolutionary years strikes had mostly been avoided. "Now the party has grown up, but what do we have, Novocherkassk", something which happened "because the party was not involved, the trade unions were on the sidelines, and the bureaucrats ruled, making announcements without preparing the workforce, and so the result is divorce and separation from the masses". However, his colleagues were not listening and when it next met on 8–9 November the Presidium accepted the resignation of Zasyadko, head of the *Gosekonomsovet* and the most prominent defender of the reform economists within the leadership.[3]

The plenum of 19–23 November did make radical changes to the way *Gosplan* operated, but not in the way the reformers had envisaged. *Gosplan* was removed from the day-to-day oversight of the planning process, and replaced the *Gosekonomsovet* as the body overseeing long-term perspective planning. Thus the body which had once been a home for reformers thinking imaginatively about the future role of perspective planning was absorbed into the conservative *Gosplan* apparatus. *Gosplan*'s previous responsibility for annual plans was transferred to a newly established Supreme *Sovnarkhoz*: this would co-ordinate the planning functions of the *Sovnarkhozy*, which were themselves reduced in number by more than a half at this time. Khrushchev still favoured the *Sovnarkhozy* having more rights, but also wanted the creation of a co-ordinating body; the creation of a Supreme *Sovnarkhoz*, however, established a stronger element of centralism than Khrushchev had in mind, for when the *Sovnarkhozy* were first established in 1957 he had specifically resisted the idea of a Supreme *Sovnarkhoz*. Re-instituting this body now might improve co-ordination, but given that it would be taking over *Gosplan*'s brief, and many of its staff, there was an obvious danger that this was the culmination of a process of recentralisation which had begun when Kosygin became *Gosplan* chairman in 1959. Despite Khrushchev's concern that the problem with planning came down to too many things going through Kosygin's hands, Kosygin's authority had risen still further with the liquidation of the *Gosekonomsovet* and its effective merger into *Gosplan*. The only crumb of comfort left for reformers at the November Plenum was the decision that enterprises should be granted greater autonomy: to this end a statute on the socialist enterprise was to be drafted, extending the rights of enterprise managers and offering workers more active participation in management; however, no clear timescale or framework for this initiative was offered.[4]

Khrushchev had not given up on the idea of more radical change. He told the November 1962 Plenum: "Our industry as a whole does not produce goods for the sake of profit, but because those goods are needed by society. It is different at the enterprise. The question of its profit takes on an important consideration as an economic signifier for its activity." This was pretty close to what Nemchinov had written about Liberman in his recent *Voprosy Ekonomiki* article.

Clearly, however, these ideas had not found favour and Khrushchev looked to other ways to bypass or weaken the powers accumulated by Kosygin's apparatus as the detail of the November 1962 reform proposals were worked through. Khrushchev explained to the Presidium on 29 November that it might be necessary to think about establishing a new body to link *Gosplan* and the new Supreme *Sovnarkhoz*. By early 1963 a number of state committees for various branches of the economy, such as the State Committee for Defence Technology, had been set up to link the work of *Gosplan* and the Supreme *Sovnarkhoz*. On 9 January 1963, the Presidium discussed a note from Khrushchev which asked: "so, what is this, is it two institutions or three?"[5]

The new committees were already acting as if they were a third body linked to the Council of Ministers. Khrushchev suggested linking these committees to *Gosplan*, while others argued forcefully that the committees should be attached to the Supreme *Sovnarkhoz*. Kosygin claimed to be backing Khrushchev, but when he suggested that the chairs of these committees would be like ministers, responsible for a branch of industry and able to attend meetings of the Council of Ministers, he seemed to be calling for the resurrection of the pre-1957 planning system with its once all-powerful ministers. When the final version of the decree establishing the Supreme *Sovnarkhoz* was discussed by the Presidium on 28 February 1963, Khrushchev again "criticised Comrade Kosygin for the way he had organised economic leadership". Because of disagreements such as these, the proposals accepted at the November Plenum were not finally implemented until 12 March 1963. With the Supreme *Sovnarkhoz* being managed by Dmitrii Ustinov, chair of the War Industry Commission of the Council of Ministers, it is not surprising that journalists at the time saw these reforms as a defeat for Khrushchev and a victory for the "steel eaters".[6]

Although Khrushchev was unable to get his way on the reform of *Gosplan*, he did succeed in pushing through the so-called "bifurcation" of the party organisation. While the aim of this reform was to improve the level of party oversight of the economy, one of its results, at least according to its critics, was to weaken the party's organisational grip on economic matters. Its origins were in Khrushchev's long-held concerns about the low intellectual level of regional party secretaries, especially in the agricultural regions such as those affected by the Ryazan Affair scandal. In his view, the decision of the November Plenum to reduce the number of *Sovnarkhozy* by half compounded the problem. When the *Sovnarkhozy* had first been set up, Khrushchev saw the strategic advantage of establishing them at regional level and allocating a leading role to regional party secretaries. By the early

1960s it was clear that the regional-level unit was too small and the total of over one hundred *Sovnarkhozy* too cumbersome to administer, especially as the regional party secretaries rarely had the economic training needed to oversee such complex organisations.

With the number of *Sovnarkhozy* cut in half, each *Sovnarkhoz* director was even more likely to be working with several regional party secretaries. Prima facie this posed a problem for the issue of party oversight, and Khrushchev took this opportunity to propose a radical organisational change. He was concerned by the constant clashes between central planners and the *Sovnarkhozy*, and in this struggle he instinctively sided with the *Sovnarkhozy*. It was, he believed, the role of the party to intervene when such clashes took place and to resolve them, and for such interventions to be successful, regional party secretaries could no longer be generalists, but would have to be specialists in either industry or agriculture. So he proposed that at regional level and below, the party would be split in two, with industrial and agricultural branches. This reform did indeed bring in new specialist talent. A study of the sixty-one regions showed that in forty cases the incumbent "generalist" secretary was shifted over to have responsibility for agriculture, while it was younger and more talented people who took up responsibility for industry.[7]

In fact, bifurcation built on a process of marginalising the regional administrative level that was already under way. In March 1962 the powers of the party's regional committees over the deployment of cadres in rural areas had been curtailed; the March 1962 Plenum transferred responsibility for cadres from the district committee to a newly established "inter-district kolkhoz–sovkhoz production administration" which bypassed the regional level and reported directly to the republican administration. In the summer Khrushchev took this initiative far further; he was developing the idea while on holiday in Crimea that August 1962. His plan to establish "more effective leadership of the economy" was discussed in the Presidium meeting of 20 August 1962, the same meeting at which he called for the *Sovnarkhozy* to be preserved and strengthened, and for *Gosplan* to be reconstructed. Khrushchev put his formal proposals to the Presidium on 10 September.[8] Almost as soon as the November Plenum had endorsed bifurcation, however, problems began to arise.

The reform involved expanding the secretariat – two secretaries for the Bureau for Industry were needed, and a further two for the Bureau for Agriculture – and some of the other practical difficulties of the reform were discussed at the Presidium meeting of 29 November 1962. Khrushchev had to clarify that the party's Regional Agricultural

Committee would be responsible for not just agriculture narrowly defined, but all factories processing agricultural products, such as hemp and linen; this meant that they would also be responsible to the local *Sovnarkhoz*, which was in turn responsible to the party's Regional Industrial Committee. Khrushchev brushed aside any suggestion that this might cause administrative confusion by saying that "double over-sight in these factories" would do no harm. As the party apparatus understood only too clearly, the reality of the bifurcation reform was to downgrade the importance of the regional party secretaries. No longer bosses over all aspects of the economy of the region, they were effectively put in a position where they carried out the will of the *Sovnarkhoz* chair-man, who now controlled a territory far larger than a region. The party body now seemed subservient to purely economic bodies. Ideological confirmation of this seemed to come in *Izvestiya* which, on 19 December 1962, talked of the party taking "a decisive turn towards production", which meant, the newspaper stressed, recognising that "the party is not the commander, but the political leader of the people".[9]

Khrushchev was helped in this change of focus for the party by the chance discovery of a forgotten essay by Lenin. On 30 September 1962 *Izvestiya* reported that a young archivist had discovered a lost chapter of Lenin's *The Immediate Tasks of Soviet Power*. Written in spring 1918, when the new Soviet state was trying to get to grips with the reduc-tion in its economic might associated with the signing of the Treaty of Brest-Litovsk and the consequent loss of Ukraine and the whole of the Donbas region, Lenin had insisted then that what the party needed were "economic organisers" not "political agitators". The comparison with the present was certainly helpful to Khrushchev, even if the eco-nomic problems of 1962 were not nearly as acute as those of 1918. The problem for Khrushchev was that Lenin had written different things at different times: soon his critics were citing the far more frequent occa-sions on which Lenin had suggested the very opposite; on 26 January 1963 an article in *Ekonomicheskaya Gazeta* turned to Lenin's writings of autumn 1920 when he attacked Trotsky and insisted very clearly that "politics cannot but have primacy over economics".[10]

De-Stalinising Ideology

If Khrushchev's push for radical economic reform had been checked at the November Plenum, that was far less clearly the case in the realm of culture and ideology. By autumn 1962, it was not uncom-mon for Komsomol leaders in universities to be using newly formed associations with bland names such as "The Club of Creative Youth" to serve as a cover for poetry readings and radical discussions; in Kiev such a group even began investigating rumours of a mass grave of Stalin's victims in a city suburb.[11] When addressing the Presidium on 5 November 1962, Khrushchev had referred to how things had changed for the better after Stalin's death, but that not everything had been pushed "to the very end". In literature he was ready to go "to the very end". Khrushchev had read Alexander Solzhenitsyn's *One Day in the Life of Ivan Denisovich* in September 1962 and, despite grumbles from ideologues like Suslov, the Presidium agreed in early October that it could be published. The mass circulation of a story describing life in one of Stalin's prison camps marked a quite extraordinary change, and it was not a one-off. On 21 October 1962, *Pravda* published the poem by Evgenii Evtushenko 'Heirs of Stalin'. This poem suggested that the Stalinist threat was not over, but hovering in the background. It talked of some "of Stalin's heirs cutting roses in retirement but secretly believing their retirement was just temporary". *Pravda* put it more bluntly, on 23 November, when it reiterated the poem's main theme by stating that "a stubborn and effective struggle needed to be waged against the remnants of the cult of personality ... they have learned nothing and forgotten nothing".[12]

    This engagement with writers was somewhat derailed on 1 December 1962 when the so-called Manezh Affair revealed Khrushchev's ultra-conservative views on abstract art. On 20 November, Khrushchev received a letter from 40 establishment artists warning that in the post-Cuba international situation attempts were being made to use modern artistic ideas to "undermine our ideology from within". And indeed, Western journalists had shown some interest in the planned art exhibition in Moscow's central Manezh gallery, since Soviet abstract artists were to have their work on show for the first time. Suslov, the KGB and other conservatives decided that this offered an ideal opportunity to force Khrushchev to halt the drift towards liberal concessions in the arts. On the eve of Khrushchev's visit, Suslov reminded Khrushchev about the dangers which could come from groups such as the Petőfi Circle, and he also whispered that most of these avant-garde artists were "homosexual". Khrushchev's response to the abstract art on display was to rant and rave in coarse street language and to deliver a verdict of the "a child could do better" variety; he also spiced things up by reminding many of the artists that they were "sponging" off state subsidies. And yet, a couple of weeks later, on 17 December, he attended a meeting with writers and artists on the Lenin Hills, which, according to the

Presidium record, was deemed to have gone very well. Journalists present recalled Khrushchev's lively exchange with Evtushenko, and how he personally introduced Solzhenitsyn to the 400 writers and artists present. In his speech on this occasion, Khrushchev repeated the line agreed after 1956: Moscow was not Budapest and "peaceful co-existence in matters of ideology" simply would not happen.[13]

Suslov had hoped that Khrushchev would summon a plenum on ideology immediately after the confrontation at the Manezh exhibition, but he opted instead for a further meeting with the intelligentsia which took place on 8 March. The speech he made on that occasion was controversial. Khrushchev had been stung by comments made by the author Ilya Ehrenburg in a recent extract from his memoirs, *People, Years, Life* published in the journal *Novyi Mir*. Ehrenburg had written of people's "silence" during Stalin's purges, looking on, knowing what was happening was wrong, but saying nothing. Khrushchev felt that he, like others, had not been silent when confronted with evidence of malpractice by the security services, but in 1937–8 it had not been clear where responsibility for such criminality lay. An article in *Izvestiya* at this time praised those, like Khrushchev, who under Stalin "made statements at public rallies" about individuals wrongfully detained. Khrushchev wanted to put the record straight about the pluses and minuses of the 1930s, which were also "bright, happy days, years of struggle and victories, of the triumph of communist ideals". Ehrenburg's concept of silence was insufficient explanation, and he reminded those present of Stalin's last years: "Do you think it was easy for us? Those last years of his life, it was madness, utter madness."[14] It is possible that on this occasion he was also tailoring his words for a rather different, Chinese, audience: on 21 February 1963 Khrushchev had sent a letter to the Chinese Communist Party proposing an unconditional reopening of dialogue, and on 9 March the Chinese appeared to welcome the idea of a resumption of bilateral talks. Whatever the reason, Khrushchev's reminiscences with the intelligentsia of the 1930s led him to make clear that before and during the revolution Stalin had played a praiseworthy role; that Bukharin's victory would have led to the restoration of capitalism, and even that Stalin had "led the struggle to rid the country of plotters". In this context Khrushchev spoke of "enemies of the people" who had used "methods such as sabotage, subversion, assassination, acts of terrorism and revolt".[15]

The hard-line reference to "plotters" was simply not in evidence when he took the very soft-line decision on 25 April 1963 that the Soviet Union should end the jamming of Western radio broadcasts:

"there will be some who listen, let them listen", he said. And by June 1963, it had become clear that reconciliation with China was impossible. Mao had no intention of letting the March proposals make progress, but simply wanted to string Khrushchev along in the hope that he would appear responsible for the eventual break in relations. On 14 June the Chinese responded to the Soviet Union's February-March initiative by issuing a document listing "twenty-five points" of dispute with Khrushchev, one of these being the new party programme. The proposed plenum on ideology got caught up with the issue of China and for this reason was repeatedly delayed. On 10 April it was set for 28 May, but then delayed again until June once the situation regarding China had become clear; when it did take place, on 21 June, it rejected the new wave of criticism from China and insisted that the new party programme was "elaborated on the basis of Marxist–Leninist theory"; if talks between the two communist leaderships were to continue, then polemics had to cease. Khrushchev's speech on this occasion made no more references to "plotters", indeed he returned to the Secret Speech and the attempts of the Anti-Party Group to prevent it being made. Reminding those present that many people had simply wanted to keep quiet about Stalin's crimes, "the issue had to be raised and discussed not for those no longer with us, but for those still alive and those who will follow". On 19 July 1963, at a broadcast rally to welcome the Hungarian leader, János Kádár, Khrushchev departed from his prepared text and issued a further attack on Stalin.[16]

The decision on 25 April to end the jamming of foreign radio stations was taken immediately after an incident concerning Yugoslavia and the May Day slogans for 1963. After the Yugoslav communists had decided in November 1957, at the very last moment, that they could not sign the joint declaration of communist and workers' parties issued to mark the 40th anniversary of the Bolshevik Revolution, relations between the Soviet Union and Yugoslavia had worsened considerably. In April 1958 the Yugoslav communists adopted a new party programme which made several criticisms of the Soviet Union and its chosen road to socialism; friendly relations between the two states were put on hold. It was only after Soviet relations with China worsened so markedly in summer 1960 that things began to change. Tito also attended the UN Assembly in New York in September 1960 and personal contact between the two leaders was restored. A trade deal was signed in March 1961 and the Yugoslav foreign minister visited in July. Although the 22nd Party Congress criticised "the ideology of revisionism most fully embodied in the Yugoslav party programme", Khrushchev's own speech to the congress called for improved relations with Yugoslavia. Unsurprisingly, the Yugoslavs warmly welcomed the decision to remove Stalin's body from Lenin's mausoleum.[17]

Khrushchev made his attitude towards Tito clear in his Varna speech of 16 May 1962. There were differences with Yugoslavia, he said, but essentially these were to do with Tito's personality: "Tito is too accustomed to making himself out to be the boss and, of course, if he returns to the socialist camp he would not have this position." However, he did not see this as a stumbling bloc to closer relations: "if Tito wants to take the position of a peacock, but is with us in great and small matters, then there will be no differences between him and the socialist camp". Tito wanted economic co-operation and "this is good, Yugoslavia is still a socialist country ... right now Yugoslavia is drawing closer to us". This was a key statement. Yugoslavia was no longer classed as a "revisionist" state but as a socialist state. When Leonid Brezhnev arrived in Yugoslavia on 24 September 1962 for the first official visit by a head of state since 1956, he was fêted royally, and at the end of the visit it was agreed that Tito would visit the Soviet Union in December. There was only one small glitch: at the end of Brezhnev's visit to Yugoslavia, Khrushchev was not in Moscow and his effective deputy, Frol Kozlov, insisted that the phrase "socialist construction in Yugoslavia" be removed from the communiqué.[18]

Tito's return visit in December 1962 was extremely high profile: both Khrushchev and Tito addressed the Supreme Soviet, and both leaders stressed that their differences were now in the past; Khrushchev specifically condemned "some people" who contended that Yugoslavia was not a socialist country. "It is impossible to deny that Yugoslavia is a socialist country," he said, "and it is from this that we proceed in our policy." On 29 January 1963 the Presidium noted that "on Yugoslavia ... the situation has changed", a line elaborated by *Pravda* on 10 February 1963 which explained that "the steps taken by the Yugoslav communist leaders in the sphere of party life, economy, home and foreign policy have rectified much of what the international communist movement regarded as erroneous and harmful to the cause of building socialism in Yugoslavia".[19] Then, while Khrushchev was on holiday, he received an emissary from Tito on 3 April 1963, who proposed that Khrushchev visit Yugoslavia. It was thus highly embarrassing when, on 8 April, *Pravda* published the proposed May Day slogans for that year which did not list Yugoslavia as a socialist state. There was a furious row. According to his son, Khrushchev exclaimed: "Again we're going back to zero!"

He immediately telephoned Kozlov and demanded a retraction. At first Kozlov refused to back down, but after further angry exchanges over the phone, he agreed to make the necessary changes; revised slogans listing Yugoslavia as a socialist state duly appeared in *Pravda* on 11 April.[20]

Reforming Again

When addressing the Presidium on 5 November 1962, Khrushchev had talked about "democratising the administration of the factories". According to his son, when Khrushchev and Tito visited Kiev at the end of Tito's visit, the two men "shared a forest hut" and talked a lot about workers' councils. The Yugoslav system of self-management was of interest to many of the reform-minded economists in the Soviet Union, and workers' councils became a theme of Khrushchev's visit to Yugoslavia, which took place from 20 August–3 September 1963. His arrival was broadcast live and Tito's greeting was effusive: in a toast on that first evening, he made clear that all conditions now existed for co-operation since any differences "would gradually disappear or lose their significance". On a factory tour, however, journalists noted the great interest Khrushchev seemed to be taking in the self-management system, telling workers that the Soviet Union was considering new forms of factory management and promising that this "progressive institution" would be studied by a delegation of party, trade union and economic council leaders who would report to the Central Committee: "our situation is now ripe for the democratisation of management in enterprises", he said.[21]

Khrushchev's private talks with Tito on his Brioni estate were extended, prompting further press speculation about what was discussed: Tito's oblique comment that "social management [of enterprises] lies at the basis of the ideas of Marx, Engels and Lenin and Comrade Nikita Sergeevich is right in paying attention to this problem", only heightened speculation that factory councils were on the agenda. Remembering this visit, Khrushchev recalled that "I wanted to look into the matter more closely" and see "to what extent they were correct and could be used in our conditions". Although the Yugoslav economic plan was still effectively determined by the government, the system deserved attention because the way things worked "suggested that the economy was not being managed by a bureaucratic upper echelon, as in the USSR, but by the people themselves", thus "there was a useful kernel of truth and correctness in the Yugoslav form of managing the economy". He now recognised the need "to make the management more dependent on the workers at enterprises and to involve the working people more actively in elaborating the plan". Back in Moscow, on 4 September, Khrushchev reassured the Presidium that Yugoslav workers' councils were essentially advisory and not so very different from the production conferences in the Soviet Union; but he was as good as his word, and called on the Soviet Trade Union Council to draw up a study of the Yugoslav experience and draft a proposal for introducing self-management into Soviet enterprises.[22]

Khrushchev's visit to Yugoslavia seems to have convinced him that Kosygin's victory in discussion about planning had to be overturned. Even before he had left for Yugoslavia, he had resumed grumbling about *Gosplan*. On 7 June he had told the Presidium that *Gosplan* had shown a complete inability to develop a coherent plan, so it was once again necessary "to interfere in its affairs". *Gosplan* was not staffed by "magicians" who could not be touched, their work was "arithmetic not magic", and often "primitive" and not based on "scientific analysis"; however he conceded that he "did not yet have a clear vision" of what to do. His vision was no clearer on 10 September when, on his return from Yugoslavia, the Presidium considered the current shortage of basic vegetables. Khrushchev was beside himself with fury: "We have socialism, but we do not have dill, potatoes, nothing. This has to come to an end. And comrades, only a lack of organisation is responsible for this." There was no need for a shortage, but there was "no system". Prices had been raised, but nothing had been done to link work to salaries. "We raised the price of meat and did meat supplies grow? Why not? The system had just remained the same." And his target was the same: "I snarled at Kosygin before, and I am snarling again for the same reason." When on 10 November 1963 the Presidium discussed the plan for 1964–5, in a report from the head of *Gosplan*, Khrushchev did not hold back. In his view "the decisions of the 21st Party Congress have been broken"; criticism of the planning process had been going on "for over two years", but new capital investments were not being reflected in increased production.[23]

Khrushchev used this speech on 10 November 1963 to announce a dramatic change of policy. Back on 28 February Khrushchev had commented in *Pravda*: "one would like to build more enterprises producing consumer goods [but] ... life dictates the need to spend enormous sums on maintaining our military might at a proper level". Now he again turned to the question of light industry and noted: "we were unable then to give money for light industry because questions of defence stood before us; now these questions do not stand before us, on the contrary, I even think that questions of defence should be squeezed". This was an expanded meeting of the Presidium and Khrushchev had been careful to invite Malinovskii, the Minister of Defence, to attend. Khrushchev was absolutely clear, he went on: "I think the time has come to return to reductions in the armed forces on the basis of the Supreme Soviet decision on 14–15 January 1960". As he warmed to his theme he wondered out loud if Soviet troops still needed to be stationed in Poland and whether so many divisions were needed in the GDR. His conclusion was equally radical: "we need to consider everything anew". A *Pravda* article by Khrushchev on 15 February 1964 confirmed that heavy industry was going to have to scale back its demands: "the officials responsible for steel production, for instance, must understand what is new and draw necessary conclusions".[24]

Khrushchev saw this reorientation of the economy as essential because by the end of 1963 it was clear that the harvest had been disastrous. At the Central Committee Plenum held in December 1963 the leadership had to report that grain deliveries had fallen from 56.6 million tons in 1962 to 44.8 million tons, the worst since the drought year of 1946. As a result the government would have no choice but to spend 372.2 tons of gold from the state reserves on the purchase of 9.4 million tons of grain. At the plenum, Khrushchev criticised "some people" who called for "belt tightening" rather than grain imports as a way of solving the crisis; he compared their approach to that of Stalin and Molotov. Khrushchev was convinced that the poor harvest was a fluke, and this turned out to be the case; in 1964 the harvest rose to 68.3 million tons. However, when the Presidium met on 23 December to consider the work of the plenum, under the formal rubric of hastening the development of the chemical fertiliser industry as the surest way to speed up agricultural development, Khrushchev was in no mood for reassuring platitudes.[25]

The Presidium discussion on 23 December ranged widely over economic matters, and at one point a minister commented that "everything is in the plan". Khrushchev could not contain himself. "That might calm down a bureaucrat," Khrushchev roared, "but the plan is a bureaucrat's dustbin." Peremptorily he told the minister concerned: "sit down and listen – we are gathered here today because we cannot go on like this". Khrushchev was clear that the system itself was no longer working. "Marx did not foresee the contradictions in a socialist economy, which are almost analogous to the capitalist ones, because bureaucrats who receive scientific information, act in a way to prevent the restructuring of production." Bureaucrats did not like "their nerves being disturbed" and would be quite happy if new discoveries took 20 years to emerge. Khrushchev's thinking was this: a capitalist style contradiction had emerged in Soviet society, the planning institutions established under Stalin seemed to be more interested in protecting their own turf than developing new methods of planning. Khrushchev did not suggest that this contradiction reflected a "class interest" but he did suggest that contradictions like this within a socialist economy were "analogous to capitalist ones", which implied at least that they were class-like.[26]

Given the systemic nature of the problem as Khrushchev now saw it, it is not surprising that he returned to the search for radical solutions. By early 1964 Liberman was back in favour again. From the end of January 1964, both *Pravda* and *Izvestiya* began once more to publish articles on the need for radical economic change, particularly to develop the sort of success indicators which would stimulate economic growth and increased productivity. When at the beginning of February a young economist wrote to Khrushchev complaining that the work of the Nemchinov Commission within the Academy of Sciences had run into the sand, Khrushchev circulated the letter to Kosygin and Ustinov. Speaking on 28 February, a speech only published in *Pravda* a week later on 7 March, Khrushchev picked up on one of the themes from the article Nemchinov had written for *Voprosy Ekonomiki* back in November 1962: planning agencies should be made financially accountable for the errors that they wrote into plans. During March 1964 Nemchinov celebrated his 70th birthday, and that month's issue of *Voprosy Ekonomiki* eulogised his achievements; later in March 1964 the mass circulation *Literaturnaya Gazeta* published an article by Nemchinov with the provocative title "The problem is still with us". Also in March, reform economists organised a conference and concluded that Liberman's ideas on profit were the key to optimising enterprise performance.[27]

Any use of profit as a success indicator required a new approach to pricing and, at a meeting of *Gosplan* on 27 May 1964, the organisation's head dismissed attempts at price reform as "harmful"; Kosygin's view that price reform needed further discussion was only slightly more enthusiastic. But the reformists fought back. On 30 May Liberman gave an interview to the *Ekonomicheskaya Gazeta* and writing in *Kommunist* in May, Nemchinov condemned *Gosplan* for continually interfering in the affairs of enterprises. This time it was not just words but deeds. From May 1964 experiments began at enterprise level to explore how a Liberman-style reform might work. Initially two clothing factories, the *Bolshevichka* in Moscow and the *Mayak* in Gorky, were chosen, but in the autumn other enterprises were added to the list, including those in machine construction and ore extraction. The *Bolshevichka* experiment was allowed to run the longest, comparing the results of the first half year, when operating according to the *Sovnarkhoz* plan, and the second half of the year, when taking full responsibility for its own affairs: production in the second half of the year went up 33% and profits 27% and, as important, if the *Sovnarkhoz* plan had remained in place, 30% of the enterprise's products would have been unsaleable and would have had to be written off.[28]

When Khrushchev addressed the Supreme Soviet on 13 July, he proposed restoring one of the original intentions of the *Sovnarkhoz* reform which had quickly fallen by the wayside. He suggested that the time really had come to change the whole basis of planning; instead of the traditional top-down approach, planning would begin with the factory and move up rather than down the hierarchy.[29] His theme was similar when on 24 July he addressed an expanded meeting of the Council of Ministers to discuss the plan for 1965–70. "We must", he said, "decide this question according to Marx and not the Chinese. The Chinese way is very simple, but following Marx, that is more complicated." So what Khrushchev proposed was to revive Liberman's ideas about the use of profit as a success indicator in planning: "if it is a question of meeting the danger of bourgeois rebirth, I want to bring forward that moment, I would be glad that it happened in my lifetime". Liberman's critics linked the concept of using profit as a success indicator to the rebirth of capitalism, and Khrushchev here was determined to face down such economic illiteracy. He was thus very clear: "on the basis of profit, capitalists get things done on time, but on the basis of a planned economy we cannot do this". So, in his view, in the next five-year plan "everything should be set out in a progressive manner, with only qualitative indicators", or "in a word, nothing should be done as it is now".[30]

On 18 August 1964, Khrushchev called a meeting of reform economists, including those who had worked with Zasyadko, Liberman and another reformist from the Academy of Sciences academic Trapeznikov; he gave them a month to draft an economic reform. The next day at the Presidium, he was again complaining about the poor quality of agricultural machinery and added: "Kosygin is not here, but it smells of Kosygin ... the threads lead back to Kosygin, who has old-fashioned views." He had told local party leaders on 8 August that he wanted increased investment in agricultural machinery but anticipated that his proposal would be resisted: "Of course, I know that in *Gosplan* I'll face some opposition, because it demands so much metal."[31] When Trapezhnikov took up his pen as a new campaigner for the profit motive in economic reform, his article in *Pravda* on 17 August was billed as the start of a new economic debate. In the article Trapezhnikov argued that enterprise directors found themselves under the petty tutelage of planners and that a financial success indicator was needed, with profit being the obvious candidate. On 1 September *Pravda* carried an article "What is Useful for the Country is Profitable for Everyone"; a further reformist article appeared in *Pravda* on 7 September, and then, just over two years after his original article had been published, on 20 September *Pravda* carried Liberman's "Once Again on Plan, Profits and Bonuses". Liberman rallied to Trapezhnikov's side, arguing that profit was an essential success indicator and making clear to critics that "what we are talking about is not a capitalist enterprise but the strengthening of initiative on the part of workers, engineers and executives". More reformist articles appeared in the first few days of October, and on 12 October an editorial in *Pravda* praised the experiment in market economics being undertaken in the *Bolshevichka* and *Mayak*: "this experiment deserves wider application, not only within the ready-made clothing industry, but also in other branches of light industry".[32]

Convincing reform economists of the need for change was one thing, changing the mind of the Presidium was quite another. On 31 August *Gosplan* presented the Presidium with the first draft of the five-year plan and it was decided to analyse that draft at a joint session of the Presidium, the Council of Ministers and other interested parties on 26 September. As that date approached, Khrushchev held a meeting with Ustinov, the head of the Supreme *Sovnarkhoz*, and advised him that "we have to wage war on the ministers", those who were unwilling to change their ways and might have to be replaced by "more progressive people". On the very eve of the joint session, 25 September, the Presidium met to discuss the plan again and Khrushchev caused consternation by commenting "let's take it over eight years". At the joint session itself, attended by four hundred people but significantly not the head of *Gosplan*, Khrushchev made clear that he considered that the five-year plans had had their day and that longer–term plans were essential, adding once again that "I would probably go for eight years". Kosygin was far less radical: he proposed planning in five-year units over a ten-year cycle; the current five-year plan would be strengthened by adding a further five-year "prognosis" plan, a proposal which effectively amounted to business as usual. As the meeting unfolded, Khrushchev again raised the fundamentals of Marxism.

Marx had predicted that socialism would replace capitalism, creating the best conditions for the development of the productive forces. But what had happened in the Soviet Union: "our labour productivity is twice to two and a half times lower than in capitalist countries". The Stalinist system was not working as Marx thought a socialist state would, so the system would have to be changed. Observers were clear, "a virtual revolution" in planning was on the cards, although it seemed significant that when on 2 October, *Pravda* reported on the joint session, it referred to a possible seven-year plan without any reference to Khrushchev's preference for an eight-year plan.[33]

Thinking the Unthinkable

If the Soviet ambassador to Norway is to be believed, Khrushchev was contemplating making dramatic constitutional changes at this time. While on a state visit to Norway, from 28 June to 4 July, the Soviet ambassador claimed that he had heard Khrushchev discuss with the editors of *Pravda* and *Izvestiya* the possibility of holding contested elections in the Soviet Union between a workers' party and a peasants' party. Certainly, when the Central Committee held a one-day plenum on 11 July, Khrushchev raised the issue of a new Soviet Constitution. Although the plenum was supposed simply to confirm the speeches to be given at the forthcoming session of the Supreme Soviet, and it was not even anticipated that Khrushchev would speak, he nevertheless spoke on a number of very broad themes and one of these was the constitution. He was clear that "the significance of the Supreme Soviet needs to be raised and given even more status", that was the essential prerequisite of any constitutional change. It was a question of democracy, he told the Central Committee, "without criticism there is no democracy; in the past someone said something, that meant an enemy of the people and he was off to a camp, with or without trial, but we have left that, condemned it". Today, not everyone was of the same opinion, "and so, for things to be more democratic, obstacles need to be removed – you sack one person and move forward another, Anastas is pleased". In this blunt and enigmatic way, Khrushchev broke to the plenum that it was his intention that at its meeting on 15 July the Supreme Soviet should replace Brezhnev as head of state with Mikoyan. Explaining his line of thinking to Mikoyan, Khrushchev made clear that Brezhnev "would not have been able to cope" with the radical enhancement of the role of the soviets which Khrushchev had planned. On 11 July, the corridor talk at the plenum was of Khrushchev's plans for multi-candidate, although not multi-party, elections and the introduction of an elected Soviet President; certainly the Constitution Commission had received lots of letters calling for precisely these two initiatives.[34]

Established after the 22nd Party Congress, the Constitution Commission had been meeting since January 1962, but progress had been slow. Khrushchev addressed it on 15 June 1962 when he suggested extending to the soviets the party's rules on the rotation of cadres, thus at least one third of the deputies would resign their seats at every election, and there would be limitations on the powers of office holders to extend their term. However, since then two years of work had produced little. That changed after the July Plenum. Khrushchev addressed the Constitution Commission on 16 July 1964 and advanced a series of new and radical proposals: he wanted the Supreme Soviet to have the right to oversee the economy, and for there to be a Standing Commission for Constitutional Oversight. The language of the all-people's state would be enshrined in the constitution since paragraph nine talked of "the all-rounded development and perfection of socialist democracy, attracting all citizens to administer the affairs of society and the state" and concluded that "in the process of developing democracy, the socialist state is gradually reborn as communist social self-administration". There would be new rights for soviets and possibly they would be renamed 'people's soviets' or 'soviets of labourers' to underline how the direct participation of people in the managing of social affairs "should receive constitutional reinforcement". "The new Constitution", he said, "will be a constitution for an all-people's socialist democracy, something as yet unseen in the history of humanity." It would guarantee "the strict observance of socialist legality and prepare the conditions for a transition to general communist self-management", Khrushchev insisted, and one such area of self-management would be the factory, where the autonomy of the factory director would be guaranteed by the constitution. At the very end of September, when Khrushchev set off for his holiday, he took all the constitution material with him; he wanted to present the draft text to the planned November Plenum, so that its implementation could begin in 1965. The process of implementation he envisaged foresaw a nationwide discussion, followed by a Supreme Soviet vote and finally endorsement in a referendum.[35]

At the July Plenum, Khrushchev also addressed the nature of the relationship which should exist between the party and the state. If he had started to recognise the need to change the Stalinist system, as he tried to do so he found himself, quite unconsciously, echoing the proposals once advanced by Trotsky in the early 1920s. In his speech to the July Plenum, Khrushchev reminisced about "the good old days" when "every district secretary knew the situation on a construction site better than the man in charge", and compared this to the situation today when the district secretary "sits like a bureaucrat, writing down statistical information". Things had to be done differently. "Let the secretary of the party committee concern himself with party work, mass educational work and the like, but specialists should be concerned with the organisation of production – that would be a force to be reckoned with ... Take the army: if the commissar [*politruk*] were to substitute for the commander, there would be no army." This really did mark a dramatic shift in Khrushchev's thinking, after all, in the years immediately after Stalin's death, when first Beria and then Malenkov had tried to argue that the party should distance itself from the economy and stick to campaigning, Khrushchev had led the opposition insisting on the party's right to strict oversight of the economy. Now, however, inspired by the discovery of Lenin's 1918 writings, he was taking the same Beria–Malenkov line and, intriguingly, the analogy he used of the Red Army commissar and the Red Army commander was very close to a military analogy once used by Trotsky who told the 11th Party Congress in March 1922 that the leading role of the party "did not mean the party directly administering every detail of every affair, especially economic issues it struggled to understand". Clarifying the relationship between the party and the state economic apparatus in a memorandum of January 1923, Trotsky said that the party played the role of the Revolutionary Military Council and the economic apparatus the role of staff headquarters: the party set the parameters for economic growth, just as the Revolutionary Military Council had set out the strategy for victory in the Russian Civil War; in the economic apparatus, the economic experts delivered the goods, just like the generals at staff headquarters were responsible for winning battles.[36]

Khrushchev was not consciously identifying with Trotsky, but he was beginning to experience something else that Trotsky had experienced, the way that the party apparatus acted as a party faction it its own right. While Stalin always maintained that the party apparatus was simply the civil service of the party, Trotsky had argued from December 1923 that the party apparatus, far from being impartial, operated a policy of "conservative bureaucratic factionalism". What Trotsky saw as the "unprecedented bureaucratisation of the party apparatus" had occurred because secretaries had been appointed because of their loyalty, and "a specific secretary's psychology" had been formed. That problem of apparatus factionalism and the secretary's psychology were issues which concerned Khrushchev over the summer of 1964. In his vision of the communist future outlined at the 22nd Party Congress, he had suggested that "the apparatus of the party administration could be reduced in size", and his concerns over the role it played were clear. The Ukrainian party secretary, Petro Shelest, recalled how towards the end of January 1964 Khrushchev railed against the "dogmatists and routiners" who surrounded him; two months later, on a visit to Budapest, Shelest recalled that it was specifically Suslov who was the target of his ire. At the start of his holiday at the very beginning of October, Khrushchev again cursed Suslov in Shelest's presence describing him as "completely divorced from reality".[37]

An example of this divorce from reality occurred in 1961, when Khrushchev and Suslov disagreed about how to portray the historical relationship between Lenin and Zinoviev. Suslov opposed publication of the story by Emmanuil Kazakevich *Blue Notebooks* because of a scene depicting the escape of Lenin and Zinoviev from the Petrograd police early in July 1917 after the July Days. Kerensky's Provisional Government had interpreted these demonstrations as an attempted Bolshevik coup, prompting both Lenin and Zinoviev to take refuge in Finland. In Kazakevich's account of the episode, Zinoviev called Lenin "comrade". Suslov's point was simple: since Zinoviev had been condemned as "an enemy of the people" in one of the 1930s show trials, he could not be portrayed addressing Lenin as "comrade". Khrushchev was amazed by Suslov's assertion, and commented: "But listen, they really were friends and were living in the same hunter's shack". For the party apparatus, however, from the point of view of the "specific secretary psychology", the myth of Soviet reality was more important than that reality itself. In retrospect Khrushchev commented that Suslov's "limited policeman's outlook does great harm" and conceded that he had made a mistake keeping him in the leadership. "I simply thought that if Suslov was working as part of our collective leadership group, we would be able to influence him ... although many people did warn me that Suslov was playing a negative role."[38]

Rather than look to Soviet ideologists for support, Khrushchev preferred to meet up with Tito. On 8 June he asked Tito, who was on a state visit to Finland, to meet him in Leningrad. What they talked about is unclear. Khrushchev told the Presidium that Tito had complained that no one ever did as he asked any more, and perhaps Khrushchev said something similar, two old communists brooding on how difficult it was to implement the ideas that had inspired their youth. Shortly afterwards, while sailing across the Baltic en route to Scandinavia, and perhaps prompted by the recent opening of the Aswan Dam which he had attended in Egypt, Khrushchev started to muse on the very dogmatic understanding of socialism that Soviet communists had. On 27 June he noted: "today, at the given stage of the struggle for socialism, the question has arisen of the role of new countries which are starting out on the road to socialism. Is the construction of socialism possible by people who do not stand on Marxist positions?" Referring to Presidents Nasser of Egypt, Ben Bella of Algeria and Nkrumah of Ghana, he was prepared to concede that they were very different, but "they talked of socialism and most of them sincerely believe and want to build that socialism".[39]

At the end of August 1964, Khrushchev telephoned Zhukov out of the blue and suggested that they meet up after his holiday. He explained how "there were people coming to me and saying that Zhukov is a dangerous man" and he believed them; now he was not so sure. He seems to have come to the conclusion that he had been "set up" by the apparatus when he was presented with the Zheltov Report. There were plenty of examples of the apparatus sabotaging policies it did not like. As Khrushchev told Castro on May Day 1963 on the podium in Red Square: "You would think that as First Secretary I could change anything in this country – like hell I can! No matter what changes I propose and carry out, everything stays the same." When Khrushchev returned from Yugoslavia and called for a report on how the Yugoslav system of factory councils might be adapted for the Soviet Union, it was deliberately sabotaged. The man assigned the task was the former ambassador to Hungary, Yurii Andropov, who was so alarmed by the political ramifications of undertaking such a project that he "took his time" and the proposals were never completed. Other cases where Khrushchev was "set up" by the apparatus were less frequent, but they did exist.[40]

In the Latvian National Communist Affair of 1959, Khrushchev was presented with an apparatus report which suggested that "bourgeois nationalism" had taken hold in the Latvian Communist Party. The report would probably have lain on the shelves of the Central Committee Secretariat if Khrushchev had not visited Riga in June 1959 where, at the instigation of the apparatus, an old war-time colleague had whispered in his ear some juicy stories about the nationalist danger. Initially Khrushchev took the report at face value and called for heads to roll, but on interrogating the Latvian leadership, eventually concluded that there was no great crisis and the Latvian

Communist Party should be left to sort out its own affairs. It was only on his return from the US and China in October 1959 that he discovered how the apparatus had carried on as if his intervention had not taken place. A new party leader had been appointed, and Khrushchev's preferred candidate for Second Secretary was on the point of being purged. Most alarming of all, the apparatus had decided that the origins of this alleged "bourgeois nationalism" could be traced back to 1953 and the report Khrushchev had written on the Russification of the Latvian Communist Party. The resolution adopted in 1953 on the basis of Khrushchev's report was now condemned as the work of "the enemy of the people Beria", even though Khrushchev had personally assured the Latvian leadership that as far as he was concerned that 1953 resolution should remain in force.[41]

The apparatus report into the Latvian National Communists had been premised on the assertion that "bourgeois nationalism" was being used to remove "experienced cadres", all of whom just happened to be Russian. In summer 1964, Brezhnev was equally concerned about the fate of "experienced cadres", perhaps because of his own dismissal as head of state. He told Shelest on 3 July 1964 that Khrushchev wanted to rejuvenate the Presidium and accused him of "gathering material to have us all got rid of ". At a Presidium meeting on 17 September, Khrushchev drew attention to the fact that there were many of its members who were "entitled to two months leave" because of their advanced years. Shelest recalled Khrushchev stating more than once over the summer that he wanted to rejuvenate the Presidium, the last time at the start of his holiday when he described the Presidium as "a society of old men". Mikoyan also recalled that shortly before leaving Moscow for his holiday, Khrushchev had promised that on his return he planned "to rejuvenate" the Presidium. While on holiday, Khrushchev told his son essentially the same thing, that he intended to add a large group of youngsters to the Presidium. The *Le Monde* journalist Michel Tatu was tipped off by what he took to be a reliable source that "there will be many changes at the top" and that "almost all the leaders except Khrushchev" would be affected; these changes would be confirmed at the planned November Plenum.[42] There were also rumours that these personnel changes would be accompanied by a new phase of de-Stalinisation. Just before he set off for his holiday, Khrushchev asked the Institute of History in the Academy of Sciences to prepare material for the November Plenum on Stalin's collectivisation campaign; the institute's new director had just produced an eight-hundred-page manuscript on collectivisation so a twenty-page analysis of the famine year 1932–3 was quickly put together.[43]

Thinking the unthinkable, however, could be petty as well as radical. If Khrushchev was an iconoclastic radical, determined to introduce an economic reform which would distance the party from the economy, and if he was also beginning to appreciate that the apparatus was a body with its own agenda which would invariably oppose such reform, he was also a product of his time. For all his new thinking, there was one alarming element of old thinking. On 13 June, and then again on 4 and 5 July, Khrushchev sent the Presidium notes on the need to intensify agricultural production. Agriculture was clearly on his mind at the July Plenum as well and here he raised a very specific issue. Khrushchev had been a lifelong supporter of the controversial biologist, Trofim Lysenko. Lysenko had made his career in the late 1920s when he proposed the theory of what he called "the phasic development of plants", if the environment in which seeds were sown was changed, the way the seeds developed could also be changed. Even from the early 1930s it was clear to most agronomists that there was no secure science behind Lysenko's theories, but Lysenko came from a peasant background and had developed his ideas in a small agricultural field station rather than the Academy of Sciences. Lysenko's background appealed to Khrushchev. and some of his techniques did appear to improve production. To someone like Khrushchev, always rather suspicious of academics in ivory towers, Lysenko seemed absolutely genuine, and just as in 1935 when his claim that new seed varieties could be created in under three years had appealed to Stalin, so, with Soviet agriculture in crisis in 1964, Lysenko seemed to offer the answers. It was at Khrushchev's insistence that Lysenko had attended the February 1964 Plenum on agriculture, and on this occasion he backed him publicly by referring to the close relationship they had developed after Khrushchev left Ukraine in 1949: "Comrade Lysenko has shown in practice that his methods produce high yields of grain, beef and milk. I was then Secretary of the Moscow Party Committee and recommended his methods to collective and state farms. And those who used them with knowledge did obtain high yield increases ... who wishes to use Lysenko's methods cannot lose."[44]

In making such an assertion, Khrushchev was entirely out of line with most Soviet scientists, who by 1964 were determined to remove the baneful influence of Lysenko on the study of genetics. They decided to put up a candidate for election to the Academy of Sciences on an anti-Lysenko ticket. Writing in *Pravda* on 2 July, Khrushchev attacked the anti-Lysenko candidate, and at the plenum on 11 July he launched a vitriolic attack on the recent behaviour of the Academy of Sciences. One of those to attack Lysenko had been the eminent physicist and future Soviet dissident Andrei Sakharov, the man who had done so much to develop Soviet nuclear technology. Khrushchev condemned Sakharov's speech and accused the Academy of Sciences of "beginning to play at politics". In what can only be called an intemperate outburst, he talked of sending the Academy of Sciences "to the devil's mother" if it continued to interfere in political affairs, and concluded that an academy of that sort was not needed "because science needed to be linked to production where it could be of use"; only "the bourgeois Russian state" needed a classic Academy of Sciences, but in socialist conditions "this appendage had played itself out". One of those present recalled that Khrushchev's outburst was met in silence, and Khrushchev himself seemed to realise he had "put his foot wrong", adding at the end of his speech "we need to think about this". On 17 September, the Presidium succeeded in shelving Khrushchev's quixotic proposal that the Soviet Agricultural Academy should be removed from Moscow and relocated at a new base on a state farm.[45]

Khrushchev's Overthrow

Plans to remove Khrushchev began to be hatched as soon as his renewed reform agenda became clear at the start of 1964. Preparations then accelerated once it became clear that Khrushchev planned to use the November Plenum to rejuvenate his team and implement a new constitution which would formalise radical economic changes. Shelest recalled that on his birthday, 14 February, Brezhnev and Podgornyi approached him tentatively and asked him about his relations with Khrushchev; they said that they were finding things difficult "because Khrushchev did not listen". The KGB chief, Vladimir Semichastnyi, was also involved from fairly early on, but refused to go along with a rather half-baked plan that Khrushchev could be arrested on his return from Scandinavia at the end of June. Brezhnev visited Shelest again on 3 July stating that Khrushchev insulted "us", took all the decisions himself and it was impossible to work with him. Yet preparations again seemed to stall, with Semichastnyi becoming increasingly edgy about possible discovery. It was only after Khrushchev had addressed the expanded meeting of the Presidium on 26 September and stated that his speech for the planned November Plenum was almost ready and that he intended finalising it while on holiday, that really determined preparations began.[46]

A key role in organising the opposition to Khrushchev was played by Nikolai Ignatov, who toured the country contacting regional leaders who bore grudges against Khrushchev. Both Mikoyan and Khrushchev's son became aware of Ignatov's activities shortly before Khrushchev departed on holiday and warned him what was happening, but Khrushchev dismissed it as bluster. Also central to the plot was Nikolai Mironov, the head of the Department of Administrative Agencies within the Central Committee. This was the heart of the apparatus; back in 1959 it had been the Department of Administrative Agencies which had frustrated Khrushchev's wishes at the time of the Latvian National Communist Affair, then, as in 1964 it had not described its actions as "plotting" but as "working for party democracy". Mironov was an associate of Brezhnev, having served with him in Dnepropetrovsk when Brezhnev was the regional secretary there. In his role as head of the Department of Administrative Agencies, Mironov was both gathering material for the November Plenum, and thus aware of Khrushchev's plans and alarmed by them, and preparing the material needed to denounce Khrushchev before the November Plenum could meet. Mironov's key role was to bring together the two strands of the conspiracy: the conservative group, led by Brezhnev, which felt the system they believed in was under threat, and the younger "Komsomol" generation of leaders such as Semichastnyi, ironically the leaders Khrushchev wanted to bring on, who were embarrassed by Khrushchev and believed that his support for Lysenko showed that he was still a prisoner of the past.[47] As preparatory work for the November Plenum got under way, so the speed of the plot accelerated; Khrushchev had to be removed before the plenum met. Yet, despite all this activity, on the very eve of the coup, a number of key figures had only recently been approached and Kosygin and Suslov, the two most frequent targets of Khrushchev's wrath, were felt to be hesitating and not certain to support the coup.[48]

On 8 October, Podgornyi informed Shelest that the material to be used in a confrontation with Khrushchev at an emergency Central Committee Plenum was ready. Shelest travelled to Moscow at once and, on 12 October, the Presidium met in Khrushchev's absence. The meeting lasted most of the day since they needed to identify an issue which would persuade Khrushchev to break off his holiday. After much discussion, they decided to ask that he return to discuss the lack of clarity about whether future economic plans were to last seven or eight years; he would also be asked to clear up confusion concerning some of his agricultural proposals. Although the idea of keeping Khrushchev on as prime minister was discussed briefly at this meeting, Brezhnev opposed it vehemently. So the Presidium decided that because of the "lack of clarity that has arisen on principled questions intended for discussion at the November Plenum and the development of the Five-Year Plan", Khrushchev should come to Moscow to discuss these issues with the Presidium on 13 October; all members and candidate members of the Central Committee would also be summoned to Moscow so that the Presidium's decision could be swiftly endorsed. Thus, at about 9 pm on the evening of 12 October, a very nervous Brezhnev phoned Khrushchev and asked him to return to Moscow the following day to discuss agriculture and other matters. At first he refused, but then relented, turning to Mikoyan, who had joined him on his holiday, saying "they don't have any problems with agriculture, apparently Sergei [Khrushchev's son] was right in his warnings".[49]

On 13 October, Khrushchev flew back to Moscow and was met at the airport by KGB chief Semichastnyi; he then went straight to the Presidium meeting, which began at 3 pm. Khrushchev sat down to chair the meeting as usual, asking what was so urgent that he had to break his holiday. Khrushchev was then presented with the Presidium Report which the General Department of the Central Committee had produced; this summed up the charges being laid against him. The document made clear that the issue was not just about clarifying things with Khrushchev, but removing him from power. Like the document produced against the Latvian leadership in 1959, or Zheltov's report on Zhukov, the Presidium Report was not an objective analysis but a list of complaints and criticisms from the perspective of an apparatus which claimed to reflect the distilled wisdom of the party. It talked of "normalising" the situation in the leadership, since "the normal working of the Presidium" had become impossible: "even major questions of principle Khrushchev decided by himself and any sensible proposal, if it did not come from him, was drowned out"; the logic was clear, "sensible proposals" came only from the "experienced cadres" of the apparatus, and Khrushchev had deliberately turned his back on such "experienced cadres". The report went on to claim that "at the same time the practice had increasingly become one of selecting cadres not on the basis of their administrative qualities but their political ones, and on the principle of personal loyalty". Khrushchev had gradually become divorced from reality by touring the country ever more frequently, but seeing only what he wanted to see: "he was putting himself above the party, striving to establish a personal dictatorship".[50]

The Presidium Report then listed failings in domestic policy, such as the need to sell gold to buy grain; the new party programme, which "in reality, no one from the Presidium took part in elaborating but nevertheless had to accept its final form"; and the bifurcation reform, which had been aimed simply at reducing the role of the party in overseeing the economy. As to foreign policy, Khrushchev was accused of "adventurism", risking war over Berlin and Cuba, and undermining the socialist bloc, in particular China. Moving back to his "personality cult", the Presidium Report stressed that he "almost never received cadres", and was determined to limit the rights of the secretariat and had "started to speak forcefully about its reorganisation". Most recently he had attacked the Academy of Sciences and suddenly proposed an eight-year plan "to hide the failure of the seven-year plan". Khrushchev had also taken de-Stalinisation too far: "the facts say that Stalin had many services and did much to strengthen and multiply the achievements of the Great October Socialist Revolution". Ignoring the Presidium, he worked through an unofficial cabinet: "just as Lenin said dismiss Stalin, now Khrushchev should be dismissed", the Presidium Report concluded.[51]

Brezhnev led the attack on Khrushchev which followed, essentially repeating elements from the Presidium Report: Khrushchev had raised the possibility of an eight-year plan without consultation; quite what was being prepared for the November Plenum was uncertain; the bifurcation of the party organisation had been disastrous; other structural changes were frequently proposed; and Khrushchev increasingly communicated with the Presidium simply by sending notes. Those who spoke after Brezhnev similarly picked up themes referred to in the Presidium Report. Shelest was concerned about the reduction in influence of party committees and insisted that the future of planning had to be agreed collectively rather than unilaterally. Shelepin accused Khrushchev of surrounding himself with "dubious" people and turning *Pravda* into a "family leaflet"; he was also worried about the material Khrushchev had started to collect on Stalin's collectivisation campaign and his "adventurism" in economic policy. Suslov commented on the "unhealthy atmosphere in the Presidium", while Kosygin felt that recent plenums had become increasingly "one-man bands", and all the talk of an eight-year plan simply masked underlying economic difficulties. Only Mikoyan spoke up in Khrushchev's support. He criticised the role of Ignatov in whipping up opposition to Khrushchev and insisted that Khrushchev was simply overworked; a man of many talents, he should be kept on in the leadership even if not in his current role. However, even Mikoyan criticised the bifurcation proposals.[52]

When Khrushchev's turn came to speak, he adopted a tone of aggrieved innocence. He ridiculed the notion that he had instituted a cult of personality, his actions had been nothing like those of Stalin, and he insisted that all foreign policy matters had been agreed collectively. "I took us for fellow thinkers not opponents; why did you not say something?", Semichastnyi recalled him demanding. Later, anger and threats took over: "You do not have a full understanding of what you are up to, the party and the people love me, the army loves me, I'll appeal to the people and you'll be thrown from the face of the earth!" But when he asked Malinovskii if the army would back him, Malinovskii answered "no". Later he asked to speak again and repeated that the party and people loved him, and suggested that they would not understand what was being done; he offered to give up the post of prime minister while remaining First Secretary, and later even suggested he could stay on as Minister of Agriculture and a mere Presidium member.[53]

The Presidium then adjourned and agreed to resume its discussion on the morning of 14 October. Khrushchev went home to his family. That evening he phoned Mikoyan and told him he would resign the next morning. Mikoyan expressed the hope that some sort of role might still be found for him. When the Presidium duly reconvened as planned, Khrushchev was conciliatory saying he would not fight his Presidium colleagues because they had all struggled together against the Anti-Party Group. He also conceded he could be rude and apologised for that, recognising that his attitude to the Academy of Sciences had lacked tact, although he could not resist the comment that science absorbed vast sums of money and much of Soviet science was far behind the West. Khrushchev concluded by saying that he was proud that "at last the party has grown up and can control any person". A relieved Brezhnev informed Semichasthyi, who was not at the Presidium meeting, that the Central Committee Plenum could now be gathered, a little later than planned, at 6 pm. Khrushchev asked if he could make a statement to the plenum, but Brezhnev and Suslov made clear that this would not be permitted. So, at the end of the Presidium session, Khrushchev began his final speech as leader of the Soviet party and state. He explained that his main mistake had been made in 1958 when "I went along with you and agreed to be both First Secretary and Prime Minister, I gave into weakness rather than opposing it". He then accepted that in recent years "he had not been coping with all the piles of work", but he had felt it worth staying on "just one little year more". His final appeal was to history: "about what is taking place now, at some point history will utter a weighty judgement". [54]

With the Presidium discussions concluded, the plenum assembled at 6 pm on 14 October. Brezhnev decided that there would be no debate or discussion, just a statement for the general public that Khrushchev had decided to resign on grounds of age and health, and a speech by Suslov to explain the real reason. Khrushchev sat through that speech in silence and then left the proceedings, saying not a word in his defence. Two active supporters of Khrushchev, Serdyuk, his old Second Secretary in Kiev in 1938, and Olga Ivashchenko, a member of the Ukrainian secretariat who had tried unsuccessfully to warn Khrushchev of the plot against him, were prevented from attending the plenum to avoid any disruption. Suslov accepted that Khrushchev had played a positive role during the Anti-Party Group struggle, but otherwise he repeated the denunciations given in the Presidium Report and articulated by various members of the Presidium the day before. As an example of Khrushchev ignoring Presidium decisions, he pointed out that at the 11 July Plenum it had not been agreed that Khrushchev would speak, but that, "unexpectedly for members of the Presidium", he had made a long speech which included "a number of serious political mistakes"; one of these mistakes was the comparison Khrushchev had made between administering the economy and administering the army; if Khrushchev was unaware he had drifted towards Trotsky's views, Suslov was not. Khrushchev, Suslov concluded, had been constantly seeking some sort of magic cure for the economy, but the calls he had made for restructuring had ended only in confusion. The solution was not dramatic experimentation but evolution, Suslov suggested, reminding the Central Committee of Lenin's advice that no action should be taken in haste. As Brezhnev settled into Khrushchev's shoes, this piece of advice was taken to heart; restoring normality quickly evolved into stability and stability became stagnation.[55]

Conclusion

Brezhnev gave Khrushchev a generous pension of 400 roubles per month, a flat in Moscow, a dacha outside the city, a modest car and access to the Kremlin hospital. Initially Khrushchev was depressed, his grandson recalled him crying frequently, but his spirit revived in 1966 when he started tape recording his memoirs. This soon became a family enterprise, with his son Sergei responsible for the transcribing and editing. In 1968 the chairman of the Party Control Commission ordered Khrushchev to stop work on the memoirs, but he refused, insisting he had a right as a Soviet citizen to write what he pleased; the request that he submit to party discipline was similarly ignored. It was after this bruising encounter with his former colleagues that Sergei Khrushchev began the process of smuggling the typescript of the memoirs abroad and getting them published in the US. After their publication there, in autumn 1970 Khrushchev was forced to sign a statement dismissing them as a fabrication. Plagued by heart problems in the last 18 months of his life, Khrushchev died on 11 September 1971.[1]

Khrushchev's reform programme was quickly undone. Just a week after his enforced resignation, the "bifurcation" of the party into industrial and agricultural branches was abolished and the Presidium took the decision in principle that the regional party committees should be reunited. The *Sovnarkhozy* survived until September 1965, when Kosygin, as part of a broader economic reorganisation which made no mention of the word "profit", reintroduced central ministries as the key bodies around which the economy would be organised. The 23rd Party Congress in March 1966 repealed the concept of the rotation of party cadres: "life has shown that it has not justified itself", Brezhnev commented. The "experienced cadres" whom Brezhnev valued so much were now entrenched in their positions with no danger they would have to surrender power once their term of office had run out.[2]

In his final statement to his Presidium colleagues on 14 October 1964, Khrushchev made clear that "history will utter a weighty judgement" on the decision to remove him from office. In the prologue to his memoirs he wrote something similar: "I place my reliance on those people who in the future, as it were, act as judges. It will be the people themselves who will judge ... I do not think that what I say is necessarily the truth. No, each person will find the truth for himself or herself comparing different points of view ... Let history itself be the judge, let the people judge."[3] So, what was Khrushchev's legacy? Writing in 1987 the eminent economic historian Alec Nove commented: "an economic or political historian in the next century is, in my view, bound to evaluate Khrushchev's record positively, but would distinguish the period of his rise, 1953–8, as the most fruitful ... He thought he could correct defects through the party machine, and then correct the party machine itself, but that was a fateful error; the machine was able to get rid of him." This verdict has stood the test of time remarkably well, although it underestimates the reforming zeal of Khrushchev in the very last period of his rule. Khrushchev's evaluation before the court of history as seen from the first quarter of the twenty-first century must be a similarly positive one: he sought to move the Soviet Union beyond Stalin's obsessions with class struggle and to get its economy serving the needs of a communist welfare state. His removal was a sign of how nervous the party apparatus had become when he decided to move against its vested interests and expectations.[4]

Khrushchev was clear about what he wanted his historic achievement to be. He told one of his closest advisers before his ouster from power that Lenin had carried out the revolution, Stalin had ensured victory against fascism, while he "gave peace and well-being to the Soviet people".[5] He was always a practical politician rather than a thinker. He was once heard to say: "of course, the ideas of Marx are good, but if they could be spread with a good layer of pork dripping that would be even better".[6] Both his concerns and his successes were practical. Even before the revolution he had been involved in running a workers' retail co-operative, striving to combat the ever rising cost of living. In the 1920s his duties as party secretary meant that he was again involved in co-operative retailing, but equally at this time his involvement in "greening" Donetsk was the first example of his commitment to urban planning. He was ultimately responsible for massive construction projects aimed at improving the standard of living of the Soviet people: the construction of the Moscow metro in the mid 1930s; the rebuilding of the *Khreshchatik* district in central Kiev at the end of the war; and, most important of all, the millions of "*Khrushchevki*" blocks of flats in the new "microdistricts" which sprang up in every major city.

When he did branch out into theory, it was in the direction of "pork dripping", a comfort food version of Marxism–Leninism. At a time when China was experiencing "the Great Proletarian Cultural Revolution", with radical bands of student activists brandishing Mao's "little red book" and assaulting "bourgeois survivals", Khrushchev was reassuring Soviet citizens that such upheavals were far in the past. The class struggle was over, and its radicalisation under Stalin was just another aspect of the dictator's criminality. As the Soviet Union moved away from socialism and towards communism, the state would, as Marx had predicted, wither away and the people would administer their own affairs. Precisely what this would mean was left unclear, but his second reconciliation with Tito in 1962–3 suggested that a version of Yugoslav self-management was on the cards. Certainly, it was partly under pressure from the Yugoslavs that Khrushchev moved from criticising Stalin the person to the edifice of Stalinism itself.

Towards the end, Khrushchev's most active supporters, like his son-in-law the editor of *Izvestiya* Aleksei Adzhubei, began to exaggerate Khrushchev's achievements, particularly his anti-Stalin stance. Addressing the June 1963 Central Committee Plenum on ideology, Adzhubei claimed that Khrushchev "was personally guiltless in the matter of Stalin's repressions and in fact had been a voice in the wilderness against the excesses of Stalinism", a reference to the way in 1937 he had discussed with Stalin whether or not to tone down the rhetoric of the resolution passed by the Moscow Provincial Party Conference. On 18 May 1964 *Izvestiya* carried an article about one of Stalin's victims, Avel Enukidze, explaining that he had been "denounced, arrested and convicted in 1937". This was corrected by *Pravda* the following day to make clear that he had been "denounced" in 1935 and later arrested and convicted in 1937; in 1935 Khrushchev had been one of those who quickly repeated Ezhov's assertion that Enukidze was a "degenerate".[7] A Central Committee report drawn up at the instigation of the last Soviet leader, Mikhail Gorbachev, in 1988 stated that Khrushchev "had personally agreed to the arrest of a considerable number of party and soviet workers".[8] However, as Khrushchev always reminded his opponents, there was to his mind a world of difference between "agreeing" to an arrest and agitating for an arrest.

Khrushchev's stance during the purges was remarkably consistent. He did not challenge the need for the purges, but from as early as August 1936 he had worries that people were being detained "to be on the safe side". As the wave of purges continued to spiral, he identified the source of the policy of arresting people "to be on the safe side" as the NKVD, which had escaped the oversight of the party. He therefore welcomed the removal of Ezhov at the end of 1938 as a sign that the NKVD had been put back in its rightful place, subservient to the party; the overweening power of the NKVD then became a constant theme in his comments from 1939 onwards. Both in 1938 and 1949, Khrushchev was prepared to challenge some of the denunciatory material prepared by Stalin, but it was only towards the very end of Stalin's life that Khrushchev recognised that it was Stalin who manipulated the NKVD rather than the other way round: "it was not Beria who invented Stalin, but Stalin who created Beria", he noted in his memoirs.[9] As soon as Stalin died, Khrushchev took up the task of atoning for Stalin's crimes. His targets were his leadership colleagues, the old members of the Politburo, Molotov and Kaganovich in particular, those who had encouraged Stalin in his decision to purge and who had joined in the process with enthusiasm, with no concerns about the fate of those arrested "just to be on the safe side".

Khrushchev's vision of the communist future was remarkably consistent. In 1934 he had sided with Stalin in ridiculing those who "fell into rapture" and spoke of the end of class struggle and the withering away of the state. Once he had come to terms with Stalin, it was precisely an end to the class struggle and the withering away of the state that he aspired to. From his address to the 13th Komsomol Congress in spring 1958 until his draft of a new constitution in summer 1964, it was the workings of an all-people's state which obsessed him. In that state, the party would always play a role; his clashes with the NKVD meant that he could never accept the Beria–Malenkov vision of a statist technocracy. However, as his clashes with the party apparatus grew, his concept of party leadership reverted to the Trotskyist flirtations of his early career.

Although leader of the Soviet Union for over a decade, Khrushchev was always a bit of an outsider. He began his revolutionary career as a working class legal activist rather than an underground committee man. During 1917 he was a member of what some historians have called the "sub elite", the middle-level leadership half way between the committee and the rank and file, the sort of activist on whom the Bolsheviks relied, but who were never brought into the heart of their organisation. Even by the time Khrushchev had become a committed

Bolshevik activist at the end of the civil war, he avoided an apparatus career, abandoning his brief apparatus job in Kharkov within a couple of months. While in Moscow in the early to mid 1930s he was very much the new boy, Stalin's favourite, but not somebody to be taken too seriously, and then he was in Kiev until 1949, spending the war years at the front. Back in Moscow in 1949 it was Malenkov and Beria who were on the inside track, and after Stalin's death he was almost sidelined for a while. Even when he had become the leader of both party and state, he was constantly on the move, travelling throughout the country and more and more frequently around the world. In 1963 he was away from Moscow for 170 days and by the time of his dismissal in October 1964 he had been away from Moscow for 150 days.[10] His colleagues suggested that this made him divorced from reality, but from his perspective it was those who were stuck in Moscow who were divorced from reality. As the Latvian National Communist Affair clearly showed, however, travelling the world meant leaving the apparatus to run the show and "stitch up" issues at home.

There is no doubt Khrushchev was an extremely effective politician. The journalist Edward Crankshaw witnessed his behaviour during his talks with the Yugoslavs in 1955: "It was impossible to watch this performance without being convinced that behind Khrushchev the showman and the extrovert there was a man born to supreme authority."[11] Frank Roberts, the British ambassador to Moscow from 1960 to 1962, was similarly effusive: "Khrushchev was a most accessible, communicative, human and stimulating leader, however adversarial, with whom to do business."[12] Semichastnyi, one of those who took a major role in removing him from power, remembered how carefully he had to prepare for meetings with Khrushchev, who would always pose the most unexpected question; Brezhnev, on the other hand, would usually be satisfied with a couple of jokes.[13]

These skills led to a certain overconfidence. One of his advisers suggested that his utter confidence in his own abilities left him too fond of flatterers and unwilling to look for allies in his reform mission.[14] Certainly in 1964, as his relationship with the Presidium became increasingly strained, he appeared to be taking on the establishment single handed. The apparatus of the Central Committee was a mammoth bureaucracy, while Khrushchev's personal staff was in fact very small. He had four assistants plus a handful of clerks and stenographers, along with a press group of five, working on speeches.[15] It was David against Goliath. And yet Khrushchev did not actively seek allies. On the contrary, he got rid of supporters like Aristov, Mukhitdinov, Ignatov and Kirichenko for reasons that had nothing to do with the battle of ideas. Kirichenko threw his weight around, Mukhitdinov drank and mistreated his wife, Aristov was too soft, but there were no points of ideological controversy, unlike with Suslov and Kosygin, both of whom he moaned about but neither of whom he would dismiss, except, perhaps, at the very end when talk about "rejuvenation" of the Presidium began. Khrushchev seems to have accepted what he told the Presidium on 13 October 1964, that those who had united to defeat the Anti-Party Group remained united thereafter.[16]

The Presidium, on the other hand, had no choice but to move against him. He was no "recidivist Trotskyist" as Kaganovich claimed, but he did want to disrupt the status quo.[17] As the contemporary political commentator Carl Linden noted soon afterwards, "he had offended too many powers within the regime too often".[18] The historian William Tompson put it the same way: "he fell because his comrades in arms had concluded that in some senses he was out of control".[19] Semichastnyi was clear, "he could not be directed".[20] Even Mikoyan felt that Khrushchev was going too far: he got carried away with new ideas, did not know the boundaries, did not want to listen to anyone, went forward like a tank.[21] Back in spring 1962 Khrushchev spoke to the Presidium about the danger of "stagnation" and he made clear that summer that "there are failings in our structures". However the outcome of the Cuban Missile Crisis and the subsequent November Plenum on the economy appeared to put an end to any radical initiatives. Then, at the start of 1964 it all began again, reform was back on the agenda, Khrushchev was behaving in the Presidium like a bull in a china shop, he knew what he did not want, but was much less clear about what he did want. One thing was clear, however, structural change was needed. As the former deputy prime minister and head of *Gosplan*, Vladimir Novikov, put it, Khrushchev understood that his new economy could not fit into the old framework and that new mechanisms were needed.[22]

How would things have turned out if Khrushchev had not been overthrown? Speculation, of course, but logic suggests that economic experimentation would have continued, experimentation that was being increasingly copied in some other Eastern European states at this time, particularly Czechoslovakia. The 23rd Party Congress would not only have endorsed a new constitution after nationwide consultation, but the discussion at the congress of the famine of 1932–3 would have opened up a whole new phase in the de-Stalinisation campaign. There could well have been a Moscow Spring before the Czechoslovak Prague Spring of 1968. Certainly, the Prague Spring of 1968 would have been allowed to follow its course. Khrushchev had got to know Alexander Dubček in summer 1964 when he attended the twentieth anniversary of the Slovak National Uprising and the two men appeared to get on well. In retirement, Khrushchev was categorical: "How could we have got into the state of affairs of the events of 1968? I cannot agree in any way that the Czechoslovaks were giving in to imperialist propaganda or wanted to restore the capitalist mode of production."[23] What the future of communism would have been if there had been no Soviet intervention in Czechoslovakia in 1968 is difficult to imagine, but there is little doubt that it would have encouraged Tito to extend still further the powers of workers' councils in Yugoslavia.[24] Whether this hypothetical Eastern Europe-wide triumph of reform communism would have produced economies dynamic enough to compete with Western capitalism is to enter the realm of fantasy, but the triumph of "experienced cadres" committed to "stability" and Lenin's watchword of doing nothing in a hurry condemned the communist system to its slow death.

Notes

Introduction

1. The ideas expressed here, and any mistakes, are entirely my own. However, I would like to thank Nataliya Kibita for reading and commenting on the manuscript.
2. I. Thatcher (2011) 'Khrushchev as Leader' in J. Smith and M. Ilič (eds) *Khrushchev in the Kremlin* (London: Routledge), p. 22.
3. This study has used: S. N. Khrushchev (2000) *Nikita Khrushchev and the Creation of a Superpower* (University Park, PA: Pennsylvania State University Press); S. N. Khrushchev (2010) *Khrushchev Reformator* (Moscow: Vremya); S. N. Khrushchev (2014) *Khrushchev in Power: Unfinished Reforms* (Boulder, CO: Lynne Riener Publishers). For the role of the apparatus, see *Reformator* p. 476.
4. W. Tompson (1995) *Khrushchev: A Political Life* (Basingstoke and New York: Palgrave), p. 246.
5. W. Taubman (2003) *Khrushchev: The Man and his Era* (London: Free Press), p. xi.
6. This work has used the English version S. N. Khrushchev (ed.) (2004) *Memoirs of Nikita Khrushchev* three volumes, (University Park, Pennsylvania: Pennsylvania State University Press), hereafter *Memoirs*, as well as the documents and articles reproduced in the four volume Russian version, N. S. Khrushchev (1999) *Vospminaniya: Vremya, Lyudi, Vlast* (Moscow: Moskovskie Novosti) hereafter *Vospminaniya*.
7. A. A. Fursenko (ed.) (2004) *Arkhivy Kremlya: Prezidium Ts K KPSS 1954-64* vol. I. *Chernovye zapisi zasedanii: stenogrammy* (Moscow: Rosspen) hereafter *Presidium*; *Nikita Sergeevich Khrushchev: Dva tsveta vremeni. Dokumenty iz Lichnogo Fonda N. S. Khrushcheva* two volumes (Moscow: Mezhdunarodnyi fond Demokratiya, 2009) hereafter *Dva Tsveta*; *Lavrentii Beriya 1953: Dokumenty* (Moscow: Mezhdunarodnyi fond Demokratiya, 1999) hereafter *Beriya*; *Reabilitatsiya: Kak Eto Bylo, Mart 1953 – Fevral' 1956: Dokumenty* (Moscow: Mezhdunarodnyi fond Demokratiya, 2000) hereafter *Reabilitatsiya*; *Doklad N S Khrushcheva o Kul'te Lichnosti Stalina na XX S"ezde KPSS: Dokumenty* (Moscow: Rosspen, 2002) hereafter *Doklad*;

Molotov, Malenkov, Kaganovich: Stenogrammy Iyunskogo Plenuma TsK KPSS i Drugie Dokumenty (Moscow: Mezhdunarodnyi fond Demokratiya, 1998) hereafter *Molotov*; *Georgii Zhukov: Dokumenty* (Moscow: Mezhdunarodnyi fond Demokratiya, 2001) hereafter *Zhukov, Dokumenty*: *Nikita Khrushchev 1964* (Moscow: Mezhdunarodnyi fond Demokratiya, 2007) hereafter *1964*; Matthew E. Lenoe (2010) *The Kirov Murder and Soviet History* (New Haven, CT and London: Yale University Press). Lenoe concludes that while Stalin used Kirov's murder to his own advantage, none of the evidence that he planned it stands up to detailed scrutiny.

8. P. Jones (ed.) (2006) *The Dilemmas of De-Stalinisation: Negotiating Cultural and Social Change in the Khrushchev Era* (London: Routledge); M. Ilič et al. (eds) (2004) *Women in the Khrushchev Era* (Basingstoke and New York: Palgrave Macmillan); M. Ilič and J. Smith (eds) (2009) *Soviet State and Society under Nikita Khrushchev* (London: Routledge); Smith and Ilič *Khrushchev*. To mention just some of the monographs: D. Kozlov (2013) *The Readers of Novyi Mir: Coming to Terms with the Stalinist Past* (Cambridge, MA: Harvard University Press); P. Jones (2013) *Myth, Memory, Trauma: Rethinking the Stalinist Past in the Soviet Union, 1953–70* (New Haven, CT and London: Yale University Press); and R. Hornsby (2013) *Protest Reform and Repression in Khrushchev's Soviet Union* (Cambridge: Cambridge University Press).

9. G. Swain (2011) *Tito: A Biography* (London: I B Tauris); G. Swain 'Before National Communism: Joining the Latvian Komsomol under Stalin' *Europe-Asia Studies* vol. 64, no. 7, 2012; G. Swain '"Come on Latvians, Join the Party – We'll Forgive you Everything": Ideological Struggle during the National Communist Affair, Summer 1959' in M. Kott and D. Smith (eds) (2016) *Latvia – A Work in Progress? 100 Years of State and Nation-building* (Hannover: *ibidem*-Verlag).

Chapter 1:   Becoming a Party Apparatchik, 1894–1929

1. For the date of birth, see Khrushchev *Reformator* p. 26. Otherwise see scattered references in *Memoirs*, vol. I, pp. 71, 247, vol. II, pp. 233, 347; also *Dva Tsveta*, p. 187.

2. *Memoirs* vol. II, pp. 47, 304.

3. P. Bogdanov et al. (eds) (1961) *Rasskaz o Pochetnom Shakhtere* (Stalino: Partizdat), p. 13; *Memoirs*, vol. II, pp. 246, 286.

4. *Rasskaz* pp. 14–15, 19–22, 203; *Memoirs* vol. III, pp. 267, 579 – *Zvezda* first appeared in December 1910; *Vospominaniya* vol. I, p. 729.

5. *Memoirs* vol. I, pp. 350, 665; *Rasskaz* pp. 19–22.

6. *Memoirs* vol. I, pp. 8, 146, vol. II, p. 245, vol. III, p. 579.

7. *Rasskaz* p. 22; Khrushchev *Reformator* p. 27; *Presidium* pp. 526, 660; *Memoirs* vol. III, p. 204.

8. *Memoirs* vol. I, p. 74, vol. II, p. 283; Khrushchev *Reformator* p. 47; *Rasskaz* pp. 14–15.

9. *Memoirs* vol. II, p. 677; *Rasskaz* pp. 25–6, 208.

10. *Memoirs* vol. I, p. 26; *Rasskaz* pp. 35–6, 210.

11. H. Kuromiya (1998) *Freedom and Terror in the Donbas* (Cambridge: Cambridge University Press), p. 91; *Rasskaz* pp. 32–4.

12. *Rasskaz* p. 39; *Memoirs* vol. II, p. 18 note 2; Kuromiya *Donbas* p. 93. For the SRs, see *Dva Tsveta*, p. 94.

13. *Memoirs* vol. I, p. 186.

14. *Memoirs* vol. II, p. 18 note 3; *Rasskaz* pp. 43–4; Kuromiya *Donbas* p. 95.

15. M. Frankland (1966) *Khrushchev* (Harmondsworth: Penguin Books), p. 25. There is some controversy about when Khrushchev joined the party – see Taubman *Khrushchev* p. 46 – but it is this author's opinion that only a committed Bolshevik would have joined a poor peasant committee.

16. *Presidium* p. 434; *1964* p. 17.

17. *Memoirs* vol. I, p. 57, vol. II, p. 80; *Zhukov* p. 195. For his wife, see Taubman *Khrushchev*, p. 52.

18. *Memoirs* vol. I, pp. 324–5.

19. The quotation is taken from Frankland *Khrushchev* p. 29. Khrushchev refers to the incident on a number of occasions, *Zhukov* p. 219; *Memoirs* vol. II, pp. 285, 501.

20. *Memoirs* vol. I, pp. 172–3, vol. II, p. 99.

21. *Rasskaz* pp. 66, 211; *Memoirs* vol. II, p. 301.

22. *Memoirs* vol. III, p. 19, 677; Taubman *Khrushchev* pp. 51, 54–5, 60.

23. *Rasskaz* p. 86.

24. Taubman *Khrushchev* p. 57; *Molotov* p. 482; *Memoirs* vol. I, pp. 127–8.

25. L. Kaganovich (1996) *Pamyatnye Zapiski* (Moscow: Vagrius), p. 565; *Rasskaz* pp. 86–7.

26. A. Adzhubei (1989) *Te Desyat'let* (Moscow: Sovetskaya Rossiya), p. 43.

27. Taubman *Khrushchev* p. 57.

28. *Memoirs* vol. I, p. 13.

29. *Memoirs* vol. I, pp. 8, 14, 19; *Vospominaniya* vol. I, p. 735.

30. *Memoirs* vol. I, p. 22; *Vospominaniya* vol. I, pp. 735, 739.

31. Kaganovich *Pamyatnye Zapiski* p. 565.

32. Taubman *Khrushchev* pp. 64–5; *Vospominaniya* vol. I, p. 740.

33. *Vospominaniya* vol. I, p. 744; *Rasskaz* pp. 128–30, 224.

34. *Memoirs* vol. I, p. 29; *Dva Tsveta* p. 95; *Vospominaniya* vol. I, pp. 745–7. Simon Petlyura was a leading figure in the Directorate, which tried to establish Ukraine as an independent state between the defeat of Germany in November 1918 and the return of Soviet rule in spring 1919.

35. *Vospominaniya* vol. I, pp. 745–7.

Chapter 2: Stalin's Favourite, 1929–41

1. *Memoirs* vol. I, p. 31; Kaganovich *Pamyatnye Zapiski*, p. 566. For his performance in English, see Khrushchev *Reformator* p. 29.

2. *Memoirs* vol. I, pp. 34–5.

3. *Memoirs* vol. I, pp. 37–8, 47, 59.

4. *Memoirs* vol. I, pp. 39–40, 51.

5. A. Ponomarev (1993) 'Nikita Khrushchev: Nachalo Karery' in *Neizvestnaya Rossiya XX Vek* vol. III (Moscow: Moskovskoe Gorodskoe Ob'edinenie Arkhivov), pp. 120–7; R. Medvedev (2006) *N. S. Khrushchev: Otets Ili Otchim Sovetskoi 'Ottepeli'* (Moscow: Yauza), p. 25; Kaganovich *Pamyatnye Zapiski* p. 425.

6. Kaganovich *Pamyatnye Zapiski* p. 566.

7. *Memoirs* vol. I, pp. 41, 47, vol. II, pp. 69–70; Adzhubei *Te Desyat'* p. 129.

8. *Memoirs* vol. I, pp. 57, 74.

9. J. V. Stalin (1955) 'Report to the 17th Party Congress' in *Collected Works of J. V. Stalin* vol. XIII (London: Lawrence and Wishart), pp. 370–1.

10. (1934) *XVII S"ezd Vsesoyuznoi Kommunisticheskoi Partii (b): Stenograficheskii Otchet* (Moscow: Partizdat), pp. 145–7.

11. *Memoirs* vol. I, pp. 91–2.

12. A. Rees (2012) *Iron Lazar* (London: Anthem Press), p. 156; Taubman *Khrushchev* p. 89; E. Crankshaw (1966) *Khrushchev* (London: Sphere), p. 85.

13. *Memoirs* vol. I, pp. 42, 74, 82, vol. II, pp. 135–6.

14. *Memoirs* vol. I, p. 17.

15. *Dva Tsveta* pp. 441–7.

16. F. Benvenuti 'Industry and Purge in the Donbas, 1936–37' *Europe-Asia Studies* vol. 45, no. 1, 1993, pp. 60, 64; J. Haslam 'Political Opposition to Stalin and the Origins of the Terror in Russia, 1932–36' *The Historical Journal* vol. 29, no. 2, 1986, p. 402.

17. *Dva Tsveta* p. 466.

18. J. V. Stalin (1937) 'Speech to the February–March Plenum 1937' in *The Moscow Trial* (London: Anglo-Russian Parliamentary Committee), pp. 262–4.

19. A. Getty (1999) *The Road to Terror* (New Haven, CT: Yale University Press), pp. 396, 402.

20. *Memoirs* vol. I, pp. 120–1.

21. Getty *Terror* p. 134; *Molotov* p. 747.

22. Tompson *Khrushchev* p. 58.

23. *Memoirs* vol. I, pp. 122–3.

24. *Memoirs* vol. I, p. 126; Tompson *Khrushchev* p. 57.

25. *Memoirs* vol. I, p. 130; Taubman *Khrushchev* p. 99.

26. *Memoirs* vol. I, pp. 127–8.

27. Ponomarev 'Nachalo Karery', p. 138; for Rykov's daughter, see T. J. Colton (1995) *Moscow: Governing the Socialist Metropolis* (Cambridge, MA: Harvard University Press), p. 289.

28. *Dva Tsveta* pp. 472–3.

29. *Memoirs* vol. I, p. 78, 98, pp. 105–7. For the reference to Chubar' see 'Speech to the Polish Workers' Party 20 March 1956' held in the Wilson Center Digital Archive Nikita Khrushchev Collection, document 111920.

30. Khrushchev *Reformator* p. 255; *Memoirs* vol. II, pp. 174, 196.

31. *Memoirs* vol. I, pp. 108–9, 121.

32. Frankland *Khrushchev* p. 52.

33. M. Jansen (2002) *Stalin's Loyal Executioner: People's Commissar Nikolai Ezhov, 1895–1940* (Stanford, CA: Hoover Institution Press), pp. 133–4; Taubman *Khrushchev* pp. 19, 116; Tompson *Khrushchev* p. 60.

34. *Politicheskoe Rukovodstvo Ukrainy, 1939–1989* (Moscow: Rosspen, 2006), p. 34.

35. Tompson *Khrushchev* p. 61; *Memoirs* vol. I, pp. 139–40.

36. Getty *Terror* p. 507; *Memoirs* vol. I, p. 13.

37. Yu. Shapoval (2000) 'The Ukrainian Years, 1894–1949' in W. Taubman, S. Khrushchev and A. Gleason (eds) *Nikita Khrushchev* (New Haven, CT: Yale University Press), p. 20.

38. *Memoirs* vol. I, pp. 148, 161.

39. *Memoirs* vol. I, pp. 115–18; *Molotov* pp. 247–8, 334.

40. *Dva Tsveta* pp. 481, 511.

41. *Memoirs* vol. I, p. 180.

42. *Memoirs* vol. I, pp. 143–4.

43. Medvedev *Khrushchev* p. 35; Taubman *Khrushchev* p. 681.

44. *Memoirs* vol. I, pp. 174–5, 194; Colton *Moscow* p. 291; Tompson *Khrushchev* p. 58.

45. *Memoirs* vol. I, p. 180, vol. III, p. 600.

46. *Memoirs* vol. I, pp. 195–6; *Vospominaniya* vol. II, p. 761.

47. *Memoirs* vol. I, pp. 168, 175–6.

48. *Dva Tsveta* p. 481.

49. *Dva Tsveta* pp. 490–1.

50. Shapoval 'The Ukrainian Years', p. 25.

51. *Memoirs* vol. I, p. 225.

52. *Memoirs* vol. I, p. 240. For collectivisation, see Taubman *Khrushchev* p. 137; for Khrushchev's family, see Khrushchev *Nikita Khrushchev* pp. 5, 19.

53. *Vospominaniya* vol. I, p. 765.

54. Frankland *Khrushchev* p. 93; Taubman *Khrushchev* p. 124.

55. *Memoirs* vol. I, pp. 299–301.

Chapter 3: Questioning Stalin, 1941–53

1. *Zhukov* p. 193.

2. E. Mawdsley (2005) *Thunder in the East: The Nazi–Soviet War, 1941–45* (London: Hodder Arnold), pp. 78–9; *Memoirs* vol. I, p. 341; Taubman *Khrushchev* p. 163.

3. Tompson *Khrushchev* pp. 79–80; *Memoirs* vol. I, p. 373; *Zhukov* pp. 193–4. As Taubman explains, *Khrushchev* p. 166, there is some disagreement between Khrushchev and Zhukov concerning these events.

4. *Memoirs* vol. I, pp. 373, 384–6; *Zhukov* pp. 193–4.

5. *Memoirs* vol. I, pp. 396, 414–20, 462–3.

6. *Memoirs* vol. I, p. 473.

7. *Memoirs* vol. I, p. 526; Mawdsley *Thunder,* p. 266. For Khrushchev's speech, see *Zhukov* p. 215.

8. *Memoirs* vol. I, pp. 325, 363, 470, 511, 561, 570.

9. *Dva Tsveta* pp. 30, 53; *Memoirs* vol. I, pp. 542–4.
10. Shapoval 'The Ukrainian Years' p. 26; Taubman *Khrushchev* p. 173 – Taubman interviewed Kostenko.
11. *Memoirs* vol. I, pp. 579–80, 585, vol. II, p. 259.
12. Shapoval 'The Ukrainian Years', pp. 28–9; Khrushchev *Reformator* p. 162.
13. *Dva Tsveta* pp. 57, 91.
14. *Memoirs* vol. I, pp. 606, 617, 624, vol. II, p. 259.
15. *Dva Tsveta* pp. 87, 91–3, 108, 112, 116.
16. *Dva Tsveta* pp. 171, 174–5, 205–12. For the personal angle, see Khrushchev *Nikita Khrushchev* p. 7.
17. *Memoirs* vol. II, pp. 5–7; *Dva Tsveta* p. 607; S. Rudenko 'Vospominaniya "Te Desyat' Let": Polemicheskie Zametki o Knige A. Adzhubeya' *Narodnyi Deputat* no. 3, 1991, p. 117.
18. *Memoirs* vol. II, p. 10; *Molotov* p. 492.
19. *Memoirs* vol. II, pp. 13–15. For the personal angle, Khrushchev *Reformator* p. 38.
20. *XXII S"ezd Kommunisticheskoi Partii Sovetskogo Soyuza: Stenograficheskii Otchet* (Moscow: Gosudarstvennoe Izdatel'stvo Politicheskoi Literatury, 1962), vol. I (in three volumes), p. 280 hereafter *22nd Party Congress Proceedings*; Kaganovich *Pamyatnye Zapiski* pp. 487–92. For Vatutin, see *Memoirs* vol. I, p. 600.
21. Khrushchev *Reformator* p. 56; *Memoirs* vol. II, pp. 15–16; Shapoval 'The Ukrainian Years' pp. 33–6.
22. Medvedev *Khrushchev*, p. 72; *Dva Tsveta* p. 506.
23. V Semichastnyi 'Nezabyvemoe' in Yu. V. Aksyutin (ed.) (1989) *Nikita Sergeevich Khrushchev: Materialy k Biorgrafii*, (Moscow: Politizdat), pp. 49, 51.
24. *Dva Tsveta* pp. 513–15.
25. *Politicheskoe Rukovodstvo Ukrainy* pp. 157–62.
26. *Dva Tsveta* pp. 223–4.
27. *Memoirs* vol. II, pp. 181–2; Kaganovich *Pamyatnye Zapiski* p. 567.
28. G. Procacci (ed.) (1994) *The Cominform: Minutes of the Three Conferences* (Milan: Fondazione Giangiacomo Feltrinelli), pp. 829–31.
29. B.Tromly 'The Leningrad Affair and Soviet Patronage Politics, 1949–1950' *Europe-Asia Studies* vol. 56, no. 5, 2004, pp. 707–29.
30. *Memoirs* vol. II, pp. 21–2, 36, 180, vol. III, p. 682.
31. *Memoirs* vol. II, p. 23.
32. R. W. Davies and M. Ilič 'From Khrushchev (1935–1936) to Khrushchev (1956–1964): Construction Policy Compared' in Smith and Ilič *Kremlin*, p. 211.
33. Medvedev *Khrushchev* p. 76. For livestock production, see N. S. Khrushchev (1962–4) *Stroitel'stvo kommunizma v SSSR i Razvitie Sel'skogo Khozyaistva: Sentyabr' 1953 Goda – Mart 1964 Goda* (Moscow: Gospolitizdat) vol. II, pp. 9–21.
34. Crankshaw *Khrushchev*, p. 178; A. V. Pyzhikov (2002) *Khrushchevskaya Ottepel'* (Moscow: Olma Press), p. 25; *22nd Party Congress Proceedings* vol. II (in three volumes), p. 183.
35. Taubman *Khrushchev* p. 226; *Memoirs* vol. II, p. 265.
36. *Memoirs* vol. I, p. 3, vol. II, pp. 62, 84. For 'madness', see Aksyutin *Materialy* p. 152.

37. *Memoirs* vol. II, p. 126. For Rykov's daughter, see *Reabilitatsiya* p. 92.
38. *Dva Tsveta* p. 388.
39. Y. Gorlizki 'Party Revivalism and the Death of Stalin' *Slavic Review* vol. 54, no. 1, 1995, pp. 4–7.
40. *Dva Tsveta* p. 412, 418.
41. *Memoirs* vol. II, pp. 110–14.
42. G. Kostyrchenko (2012) *Tainaya Politka Khrushcheva* (Moscow: Mezhdunarodnye Otnosheniya), p. 23.
43. *Reabilitatsiya* p. 129; Khrushchev *Nikita Khrushchev* p. 26; Khrushchev *Reformator* p. 92.
44. Taubman *Khrushchev* pp. 236, 239; Adzhubei *Te Desyat'* p. 132.

Chapter 4:   Dethroning Stalin, 1953–6

1. Yu. V. Aksyutin (2004) *Khrushchevskaya 'Ottepel' i Obshchestvennye Nastroenniya v SSSR v 1953–64 gg* (Moscow: Rosspen), pp. 17–18, 35; Pyzhikov *Ottepel'*, p. 87; N. Mukhitdinov (1994) *Gody Provedennye v Kremle* (Tashkent: Izdatel'stvo Narodnogo Naslediya Imeni Abdully Kadyri), p. 101.
2. Pyzhikov *Ottepel'* p. 41; Mukhitdinov *Gody* p. 101.
3. Kostyrchenko *Tainaya Politika* pp. 16–17; *Beria* p. 25; Taubman *Khrushchev* p. 246.
4. M. Dobson (2009) *Khrushchev's Cold Summer: Gulag Returnees, Crime and the Fate of Reform after Stalin* (Ithaca, NY and London: Cornell University Press), p. 51.
5. Aksyutin *Khrushchevskaya* p. 37; *Reabilitatsiya* p. 19; *Shepilov i Primknuvshii k Nim* (Moscow: Evonnitsa-MG, 1998), p. 118.
6. T. Tannenberg (2008) *Politka Moskvy v Respublikakh Baltii v Poslevoennye Gody (1944–1956): Issledovaniya i Dokumenty* (Tartu: Tartu University Press), p. 81; Mukhitdinov *Gody* pp. 109–11; Khrushchev *Reformator* p. 114.
7. *Beria* pp. 88, 157.
8. Tannenberg *Politika* p. 83; V. Krumin'sh 'Dolgaya Doroga k Demokratii' *Kommunist Sovetskoi Latvii* no 3, 1990 p. 90; *Latvija Padomju Režīma Varā: 1945–1986: Dokumentu Krājums* (Riga: Latvijas Vēstures Institūta Apgāds, 2001), p. 193; *Memoirs* Vol. II, p. 189.
9. Aksyutin *Khrushchevskaya* p. 33; S. Beria (1999) *Beria: My Father. Inside Stalin's Kremlin* (London: Duckworth), p. 253. For the sacking of the minister, Khrushchev *Reformator* p. 115.
10. *Beria* p. 59; *Memoirs* Vol. II, pp. 183–4. They never did address each other in this way.
11. Aksyutin *Khrushchevskaya* p. 42; *Beria* p. 88.
12. A. B. Edemskii (2008) *Ot Konflikta k Normalizatsii: Seveetsko-Yugoslavskie Otnosheniya v 1953–56 Godakh* (Moscow: Nauka), pp. 83, 89, 107.
13. *Memoirs* Vol. II, p. 189.
14. Kostyrchenko *Tainaya politika* pp. 16–17.
15. *Memoirs* Vol. II, p. 150; Khrushchev *Nikita Khrushchev* p. 35.

16. *Beria* pp. 69, 73.
17. D. Volkogonov (1996) *Sem' Vozhdei* vol. I (Moscow: Novosti), pp. 352–9; Aksyutin *Khrushchevskaya* p. 75. There is also discussion of this in E. Yu. Zubkova (1993) *Obshchestvo i Reform, 1945–1964* (Moscow: Izdatel'skii Tsentr "Rossiya Molodaya"), pp. 128–30.
18. Aksyutin *Khrushchevskaya* p. 45; *Beria* p. 88.
19. Medvedev *Khrushchev*; Khrushchev *Reformator* p. 137; Crankshaw *Khrushchev* p. 192; V. A. Shestakov (2006) *Sotsialno-ekonomicheskaya Politika Sovetskogo Gosudarstva vo 50-e i Seredine 60-kh Godov* (Moscow: Nauka), p. 168.
20. Aksyutin *Materialy* p. 75; Kaganovich *Pamyatnye Zapiski* p. 498. For the joint signatures, Khrushchev *Nikita Khrushchev* p. 62.
21. A. Strelyanin (1989) 'Poslednii Romantik' in L. A. Kirshner et al. (eds.) *Svet i Teni "Velikovogo Desyatiletiya": N S Khrushchev i Ego Vremya* (Leningrad: Lenizdat), p. 196.
22. For the Virgin Lands, see Taubman *Khrushchev* p. 261 and Tompson *Khrushchev* p. 135. See also Khrushchev's speech reproduced in *Svet i Teni* p. 22
23. Khrushchev *Reformator* p. 151; *Memoirs* vol. II, p. 333. It should be noted that transport costs from Kazakhstan and the lack of adequate storage facilities mitigated against Khrushchev's confident comments on the economic success of the scheme long term. However, Shestakov (*Sotsialno-ekomicheskaya Politika* p. 232) confirms that because of the shortage of investment funds, in the short term extensive agricultural development was the only way forward.
24. Taubman *Khrushchev* p. 264; Tompson *Khrushchev* p. 136; Khrushchev *Reformator* pp. 165–6. Khrushchev is quoted from G. Roberts (2008) 'A Chance for Peace? The Soviet Campaign to End the Cold War, 1953–55' *Cold War International History Project* Working Paper 57, p. 29.
25. *Reabilitatsiya* pp. 9, 56–8, 72.
26. Aksyutin *Khrushchevskaya* pp. 77–8.
27. *Reabilitatsiya* pp. 74, 111, 115.
28. *Reabilitatsiya* pp. 129–41; *Dva Tsveta* pp. 504, 511.
29. M. E. Lenoe (2010) *The Kirov Murder and Soviet History* (New Haven, CT and London: Yale University Press), pp. 563–4.
30. Taubman *Khrushchev* p. 264; Crankshaw *Khrushchev* p. 200; Tompson *Khrushchev* p. 130; Kostyrchenko *Tainaya Politika* p. 20.
31. Tompson *Khrushchev* pp. 140–1.
32. *Presidium* p. 35; *Molotov* p. 394; Aksyutin *Khrushchevskaya* pp. 90–2.
33. *Presidium* pp. 37–40.
34. *Dva Tsveta* p. 528.
35. Edemskii *Ot Konflikta* pp. 197–9, 202–3.
36. Edemskii *Ot Konflikta* pp. 229–30.
37. Edemskii *Ot Konflikta* pp. 249, 252, 268–70.
38. Edemskii *Ot Konflikta* pp. 297–300, 325.
39. Edemskii *Ot Konflikta* pp. 343, 348–51.

40. Edemskii *Ot Konflikta* pp. 371, 383, 407.
41. *Presidium* pp. 41–6.
42. Edemskii *Ot Konflikta* pp. 438, 441, 445–6, 449, 457.
43. Edemskii *Ot Konflikta* pp. 467, 477–82.
44. S. Rajak 'Yugoslav–Soviet Relations 1953–1957: Normalisation, Comradeship, Confrontation' London School of Economics and Political Science PhD (2004), p. 194.
45. *Presidium* pp. 489–504; Aksyutin *Khrushchevskaya* pp. 126–39.
46. *Memoirs* vol. II, p. 215, vol. III, pp. 353, 356. Also Taubman *Khrushchev* p. 277.
47. Edemskii *Ot konflikta* p. 449; *Dva Tsveta* pp. 544, 547.
48. *Reabilitatsiya* p. 217, 224.
49. *Dva Tsveta* pp. 555–6.
50. *Reabilitatsiya* p. 266; *Presidium* p. 57. It is noteworthy that Kaganovich used the intimate form of "you" [s toboi] when referring to Khrushchev.
51. *Reabilitatsiya* p. 294.
52. Aksyutin *Khrushchevskaya* p. 155; A. Mikoyan (1999) *Tak Bylo: Razmyshlenie o Minuvshem* (Moscow: Vagrius), pp. 590–2; *Presidium* pp. 79–80; Lenoe *Kirov* p. 568. For Khrushchev's involvement, see Mukhitdinov *Gody* p. 172.
53. *Memoirs* vol. II, p. 206; *Reabilitatsiya* p. 303.
54. Khrushchev *Reformator* p. 263; *Presidium* p. 95.
55. *Presidium* p. 95. For the opposition of Molotov, Kaganovich and Malenkov, see *22nd Party Congress Proceedings* vol. II (in three volumes), pp. 253–4.
56. Aksyutin *Khrushchevskaya* p. 159; *Reabilitatsiya* pp. 325–6, 347.
57. Aksyutin *Khrushchevskaya* pp. 160–2; *Presidium* pp. 100–2, 106.
58. Volkogonov *Sem' Vozhdei* vol. I, p. 375; *22nd Party Congress Proceedings* vol. II (in three volumes), pp. 253–4.
59. Khrushchev *Nikita Khrushchev* p. 98; Taubman *Khrushchev* p. 281; Jones *Myth* p. 21.
60. *Doklad* pp. 41–2, 56, 58, 73; Jones *Myth* pp. 22–3.
61. *Doklad* pp. 74, 81, 99. See also *Reabilitatsiya* p. 379. For Kaganovich, see Mukhtidinov *Gody* p. 180.

Chapter 5:   Ousting Stalinists

1. S. Schattenberg (2006) '"Democracy or Despotism": How the Secret Speech was Translated into Everyday Life' in Jones *Dilemmas* p. 65; Jones *Myth* p. 27; I. Caşu and M. Sandle 'Discontent and Uncertainty in the Borderland: Soviet Moldavia and the Secret Speech 1956–57' *Europe-Asia Studies* vol. 66, no. 4, 2014, p. 620.
2. Zubkova *Oshchestvo* p. 141; K. E. Loewenstein 'Re-emergence of Public Opinion in the Soviet Union: Khrushchev and Responses to the Secret Speech' *Europe-Asia Studies* vol. 58, no. 8, 2006, p. 1337.

3. Medvedev *Khrushchev* p. 150; *Presidium* p. 116. The summary of events in Poland at this time is taken from A. Kemp-Welch 'Khrushchev's "Secret Speech" and Polish Politics: The Spring of 1956' *Europe-Asia Studies* vol. 48, no. 2, 1996, pp. 181–206.

4. Pyzhikov *Ottepel'* p. 52; Taubman *Khrushchev* p. 287; *Presidium* p.121. For Mikoyan, see *22nd Party Congress Proceedings* vol. I (in three volumes), p. 448.

5. *Doklad* p. 294; *Presidium* pp. 124–5.

6. *Memoirs* vol. III, p. 528.

7. *Presidium* pp. 136–8.

8. For Tito's arrival, see Khrushchev *Nikita Khrushchev*, p. 147; Medvedev *Khrushchev* p. 149. Otherwise these events are covered in G. Swain and N. Swain (2009) *Eastern Europe since 1945* (Basingstoke and New York: Palgrave Macmillan), pp. 96–7.

9. *Presidium* p. 139. For Zhukov, see *Doklad* p. 347 and *Zhukov* p. 139.

10. Mukhitdinov *Gody* p. 137; *Doklad* p. 351.

11. *Presidium* p. 147.

12. *Doklad* pp. 352–68, 381.

13. *Presidium* p. 149.

14. For the Petőfi Circle, see A. B. Hegedus (1997) 'The Petőfi Circle: The Forum of Reform in 1956' in T. Cox (ed.) *Hungary 1956 – Forty Years On* (London: Frank Cass), pp. 108–33.

15. *Presidium* p. 951; Swain and Swain *Eastern Europe* pp. 97–9.

16. Swain and Swain *Eastern Europe* pp. 100, 109.

17. *Presidium* p. 168; *Memoirs* vol. II, p. 223, vol. III, p. 624.

18. *Memoirs* vol. III, p. 628.

19. *Memoirs* vol. III, p. 629; *Presidium* p. 168.

20. *Presidium* p. 168.

21. *Presidium* pp. 176–7.

22. *Presidium* p. 180.

23. *Presidium* p. 185.

24. *Presidium* pp. 178, 187–8.

25. *Memoirs* vol. III, pp. 431, 647; *Presidium* pp. 191–2.

26. *Presidium* p. 195; *Memoirs* vol. III, p. 661.

27. Swain and Swain *Eastern Europe* p. 106.

28. *Presidium* pp. 201–4; *Memoirs* vol. III, p. 657.

29. G. Swain (2011) *Tito* (London: I B Tauris), p. 125; Rajak 'Yugoslav-Soviet Relations' p. 293; L. Gibianskii (1998) 'Soviet-Yugoslav Relations in the Hungarian Revolution of 1956' *Cold War International History Project Bulletin* no. 10, p. 146.

30. Swain *Tito* p. 127; *Presidium* p. 210.

31. *Presidium* p. 213; Aksyutin *Khrushchevskaya* p. 196.

32. Kozlov Readers pp. 89, 91; Jones *Myth* p. 58; Schattenberg 'Democracy' p. 68; Loewenstein 'Re-emergence' p. 1339.

33. Zubkova *Obshchestvo* p. 151; Kostyrchenko *Tainaya Politka* p. 105; Aksyutin *Khrushchevskaya* p. 195.

34. R. Hornsby (2014) 'A "Merciless Struggle": De-Stalinisation and the 1957 Clampdown on Dissent' in T. M. Bohn et al. (eds) *De-Stalinisation Reconsidered: Persistence and Change in the Soviet Union* (Frankfurt: Campus Verlag), p. 98, pp. 101–2; *Doklad* pp. 395–6; Aksyutin *Khrushchevskaya* p. 195.

35. *Presidium* pp. 209, 211, 214–15; *1964* p. 69; Khrushchev *Nikita Khrushchev* pp. 366–7.

36. *Presidium* pp. 211, 221–3.

37. *22nd Party Congress Proceedings* vol. I (in three volumes), pp. 396, 436; V. Vasiliev 'Failings of the *Sovnarkhoz* reform: The Ukrainian Experience' in Smith and Ilič *Kremlin*, p. 120.

38. *Presidium* p. 239; *Shepilov i Primknuvshii*, p. 129.

39. *Presidium* pp. 140–5, 999–1000; Aksyutin *Khrushchevskaya* pp. 205, 212.

40. *Presidium* p. 254; *Molotov* pp. 245–6; Kaganovich *Pamyatnye Zapiski* pp. 519–20.

41. *Molotov* p. 471; Kostyrchenko *Tainaya Politika* pp. 89–93; Jones *Myth* p. 86. For the underground cell in the Komsomol see J. Fürst 'The Arrival of Spring? Changes and Continuities in Soviet Youth Culture and Policy between Stalin and Khrushchev' in Jones *Dilemmas* p. 141.

42. Kirshner *Svet i Teni* pp. 126–33; Aksyutin *Khrushchevskaya* pp. 217–21; Jones *Myth* p. 84.

43. *Molotov* pp. 188–92; *Vneocherednoi XXI S''ezd Kommunisticheskoi Partii Sovetskogo Soyuza: Stenograficheskii Otchet* (Moscow: Gosudarstvennoe Izdatel'stvo Politicheskoi Literatury, 1959) vol. II (in two volumes), pp. 290–1 hereafter *21st Party Congress Proceedings*; *Presidium* p. 257.

44. *Molotov* pp. 167–9; *21st Party Congress Proceedings* vol. II (in two volumes), pp. 14, 203–5.

45. *Molotov* pp. 26–31; Taubman *Khrushchev* p. 318; Kaganovich *Pamyatnye Zapiski* p. 520.

46. *Zhukov* pp. 154–5, 380, 333; *Molotov* pp. 33, 75, 110.

47. Adzhubei *Te Desyat'* p. 275; *22nd Party Congress Proceedings* vol. II (in three volumes), pp. 106–7.

48. Medvedev *Khrushchev* p. 172; Aksyutin *Materialy* p. 44; Mukhitdinov *Gody* pp. 265–74; Taubman *Khrushchev* p. 320.

49. *Molotov* pp. 26–31, 37–41; *Zhukov* pp. 158–61.

50. *Molotov* pp. 47–9, 275, 289.

51. *Molotov* pp. 68–70.

52. *Molotov* pp. 119–21.

53. *Molotov* pp. 293, 329, 431, 491.

54. *Molotov* pp. 188–92.

55. Swain *Tito* p. 129.

56. *Zhukov* pp. 86–7, 134–5, 649; Pyzhikov *Ottepel'* p. 97; Beria *My Father* p. 252.

57. *Zhukov* pp. 114, 216–17, 376, 651; *Presidium* pp. 269–73.

58. Mukhitdinov *Gody* pp. 286–91; *Presidium* p. 278; *Zhukov* pp. 190–1, 194–6. For Party cells in the army, *22nd Party Congress Proceedings* vol. III (in three volumes), p. 68.

59. *Presidium* pp. 300–1; *Memoirs* vol. I, pp. 238–9.

Chapter 6: Constructing Communism at Home, 1958–62

1. N.S.Khrushchev *Stroitel'stvo kommunisma v SSSR i razvitie sel'skogo khozyaistva: sentyabr' 1953 goda - mart 1964 goda* (Moscow: Gospolitizdat 1962–64), vol. 2 (in three volumes), p. 37.; Taubman *Khrushchev* pp. 364–5; F. A. Durgin 'The Virgin Lands Programme, 1952–1960' *Soviet Studies* vol. 13, no. 3, 1962, pp. 260–1, 269.

2. *21st Party Congress Proceedings* vol. I (in two volumes) pp. 42–3; Durgin 'Virgin Lands' p. 273; Medvedev *Khrushchev* pp. 206–7.

3. T. Bohn '"Closed Cities" versus "Open Society"? The Interaction of De-Stalinisation and Urbanisation' in Bohn *De-Stalinisation Reconsidered* p. 120; M. Smith (2009) 'Khrushchev's Promise to Eliminate the Urban Housing Shortage' in M. Ilič and J. Smith (eds) *Soviet State and Society under Nikita Khrushchev* (London: Routledge), pp. 26, 33; G. D. Andrusz (1984) *Housing and Urban Development in the USSR* (Basingstoke: Macmillan), pp. 19, 150.

4. Andrusz *Housing* pp. 144, 177, 183; *Memoirs* vol. II, p. 283.

5. L. Attwood 'Housing in the Khrushchev Era' in M. Ilič *Women* p. 182, 188; S. E. Reid 'The Khrushchev Kitchen: Domesticating the Scientific–Technical Revolution' *Journal of Contemporary History* vol. 40, no. 2, 2005, p. 314; Reid 'Cold War in the Kitchen: Gender and De-Stalinisation of Consumer Taste in the Soviet Union under Khrushchev' *Slavic Review* vol. 61, no. 2, 2002, pp. 227, 244.

6. G. Ivanova (2011) '"A Question of Honour": Socialist Welfare State versus the Stalinist Apparatus of Repression' in Bohn *De-Stalinisation* p. 136, 139; G. M. Ivanova 'Na Poroge "Gosudarstva Vseobshchego Blagosostoyaniya": Sotsial'naya Politika v SSSR (Seredina 1950x – Nachalo 1970x Godov' PhD Thesis, Moscow, Institute of History, Russian Academy of Sciences, p. 101, 103.

7. Ivanova 'Na Poroge' pp. 118, 154, 162.

8. Ivanova 'Na Poroge' pp. 108, 285.

9. Ivanova 'Na Poroge' p. 92; L. Coumel 'The Scientist, the Pedagogue and the Party Official' in Ilič and Smith *Soviet State* pp. 67–73; *21st Party Congress Proceedings* vol. I (in two volumes), pp. 59–60.

10. J. Jo 'Dismantling Stalin's Fortress: Soviet Trade Unions in the Khrushchev Era' in Ilič and Smith *Soviet State* pp. 125–6, 128–9, 134.

11. Pyzhikov *Ottepel'* p. 120.

12. M. Ilič 'Contesting Inequality: Khrushchev and the Revival of the "Woman Question"' in Bohn *De-Stalinisation* p. 185; Khrushchev *Reformator* p. 624.

13. Khrushchev *Reformator* pp. 571, 573; Aksyutin *Materialy* p. 18; O. Grinevskii (1998) *Tysyacha i Odin den' Nikity Sergeevicha* (Moscow: Vagrius), p. 156; G. A. Brinkley 'Khrushchev Remembered: On the Theory of Soviet Statehood' *Soviet Studies* vol. 24, no. 3, 1973, p. 388.

14. *Presidium* p. 336.

15. *21st Party Congress Proceedings* vol. I (in two volumes), pp. 20, 39, 48, 52, 63.

16. *21st Party Congress Proceedings* vol. I (in two volumes), pp. 94–5, 98, 102–3.

17. *21st Party Congress Proceedings* vol. I (in two volumes), pp. 106, 117.

18. *21st Party Congress Proceedings* vol. I (in two volumes), pp. 494, 540. For Suslov, see vol. I, pp. 13, 362.

19. *21st Party Congress Proceedings* vol. I (in two volumes), pp. 13, 87–9, vol. II p. 47. On Unità, see Crankshaw *Khrushchev* p. 261.

20. Khrushchev *Reformator* p. 630; N. Davis (1995) *A Long Walk to Church* (Boulder, CO: Westview Press), pp. 34–40; M. Froggatt '"Renouncing the Dogma, Teaching Utopia": Science in Schools under Khrushchev' in Jones *Dilemmas* p. 258.

21. *Presidium* pp. 267, 420.

22. M. Tatu (1969) *Power in the Kremlin* (London: Collins), pp. 117–21; E. Zaleski (1967) *Planning Reforms in the Soviet Union* (Chapel Hill, NC: University of North Caroline Press), p. 28.

23. Khrushchev *Reformator* pp. 710–12; see also the English version of this, S. Khrushchev (2014) *Khrushchev in Power: Unfinished Reforms, 1961–64* (Boulder, CO: Lynne Riener Publishers), p. 139.

24. Taubman *Khrushchev* pp. 480–1; *Presidium* pp. 453–66.

25. O. Khlevnyuk 'The Economy of Illusions: the Phenomenon of Data Inflation in the Khrushchev Era' in Smith and Ilič *Kremlin* pp. 171–4.

26. C. A. Linden (1966) *Khrushchev and the Soviet Leadership 1957–1964* (Baltimore, MD: Johns Hopkins Press), pp. 50, 60.

27. Linden *Soviet Leadership* pp. 69, 105; Strelyanin 'Poslednii' p. 255.

28. Linden *Soviet Leadership* pp. 106–7; Tatu *Power* p. 168.

29. *Presidium* pp. 479, 485, 488; Tatu *Power* p. 169; Linden *Soviet Leadership* p. 108.

30. *Presidium* pp. 522–5.

31. *Presidium* pp. 389, 399–400.

32. Tatu *Power* p. 131; Pyzhikov *Ottepel'* pp. 343–4; A. Titov 'The 1961 Party Programme and the Fate of Khrushchev's Reforms' in Ilič and Smith *Soviet State* p. 10.

33. Taubman *Khrushchev* p. 5111; *Presidium* pp. 513–15.

34. Tatu *Power* p. 182; Pyzhikov *Ottepel'* p. 292.

35. *22nd Party Congress Proceedings* vol. I (in three volumes), pp. 57, 110.

36. *22nd Party Congress Proceedings* vol. I (in three volumes), pp. 114–15, 119.

37. *22nd Party Congress Proceedings* vol. I (in three volumes), pp. 145, 151, 165, 167.

38. *22nd Party Congress Proceedings* vol. I (in three volumes), pp. 210–12, 215–17.

39. *22nd Party Congress Proceedings* vol. I (in three volumes), pp. 241, 524. For Lassalle and Molotov see vol. II, pp. 353, 461, vol. III, p. 19.

40. Lenoe *Kirov* pp. 606–7, 631; *Presidium* p. 497.

41. *22nd Party Congress Proceedings* vol. I (in three volumes), pp. 102–3, 105, for Spirdonov and Podgornyi pp. 281, 284.

42. *22nd Party Congress Proceedings* vol. II (in three volumes), pp. 215–16, 353, 403–4.

43. *22nd Party Congress Proceedings* vol. II (in three volumes), pp. 579, 583–4, 587; Lenoe *Kirov* p. 639.

44. Mukhitdinov *Gody* p. 214; Otchet N. M. Shvernika *Istochnik* no. 1, 1995, p. 119; Mikoyan *Tak Bylo* p. 610.
45. W. Taubman 'Khrushchev at his most Khrushchevian' *Cold War International History Project* e-dossier no. 8, Document 7, Speech in Varna, 16 May 1962; Lenoe *Kirov* p. 639.
46. *22nd Party Congress Proceedings* vol. I (in three volumes), pp. 62, 66, 205–6; for Spiridonov and Podgornyi, pp. 271, 287.
47. Tatu *Power* p. 208; Khrushchev *Unfinished Reforms* p. 139.
48. *Presidium* p. 530; Linden *Soviet Leadership* p. 140; Tatu *Power* p. 216; Taubman *Khrushchev* p. 518.
49. *Presidium* pp. 550–1.
50. *Presidium* p. 561.
51. D. Filtzer 'The Soviet Wage Reform of 1956–62' *Soviet Studies* vol. 41, no. 1, 1989, pp. 89–101.
52. J. C. Andy 'The Soviet Military at Novocherkassk' in Ilič and Smith *Soviet State* pp. 181–9.
53. Khrushchev *Nikita Khrushchev* p. 581; Mikoyan *Tak Bylo*, p. 610; *Presidium* p. 568, 581. Whether the director actually referred to liver sausage or cabbage is hard to say, but Khrushchev was prone to exaggeration when worked up.
54. *Presidium* pp. 571, 573, 575, 592.
55. Zaleski *Planning Reforms* p. 77; G. R. Feiwel (1967) *The Soviet Quest for Economic Efficiency* (New York: Praeger), p. 217; Khrushchev *Reformator* p. 811.
56. M. E. Sharpe (ed.) (1966) *Planning, Profit and Incentives in the USSR* (White Plains, NY: International Arts and Science Press), pp. 71. 83; J. L. Felker (1966) *Soviet Economic Controversies* (Massachusetts: MIT Press), p. 109.
57. Zaleski *Planning Reforms* pp. 78–9; Feiwel *Quest* pp. 205–6.
58. *Presidium* pp. 611–12.

Chapter 7:   Confronting Capitalism

1. Taubman *Khrushchev* p. 379; D. Deletant and M. Ionescu (2011) 'Romania and the Warsaw Pact' *Cold War International History Project* Working Paper no. 43, p. 14; *Memoirs* vol. II, pp. 483, 513.
2. Roberts 'A Chance for Peace?' pp. 50–7.
3. V. Zubok (1993) 'Khrushchev and the Berlin Crisis' *Cold War International History Project* Working Paper no. 6, pp. 7–12.
4. *Presidium* pp. 338–9; H. M. Harrison (1993) 'Ulbricht and the Concrete "Rose": New Archival Evidence on the Dynamics of Soviet–East German Relations and the Berlin Crisis, 1958–61' *Cold War International History Project* Working Paper no. 5, p. 6, 22.
5. *Presidium* p. 346; Tompson *Khrushchev* p. 204.
6. *Presidium* p. 352; Harrison 'Ulbricht' p. 26.
7. Zubok 'Berlin Crisis' p. 13; *21st Party Congress Proceedings* vol. II (in two volumes), p. 406; Taubman *Khrushchev* pp. 413–15.

8. Taubman *Khrushchev* pp. 435–9; Grinevskii *Tysyacha i Odin,* pp. 93, 107.

9. Tompson *Khrushchev* pp. 137–8; N. S. Khrushchev (1971) *Khrushchev Remembers* (London: Sphere), p. 427; D. Shepilov (2007) *The Kremlin's Scholar* (New Haven, CT: Yale University Press), p. 381.

10. *Memoirs* vol. III, p. 423, 431, 440. For the Anti-Party Group, see M. McCauley (1991) *Nikita Khrushchev* (London: Cardinal), p. 73.

11. Taubman *Khrushchev* p. 391.

12. *Presidium* pp. 316, 1038; Taubman *Khrushchev* p. 389; D. Wolff (2011) '"The Finger's Worth of Historical Events": New Russian and Chinese Evidence on the Sino-Soviet Alliance and Split, 1950–59' *Cold War International History Project* Working Paper no. 30, p. 14; D. Wolff (1998) 'The Drama of the Plenums: A Call to Arms' *Cold War International History Project* Bulletin no. 10, pp. 52–4.

13. Aksyutin *Khrushchevskaya* pp. 315–16; D. Wang (2011) 'Quarrelling Brothers: New Chinese Archives and a Reappraisal of the Sino-Soviet Split, 1959–62' *Cold War International History Project* Working Paper no. 49, p. 17.

14. Wang 'Quarrelling Brothers' pp. 22, 27; Aksyutin *Khrushchevskaya* pp. 317–20. For Kars, see Volkogonov *Sem' Vozhdei* p. 414.

15. Wolff 'Finger's Worth' p. 17, 57, 65.

16. Aksyutin *Khrushchevskaya* pp. 317–20; Wang 'Quarrelling Brothers', p. 22, 27; *Presidium* p. 389; Wolff 'Finger's Worth' p. 17.

17. Wang 'Quarrelling Brothers' pp. 30, 35–40; Tatu *Power* p. 108. For "galoshes", see L. M. Lüthi (2008) *The Sino-Soviet Split: Cold War in the Communist World* (Princeton, NJ and Oxford: Princeton University Press), p. 162.

18. Wang 'Quarrelling Brothers' pp. 47–52, 60–1; Aksyutin *Khrushchevskaya* p. 322. For the wreath, see Lüthi *The Sino-Soviet Split* p. 207.

19. Grinevskii *Tysyacha i Odin,* p. 93, 107; *Vospominaniya* vol. IV, p. 546; Kirshner *Svet i Teni* p. 155; Linden *Soviet Leadership* pp. 92–3.

20. Medvedev *Khrushchev* pp. 246–7; Linden *Soviet Leadership* p. 93; Grinevskii *Tysyacha i Odin* pp. 150–1; *Presidium* p. 441.

21. Tatu *Power* p. 49.

22. Taubman *Khrushchev* p. 455.

23. Grinevskii *Tysyacha i Odin* pp. 251–88, 292; Taubman *Khrushchev* p. 465.

24. Tatu *Power* pp. 44, 69, 71, 75.

25. Mikoyan *Tak Bylo* p. 605; Taubman *Khrushchev* p. 475.

26. Grinevskii *Tysyacha i odin* p. 346.

27. Zubok 'Berlin Crisis' pp. 18–19, 22.

28. Zubok 'Berlin Crisis' pp. 22–3.

29. Zubok 'Berlin Crisis' p. 23; Taubman *Khrushchev* pp. 499–500; Grinevskii *Tysyacha i Odin* p. 353.

30. Zubok 'Berlin Crisis' pp. 25–6; Taubman *Khrushchev* p. 502.

31. Harrison 'Ulbricht' pp. 39, 52–62; Zubok 'Berlin Crisis' p. 28.

32. *Presidium* p. 546; Zubok 'Berlin Crisis' p. 29; Taubman *Khrushchev* p. 536.

33. Taubman *Khrushchev* p. 536; Tompson *Khrushchev* p. 248; *Presidium* pp. 535–7.

34. Tompson *Khrushchev* p. 247; Taubman *Khrushchev* p. 541; Khrushchev *Khrushchev Remembers* pp. 454–5.
35. Khrushchev *Khrushchev Remembers* pp. 454–5; Mikoyan *Tak Bylo* p. 605; *Presidium* p. 556; Taubman *Khrushchev* pp. 551–2; Tompson *Khrushchev* pp. 248–9.
36. Taubman *Khrushchev* p. 553.
37. Taubman *Khrushchev* p. 551.
38. Khrushchev *Khrushchev Remembers* pp. 456–7; Taubman *Khrushchev* pp. 561–2.
39. Taubman *Khrushchev* p. 563, 566.
40. The Kennedy–Khrushchev correspondence during the height of the Cuban Missile Crisis was published in a special issue of the Moscow journal *International Affairs* in summer 1992 to mark the thirtieth anniversary of those events. The letters are reproduced in date order.
41. Taubman *Khrushchev* pp. 571–2.
42. Taubman *Khrushchev* p. 575; Kirshner *Svet i Teni* pp. 177–80; *Presidium* p. 623.
43. Taubman *Khrushchev* pp. 531, 552; Tompson *Khrushchev* p. 253.

Chapter 8: The Reformer Ousted

1. Khrushchev *Reformator* p. 811; Zaleski *Planning Reforms* pp. 95–6; Felker *Controversies* pp. 143, 162.
2. *Presidium* p. 628.
3. *Presidium* pp. 634, 347; Tatu *Power* p. 285.
4. N. Kibita 'Moscow–Kiev Relations and the *Sovnarkhoz* Reform' in Smith and Ilič *Kremlin* p. 107; Khrushchev *Reformator* p. 812; Zaleski *Planning Reforms* p. 89.
5. Khrushchev *Reformator* p. 811; *Presidium* pp. 649, 1130.
6. *Presidium* pp. 682–3, 690, 699–700; Tatu *Power* pp. 228, 230.
7. J. A. Armstrong 'Party Bifurcation and Elite Interests' *Soviet Studies* vol. 17, no. 4, 1966, pp. 418–19.
8. Khrushchev *Reformator* pp. 13–14, 780, Khrushchev *Unfinished Reforms* pp. 151–2; *Presidium* p. 577; Taubman *Khrushchev* p. 523.
9. Linden *Soviet Leadership* pp. 150–1; *Presidium* pp. 657, 661; Khrushchev *Reformator* pp. 13–14, 813; J. Hazard (1967) 'The Politics of Soviet Economic Reform' in A. Balinsky et al. (eds) *Planning and the Market in the USSR: The 1960s* (New Brunswick, NJ: Rutgers University Press), pp. 68, 72.
10. Linden *Soviet Leadership* p. 169.
11. B. Tromly 'An Unlikely National Revival: Soviet Higher Learning and the Ukrainian "Sixties", 1953–65' *Russian Review* vol. 68, no. 4, 2009, pp. 616–18.
12. Tatu *Power* p. 283.
13. *Presidium* p. 669; Tatu *Power* pp. 303, 307; M. Romm "Chetyre Vstrechi s N. S. Khrushchevym" in Aksyutin *Materialy* p. 141. The Manezh Affair is fully described in V. Zubok (2009) *Zhivago's Children: The Last Russian*

Intelligentsia (Cambridge, MA: Belknap Press of Harvard University Press), pp. 193, 209.

14. Kozlov *Readers* p. 188; Jones *Myth* p. 153; Romm 'Chetyre' p. 152.

15. Tatu *Power* pp. 320–2; Volkogonov *Sem' Vozhdei* p. 398.

16. *Presidium* p. 715; Tatu *Power* pp. 337, 349; Kirshner *Svet i teni* p. 185; Yu. Aksyutin 'N. S. Khrushchev: "My Dolzhny Skazat' Pravdu o Kul'te Lichnosti"' in Aksyutin *Materialy* p. 41; Linden *Soviet Leadership* p. 181. Lüthi (*Sino–Soviet Split* p. 239) is clear that Mao was deliberately provoking Khrushchev at this time.

17. Swain *Tito* p. 134.

18. Khrushchev Collection, Wilson Center Digital Archive "Speech of N. S. Khrushchev at a friendly dinner in Yevksinograd (Varna), 16 May 1962"; Adzhubei *Te Desyat'* p. 207.

19. Swain *Tito* p. 135; *Presidium* p. 1128.

20. Khrushchev *Reformator* p. 931; Khrushchev *Nikita Khrushchev* p. 680.

21. Khrushchev *Unfinished Reforms* pp. 28, 180; British Broadcasting Corporation *Summary of World Broadcasts 2 (Eastern Europe)* 21.8.1963 hereafter *SWB*; *Radio Free Europe Bulletin* 15.3.1964; *Keesings Contemporary Archives* p. 19660.

22. *SWB* 2.9.1963; *Memoirs* vol. III, pp. 544–5; *Presidium* p. 735; Yu. V. Bernov (1995) *Zapiski Diplomata* (Moscow: Parusa), p. 82.

23. *Presidium* pp. 731, 747–51.

24. Linden *Soviet Leadership* p. 194; *Presidium* p. 767, 772; Tatu *Power* pp. 370–1.

25. Pyzhikov *Ottepel'* p. 161; Linden *Soviet Leadership* p. 189; Volkogonov *Sem' Vozhdei* p. 384.

26. *Presidium* p. 788.

27. Khrushchev *Reformator* pp. 710–12, 1003; Zaleski *Planning Reforms* pp. 85–7, 97.

28. Khrushchev *Reformator* pp. 712, 1005; Felker *Controversies* pp. 86, 178–9; Feiwel *Quest* pp. 228–9. See also Zaleski *Planning Reforms* pp. 125–6 – in the Gorky experiment, the *Sovnarkhoz* broke the rules and during the second half of the year insisted an unwanted order be fulfilled.

29. There was a strong element of planning from below in the original *Sovnarkhoz* proposals, but these had been progressively watered down after 1958, see Nataliya Kibita (2013) *Soviet Economic Management under Khrushchev* (London: Routledge), pp. 56–8, 76, 132.

30. Khrushchev *Reformator* p. 1005; *1964* pp. 70–4.

31. Khrushchev *Reformator* p. 1107; *Presidium* pp. 839–49; *1964* p. 82.

32. Feiwel *Quest* p. 218; Felker *Controversies* pp. 79, 193–6, 213–15, 218; Khrushchev *Reformator* p. 1008; Tatu *Power* p. 437.

33. *Presidium* p. 860, 1178; *1964* pp. 137, 145–9; Linden *Soviet Leadership* pp. 198–200; Tatu *Power* pp. 391–2.

34. Khrushchev *Unfinished Reforms* p. 476; *1964* p. 53; Mikoyan *Tak Bylo* pp. 95–6; Pyzhikov *Ottepel'* p. 310.

35. Pyzhikov *Ottepel'* pp. 302–13; *1964* pp. 66–8; Khrushchev *Reformator* pp. 998–9; W. Tompson 'The Fall of Nikita Khrushchev' *Soviet Studies* vol. 43, no. 6, p. 1110.

36. *1964* p. 58; G. Swain (2006) *Trotsky* (Harlow: Pearson Longman), pp. 136–8.
37. Swain *Trotsky* p. 146, 155; *Vospominaniya* vol. IV, pp. 610, 623.
38. *Memoirs* vol. II, pp. 255–6.
39. *Presidium* p. 855; *1964* p. 43.
40. Khrushchev *Nikita Khrushchev* p. 256; Taubman *Khrushchev* p. 598; Bernov *Zapiski* p. 82.
41. For detailed discussion of the Latvian National Communist Affair see W. Prigge 'The Latvian Purges of 1959: A Revision Study' *Journal of Baltic Studies* no. 3, 2004 and G. Swain 'Come on Latvians'.
42. *Vospominaniya* vol. IV, pp. 615–6, 623; *1964* p. 9; Mikoyan *Tak Bylo* p. 614; Khrushchev *Nikita Khrushchev* p. 713; Tatu *Power* p. 398.
43. Aksyutin *Khrushchevskaya* p. 437; Khrushchev *Reformator* p. 16; R. D. Markwick 'Thaws and Freezes in Soviet Historiography, 1953–64' in Jones *Dilemmas*, p. 184.
44. *1964* pp. 14, 44, 48; Medvedev *Khrushchev* p. 363.
45. Tatu *Power* p. 379; *1964* p. 61; V. N. Novikov 'V Gody Rukovodstva N. S. Khrushcheva' *Voprosy Istorii* no. 2, 1989 p. 107; *Presidium* p. 857.
46. Yu. Shapoval (2003) *Petro Shelest* (Kiev: Ukrainian Academy of Sciences), p. 682.
47. S. Rudenko p. 117; *1964* pp. 154–50; '"Sobiraya Griby" Reshali Sud'bu Khrushcheva' *Argumenty i Fakty* no. 43, 1995.
48. Tompson 'The Fall' p. 1106; Novikov 'V Gody' pp 114–15; *Vospominaniya* vol. IV, pp. 619–20.
49. *Vospominaniya* vol. IV, pp. 626–7; *1964* pp. 181–2; Khrushchev *Nikita Khrushchev* p. 731.
50. *Vospominaniya* vol. IV pp. 626–7; *1964* pp. 182–4.
51. *1964* pp. 184–214.
52. *Presidium* p. 1181 et seq.
53. *Vospominaniya* vol. IV, pp. 626–7; Rudenko 'Vospominaya' p. 117.
54. Tompson 'The Fall' p. 1109, 1112; Khrushchev *Reformator* p. 18, 21; *1964* p. 226; Adzhubei *Te Desyat'* p. 291; *Presidium* pp. 862, 872; V. E. Semichastnyi "V svete glasnosti. Kak smeshali N. S.Khrushcheva" *Argumenty i Fakty* no. 20, 1989; Adzhubei *Te Desyat'* p. 291.
55. G. I. Voronov 'Ot Ottepeli do Zastoya' in Aksyutin *Materialy* p. 219; Khrushchev *Reformator* p. 23; *1964* pp. 242–50.

Conclusion

1. Tompson *Khrushchev* p. 281.
2. *Presidium* p. 873; B. Levytzkys 'Generations in Conflict' *Problems of Communism* no. 1, 1967, p. 38.
3. *Memoirs* vol. I, p. 3.
4. A. Nove (1987) 'Industry' in M. McCauley *Khrushchev and Khrushchevis* (Basingstoke: Macmillan), p. 70.

5. F. Burlatskii 'Khrushchev, Shtrikhi k Politicheskomu Portretu' in Aksyutin *Materialy* p. 16.

6. Romm 'Chetyri Vstrechi' in Aksyutin *Materialy* p. 137.

7. Linden *Soviet Leadership* pp. 179, 186.

8. Otchet N. M. Shvernika *Istochnik* no. 1, 1995, p. 127.

9. *Memoirs* vol. II, p. 163.

10. Taubman *Khrushchev* p. 617.

11. Crankshaw *Khrushchev* p. 24.

12. F. K. Roberts 'Encounters with Khrushchev' in McCauley *Khrushchevism*, p. 228.

13. Semichastnyi 'V Svete', *Argumenty i Fakty*, 20 May 1989.

14. Burlatskii 'Shtrikhi' in Aksyutin *Materialy* p. 19.

15. Taubman *Khrushchev* p. 366.

16. *1964* p. 226.

17. Kaganovich *Pamyatnye Zapiski* p. 568.

18. Linden *Soviet Leadership* p. 208.

19. Tompson 'The Fall' p. 1111.

20. See note 13.

21. Mikoyan *Tak Bylo* p. 597.

22. Novikov 'V Gody' p. 105.

23. *Memoirs* vol. III, p. 694.

24. Swain *Tito* pp. 162, 190–1.

Bibliography

Documentary Collections

Arkhivy Kremlya: Prezidium Ts K KPSS 1954-64 vol. I. *Chernovye Zapisi Zasedanii: Stenogrammy* (Moscow: Rosspen, 2004).

Doklad N S Khrushcheva o Kul'te Lichnosti Stalina na XX s"ezde KPSS: Dokumenty (Moscow: Rosspen, 2002).

Dokumenty: Nikita Khrushchev 1964 (Moscow: Mezhdunarodnyi fond Demokratiya, 2007).

Georgii Zhukov: Dokumenty (Moscow: Mezhdunarodnyi fond Demokratiya, 2001).

Lavrentii Beriya 1953: Dokumenty (Moscow: Mezhdunarodnyi fond Demokratiya, 1999).

Molotov, Malenkov, Kaganovich: Stenogrammy Iyunskogo Plenuma TsK KPSS i Drugie Dokumenty (Moscow: Mezhdunarodnyi fond Demokratiya, 1998).

Nikita Sergeevich Khrushchev: Dva Tsveta Vremeni. Dokumenty iz Lichnogo Fonda N. S. Khrushcheva two volumes (Moscow: Mezhdunarodnyi fond Demokratiya, 2009).

Politicheskoe Rukovodstvo Ukrainy, 1939–1989 (Moscow: Rosspen, 2006).

Reabilitatsiya: Kak eto Bylo, Mart 1953–Fevral' 1956: Dokumenty (Moscow: Mezhdunarodnyi fond Demokratiya, 2000).

Congress Proceedings

XVII S"ezd Vsesoyuznoi Kommunisticheskoi Partii (b): Stenograficheskii Otchet (Moscow: Partizdat, 1934).

Vneocherednoi XXI S"ezd Kommunisticheskoi Partii Sovetskogo Soyuza: Stenograficheskii Otchet (Moscow: Gosudarstvennoe Izdatel'stvo Politicheskoi Literatury, 1959).

XXII S"ezd Kommunisticheskoi Partii Sovetskogo Soyuza: Stenograficheskii Otchet (Moscow: Gosudarstvennoe Izdatel'stvo Politicheskoi Literatury, 1962).

The Writings of Khrushchev's Son

S. N. Khrushchev (2000) *Nikita Khrushchev and the Creation of a Superpower* (University Park, PA: Pennsylvania State University Press).

S. N. Khrushchev (2010) *Khrushchev Reformator* (Moscow: Vremya).

S. N. Khrushchev (2014) *Khrushchev in Power: Unfinished Reforms* (Boulder, CO: Lynne Riener Publishers).

Khrushchev's Memoirs

N. S. Khrushchev (1971) *Khrushchev Remembers* (London: Sphere).

N. S. Khrushchev (1999) *Vospminaniya: Vremya, Lyudi, Vlast* (Moscow: Moskovskie Novosti).

S. N. Khrushchev (ed.) (2004) *Memoirs of Nikita Khrushchev* three volumes, (University Park, PA: Pennsylvania State University Press).

Other Memoirs

A. Adzhubei (1989) *Te Desyat'let* (Moscow: Sovetskaya Rossiya).

L. Kaganovich (1996) *Pamyatnye Zapiski* (Moscow: Vagrius).

A. Mikoyan (1999) *Tak Bylo: Razmyshlenie o Minuvshem* (Moscow: Vagrius).

N. Mukhitdinov (1994) *Gody Provedennye v Kremle* (Tashkent: Izdatel'stvo Narodnogo Naslediya Imeni Abdully Kadyri).

V. N. Novikov 'V Gody Rukovodstva N. S. Khrushcheva' *Voprosy Istorii* vol. 2, 1989, pp. 106–17.

D. Shepilov (2007) *The Kremlin's Scholar* (New Haven, CT: Yale University Press).

Biographies of Khrushchev

E. Crankshaw (1966) *Khrushchev* (London: Sphere).

M. Frankland (1966) *Khrushchev* (Harmondsworth: Penguin Books).

M. McCauley (1991) *Nikita Khrushchev* (London: Cardinal).

R. Medvedev (2006) *N. S. Khrushchev: Otets ili Otchim Sovetskoi 'Ottepeli'* (Moscow: Yauza).

W. Taubman (2003) *Khrushchev: The Man and his Era* (London: Free Press).

W. Tompson (1995) *Khrushchev: A Political Life* (Basingstoke and New York: Palgrave).

Other Works

Yu. V. Aksyutin (ed.) (1989) *Nikita Sergeevich Khrushchev: Materialy k Biogrgafii*, (Moscow: Politizdat).

Yu. V. Aksyutin (2004) *Khrushchevskaya 'Ottepel' i Obshchestvennye Nastroenniya v SSSR v 1953–64 gg* (Moscow: Rosspen).

G. D. Andrusz (1984) *Housing and Urban Development in the USSR* (Basingstoke: Macmillan).

J. A. Armstrong 'Party Bifurcation and Elite Interests' *Soviet Studies* vol. 17, no. 4, 1966.

A. Balinsky et al. (eds) (1967) *Planning and the Market in the USSR: The 1960s* (New Brunswick, N J: Rutgers University Press), pp. 417–30.

F. Benvenuti 'Industry and Purge in the Donbas, 1936–37' *Europe-Asia Studies* vol. 45, no. 1, 1993, pp. 57–78.

S. Beria (1999) *Beria: My Father. Inside Stalin's Kremlin* (London: Duckworth).

Yu. V. Bernov (1995) *Zapiski Diplomata* (Moscow: Parusa).

P. Bogdanov et al. (eds) (1961) *Rasskaz o Pochetnom Shakhtere* (Stalino: Politizdat).

T. M. Bohn et al. (eds) (2014) *De-Stalinisation Reconsidered: Persistence and Change in the Soviet Union* (Frankfurt: Campus Verlag).

G. A. Brinkley 'Khrushchev Remembered: On the Theory of Soviet Statehood' *Soviet Studies* vol. 24, no. 3, 1973, pp. 387–401.

I. Caşu and M. Sandle 'Discontent and Uncertainty in the Borderland: Soviet Moldavia and the Secret Speech 1956–57' *Europe-Asia Studies* vol. 66, no. 4, 2014, pp. 612–44.

T. Cox (ed.) (1997) *Hungary 1956 – Forty Years On* (London: Frank Cass).

N. Davis (1995) *A Long Walk to Church* (Boulder, CO: Westview Press).

D. Deletant and M. Ionescu (2011) 'Romania and the Warsaw Pact' *Cold War International History Project* Working Paper no. 43.

M. Dobson (2009) *Khrushchev's Cold Summer: Gulag Returnees, Crime and the Fate of Reform after Stalin* (Ithaca, N Y and London: Cornell University Press).

F. A. Durgin 'The Virgin Lands Programme, 1952–1960' *Soviet Studies* vol. 13, no. 3, 1962.

A. B. Edemskii (2008) *Ot Konflikta k Normalizatsii: Seveetsko-Yugoslavskie Otnosheniya v 1953–56 Godakh* (Moscow: Nauka), pp. 255–80.

G. R. Feiwel (1967) *The Soviet Quest for Economic Efficiency* (New York: Praeger).

J. L. Felker (1966) *Soviet Economic Controversies* (Cambridge, MA: MIT Press).

D. Filtzer 'The Soviet Wage Reform of 1956–62' *Soviet Studies* vol. 41, no. 1, 1989, pp. 88–110.

A. Getty (1999) *The Road to Terror* (New Haven, CT: Yale University Press).

L. Gibianskii (1998) 'Soviet-Yugoslav Relations in the Hungarian Revolution of 1956' *Cold War International History Project* Bulletin no. 10.

Y. Gorlizki 'Party Revivalism and the Death of Stalin' *Slavic Review* vol. 54, no. 1, 1995, pp. 1–22.

O. Grinevskii (1998) *Tysyacha i Odin den' Nikity Sergeevicha* (Moscow: Vagrius).

H. M. Harrison (1993) 'Ulbricht and the Concrete "Rose": New Archival Evidence on the Dynamics of Soviet–East German Relations and the Berlin Crisis, 1958–61' *Cold War International History Project* Working Paper no. 5.

J. Haslam 'Political Opposition to Stalin and the Origins of the Terror in Russia, 1932–36' *The Historical Journal* vol. 29, no. 2, 1986, pp. 395–418.

R. Hornsby (2013) *Protest Reform and Repression in Khrushchev's Soviet Union* (Cambridge: Cambridge University Press).

M. Ilič et al. (eds) (2004) *Women in the Khrushchev Era* (Basingstoke and New York: Palgrave Macmillan).

M. Ilič and J. Smith (eds) (2009) *Soviet State and Society under Nikita Khrushchev* (London: Routledge).

M. Jansen (2002) *Stalin's Loyal Executioner: People's Commissar Nikolai Ezhov, 1895–1940* (Stanford, CA: Hoover Institution Press).

P. Jones (ed.) (2006) *The Dilemmas of De-Stalinisation: Negotiating Cultural and Social Change in the Khrushchev Era* (London: Routledge).

P. Jones (2013) *Myth, Memory, Trauma: Rethinking the Stalinist Past in the Soviet Union, 1953–70* (New Haven, CT and London: Yale University Press).

A. Kemp-Welch 'Khrushchev's "Secret Speech" and Polish Politics: The Spring of 1956' *Europe-Asia Studies* vol. 48, no. 2, 1996, pp. 181–206.

N. Kibita (2013) *Soviet Economic Management under Khrushchev* (London: Routledge).

L. A. Kirshner et al. (eds) (1989) *Svet i Teni "Velikovogo Desyatiletiya": N S Khrushchev i Ego Vremya* (Leningrad: Lenizdat).

G. Kostyrchenko (2012) *Tainaya Politka Khrushcheva* (Moscow: Mezhdunarodnye Otnosheniya).

D. Kozlov (2013) *The Readers of Novyi Mir: Coming to Terms with the Stalinist Past* (Cambridge, MA: Harvard University Press).

H. Kuromiya (1998) *Freedom and Terror in the Donbas* (Cambridge: Cambridge University Press).

M. E. Lenoe (2010) *The Kirov Murder and Soviet History* (New Haven, CT and London: Yale University Press).

C. A. Linden (1966) *Khrushchev and the Soviet Leadership 1957–1964* (Baltimore, MD: Johns Hopkins Press).

K. E. Loewenstein 'Re-emergence of Public Opinion in the Soviet Union: Khrushchev and Responses to the Secret Speech' *Europe-Asia Studies* vol. 58, no. 8, 2006, pp. 1329–45.

L. M. Lüthi (2008) *The Sino-Soviet Split: Cold War in the Communist World* (Princeton, NJ and Oxford: Princeton University Press).

E. Mawdsley (2005) *Thunder in The East: The Nazi-Soviet War, 1941–45* (London: Hodder Arnold).

M. McCauley (1987) *Khrushchev and Khrushchevis* (Basingstoke: Macmillan), p. 70.

A. Ponomarev (1993) 'Nikita Khrushchev: Nachalo Karery' in *Neizvestnaya Rossiya XX Vek* vol. III (Moscow: Moskovskoe Gorodskoe Ob'edinenie Arkhivov).

W. Prigge 'The Latvian Purges of 1959: A Revision Study' *Journal of Baltic Studies* vol. 35, no. 3, 2004, pp. 211–30.

A. V. Pyzhikov (2002) *Khrushchevskaya Ottepel'* (Moscow: Olma Press).

A. Rees (2012) *Iron Lazar* (London: Anthem Press).

S. E. Reid 'Cold War in the Kitchen: Gender and De-Stalinisation of Consumer Taste in the Soviet Union under Khrushchev' *Slavic Review* vol. 61, no. 2, 2002, pp. 211–52.

S. E. Reid 'The Khrushchev Kitchen: Domesticating the Scientific–Technical Revolution' *Journal of Contemporary History* vol. 40, no. 2, 2005, pp. 289–316.

G. Roberts (2008) 'A Chance for Peace? The Soviet Campaign to End the Cold War, 1953–55' *Cold War International History Project* paper 57.

S. Rudenko 'Vospominaniya "Te Desyat' Let": Polemicheskie Zametki o Knige A. Adzhubeya' *Narodnyi Deputat* no. 3, 1991.

Yu. Shapoval (2003) *Petro Shelest* (Kiev: Ukrainian Academy of Sciences).

M. E. Sharpe (ed.) (1966) *Planning, Profit and Incentives in the USSR* (White Plains, NY: International Arts and Science Press).

V. A. Shestakov (2006) *Sotsialno-ekonomicheskaya Politika Sovetskogo Gosudarstva vo 50-e i Seredine 60-kh Godov* (Moscow: Nauka).

J. Smith and M. Ilič (eds) (2011) *Khrushchev in the Kremlin* (London: Routledge).

G. Swain (2006) *Trotsky* (Harlow: Pearson Longman).

G. Swain (2011) *Tito: A Biography* (London: I B Tauris).

G. Swain 'Before National Communism: Joining the Latvian Komsomol under Stalin' *Europe-Asia Studies* vol. 64, no. 7, 2012, pp. 1239–70.

G. Swain '"Come on Latvians, Join the Party – We'll Forgive you Everything": Ideological Struggle during the National Communist Affair, Summer 1959' in M. Kott and D. Smith (eds) (2016) *Latvia – A Work in Progress? 100 Years of State and Nation-building* (Hannover: *ibidem*-Verlag).

G. Swain and N. Swain (2009) *Eastern Europe since 1945* (Basingstoke and New York: Palgrave Macmillan).

T .Tannenberg (2008) *Politka Moskvy v Respublikakh Baltii v Poslevoennye Gody (1944–1956): Issledovaniya i Dokumenty* (Tartu: Tartu University Press).

M. Tatu (1969) *Power in the Kremlin* (London: Collins).

W. Taubman, S. Khrushchev and A. Gleason (eds) (2000) *Nikita Khrushchev* (New Haven, CT: Yale University Press).

W. Tompson (1991) 'The Fall of Nikita Khrushchev' *Soviet Studies* vol. 43, no. 6, pp. 1101–21.

B. Tromly 'The Leningrad Affair and Soviet Patronage Politics, 1949–1950' *Europe-Asia Studies* vol. 56, no. 5, 2004.

B. Tromly 'An Unlikely National Revival: Soviet Higher Learning and the Ukrainian "Sixties", 1953–65' *Russian Review* vol. 68, no. 4, 2009.

D. Volkogonov (1996) *Sem' Vozhdei* (Moscow: Novosti).

D. Wang (2011) 'Quarrelling Brothers: New Chinese Archives and a Reappraisal of the Sino-Soviet Split, 1959–62' *Cold War International History Project* Working Paper no. 49.

D. Wolff (2011) '"The Finger's Worth of Historical Events": New Russian and Chinese Evidence on the Sino-Soviet Alliance and Split, 1950–59' *Cold War International History Project* Working Paper no. 30.

D. Wolff (1998) 'The Drama of the Plenums: A Call to Arms' *Cold War International History Project* Bulletin no. 10.

E. Zaleski (1967) *Planning Reforms in the Soviet Union* (Chapel Hill, NC: University of North Carolina Press).

E. Yu. Zubkova (1993) *Obshchestvo i Reform, 1945–1964* (Moscow: Izdatel'skii Tsentr "Rossiya Molodaya").

V. Zubok (1993) 'Khrushchev and the Berlin Crisis' *Cold War International History Project* Working Paper no. 6.

Index